ZHOU ENLAI

The Early Years

Zhou Enlai

THE EARLY YEARS

Chae-Jin Lee

Stanford University Press
Stanford, California

Stanford University Press
Stanford, California

Printed in the United States of America

CIP data appear at the end of the book

Stanford University Press publications
are distributed exclusively by Stanford
University Press within the United States,
Canada, Mexico, and Central America;
they are distributed exclusively by
Cambridge University Press throughout
the rest of the world.

To
William P. Gerberding
and Theodore J. Lee

Preface

After having carefully read a number of biographical studies on Zhou Enlai, I came to realize that many important questions about his intellectual growth and political development were still unanswered. Hence I decided to undertake research on his early years, focusing on these critical questions, and to present an objective and balanced account and assessment. Although there are numerous methodological constraints, especially the limited access to archival sources in China and to Zhou Enlai's relatives and contemporaries, I have drawn upon primary documents and reliable data concerning his childhood and young adulthood. My findings and analyses are largely based on previously unknown or underutilized sources that shed new light on Zhou Enlai's educational experience, literary and journalistic activities, nationalistic commitment, progressive orientation, and communist leadership. This book is the modest outcome of my research, which has been conducted for over a decade.

For my field research in China, I have relied heavily upon a number of persons at Nankai University who gave me generous help in locating old books and journals, arranging appropriate interviews, and freely sharing their knowledge and insights. In particular, I wish to express my deep appreciation to Liu Xi, Wang Yongxiang, Wei Hongyun, Lai Xinxia, Mu Guoguang, Teng Weizao, Pang Songfeng, Yu Xinchun, and Feng Chengbai. At Beijing University I received important advice and support from Yan Rengeng, Yang Tongfang, Ye Yifen, and Zhou Erliu. I am also grateful to Liao Yongwu and Wang Shujin for allowing me on several occasions to visit the Zhou Enlai Memorial Museum in Tianjin and to use its oral history projects and photographic collections.

Among Zhou Enlai's contemporaries at Nankai Middle School, it was my privilege to spend a delightful afternoon with Wu Guozhen (K. C. Wu) in Savannah, Georgia, to interview Yan Renzeng (Louis Yen) in Tianjin, and to exchange useful correspondence with Meng Zhi (Chih Meng) and Mei Yibao (Y. P. Mei). I learned much from several of Zhou Enlai's close relatives, but they remain anonymous at their request.

I should like to thank Dick Wilson for inviting me to his London home and allowing me to peruse his substantial research notes on Zhou Enlai, Henry R. Lieberman for responding to questions about his extensive interviews with Zhou Enlai, and Arthur L. Rosenbaum for his critical reading of my manuscript. In Tokyo, I greatly benefited from Sanetō Keishū's detailed explanations about the history of Chinese students in Japan and from Ogawa Heishirō's remarkable knowledge of Zhou Enlai's family background. I am very appreciative of the cooperation and encouragement from Daniel Bays, Philip West, Jin Chongji, Zhang Wenjin, Cui Longhao, Kang Tiejuan, Yan Wenpu, Julia Yen, Kyung S. Lee, Miura Isamu, and Y. F. Chang. My thanks go to Jack Stark, Anthony Fucaloro, and Ralph Rossum, who offered funds for my research at Claremont McKenna College. I gratefully acknowledge the able assistance provided by Mary Anderson, Shari Anderson, Cao Qizhen, Therese Mahoney, Tang Wenfang, Yoshida Kazunori, and Wang Li. Muriel Bell, Peggy Berg, Karen Brown Davison, Amy Klatzkin, and Shirley Taylor at Stanford University Press guided me well in revising and completing the manuscript. I acknowledge permission to use excerpts from *In Quest: Poems of Chou En-lai*, translated by Nancy T. Lin, © 1979 by Joint Publishing (Hong Kong) Co., Ltd.

I am pleased to dedicate this book to my mentor, William P. Gerberding, and to my son, Theodore J. Lee. It should be made clear that I am solely responsible for the interpretations and any inaccuracies contained in the book.

C.J.L.

Contents

Figure and Tables

ZHOU ENLAI

The Early Years

Introduction

It is widely believed that the late Chinese Premier Zhou Enlai (Chou En-lai, 1898–1976) was a sophisticated intellectual, pragmatic Marxist, able political leader, and skillful diplomatic negotiator. Many Chinese and foreign observers have attested to this general assessment at various stages in his illustrious political career. For example, Edgar Snow, who interviewed the major leaders of the Chinese Communist Party in the caves of Yanan in 1936, described Zhou Enlai as a "pure intellectual in whom action was coordinated with knowledge and conviction."[1] "There was certainly," he said, "a kind of magnetism about him that seemed to derive from a curious combination of shyness, personal charm and complete assurance of command." Theodore H. White, who became a friend of Zhou Enlai at Chongqing during the Sino-Japanese War in 1941, called him a brilliant, warm, and elastic man and praised his analytical, clinical, and logical mind.[2] Henry A. Kissinger, who participated in a series of intensive negotiations with Zhou at Beijing in 1971 and 1972, said: "His gaunt, expressive face was dominated by piercing eyes, conveying a mixture of intensity and repose, of wariness and calm self-confidence. . . . He was equally at home in philosophy, reminiscence, historical analysis, tactical probes, humorous repartee. . . . Chou Enlai, in short, was one of the two or three most impressive men I have ever met."[3] And Richard M. Nixon, who issued the historic Shanghai Communiqué with Zhou Enlai in 1972, characterized him, among other things, as "a very complex, subtle man" and a "grand conciliator."[4]

Yet Zhou's major biographers—Chinese as well as non-Chinese —have not made an adequate effort to explain how Zhou Enlai acquired and developed these notable intellectual and personal attributes. Most of his biographers in the People's Republic of China are inclined toward a degree of hagiography about their beloved revolutionary leader,[5] but in Taiwan and Hong Kong, his critics are largely negative in assessing his personality and leadership.[6] Outside China, a number of authors, notably Kai-yu Hsu in the United States and Dick Wilson in the United Kingdom, wrote pioneering books on Zhou Enlai,[7] but until recently his non-Chinese biographers have suffered from limited access to the important primary sources about Zhou Enlai's personal life and political activities.

My decade-long study of the extensive records of Zhou Enlai's life and career has convinced me that his rich and diverse personal, educational, and political experiences during his formative years laid a solid foundation for his intellectual and ideological sophistication, and, furthermore, established the clear patterns of his personal and political orientations. His formative years can be divided into four phases: his upbringing in Jiangsu province and Manchuria (1898–1913), his education at Nankai Middle School (1913–17), his experience in Japan (1917–19), and his political activism during the May Fourth era (1919–20) and in Europe (1921–24).

As the firstborn son of a prominent gentry family in Jiangsu province, the young Zhou was initially exposed to a gentle, cultured, and protected Confucian environment; this Confucian factor remained a significant determinant of his ethical and behavioral attitudes throughout his early life. After he moved to the rugged Manchurian frontier at the age of twelve, he encountered the dynamic political and cultural crosscurrents within China's northeastern region and witnessed foreign exploitation, patriotic movements, and revolutionary upheavals. At Nankai Middle School in Tianjin, he received "Western learning" from Zhang Boling, refined his nascent nationalistic consciousness, exercised organizational leadership, and acquired literary, journalistic, and dramatic training. He studied Shakespeare, Spencer, Huxley, Darwin, Rousseau, Montesquieu, Jefferson, and Lincoln, along with modern Chinese thinkers such as Liang Qichao. His Nankai education was therefore broad but not anti-Confucian, since many basic attitudes and orientations taught at Nankai were derived from Confucian principles.

During his two-year sojourn in Japan Zhou learned a great deal about the Taishō democracy, the Bolshevik Revolution, Chinese student politics, and socialist and anarchist perspectives. Most importantly, he was influenced by Kawakami Hajime's authoritative interpretations of Karl Marx. His Nankai University years (1919–20) were also the years of the May Fourth Movement, and he had an increasingly important part in radical student activities and publications. He cultivated close associations with Li Dazhao and other *Xinqingnian* (New Youth) intellectuals, and spent six months in prison. By the time he left China in November 1920 intending to study at the University of Edinburgh, the extent and depth of his activities were already impressive: he had grafted concepts and practices derived from modern enlightenment onto his Confucian background, had undergone a socialist transformation, had acquired organizational and journalistic experience, and had lived in Japan. As a logical extension of his work in the May Fourth Movement, he assumed a leading role in the initiation of the communist movement among Chinese students in Europe.

The commonly held view about Zhou Enlai's early years is that the young Zhou, abandoned by his parents and held back by family misfortunes, was angry and sullen. Zhou's early childhood was indeed disturbed by adoption, family tragedies, and frequent moves, but he seems nonetheless to have grown up in a family environment that was warm and supportive, and despite the unusual circumstances of his adoption, he remained fairly close to his natural parents. Always, too, he had the support of his paternal uncles. During his Nankai Middle School years especially, he benefited from a variety of mentors. Zhang Boling's Western, Christian, and scientific teachings were supplemented by the neotraditionalist example of Yan Xiu, the school's founder, and by Liang Qichao and their political and intellectual associates. From Yan Xiu in particular, with whom Zhou established a long-standing connection, Zhou learned the importance of moral integrity, public service, and dedication to country.

There is no evidence to support the statements of some biographers that Zhou Enlai while in Japan attended Waseda, Hosei, Nihon, or Kyoto Imperial universities or that he assumed a central political leadership role during the Chinese student demonstrations there. Zhou did learn from the writings of Kawakami Hajime the rudimentary principles of Karl Marx's historical materialism, economic determinism, and class analysis, but, contrary to the contentions of several biographers, he did not return to China in 1919 because of the impending May Fourth Movement. His reasons seem to have been only practical ones—failing the entrance examinations for the Tokyo Higher Normal School and the First Higher School, and a lack of money.

After returning to China, it took some time for Zhou to become part of the May Fourth Movement in Tianjin. Archival materials indicate that his political activities in Tianjin started toward the end of June 1919. As the movement began to develop, he gradually assumed an important leadership position in student organizations and formed an intimate ideological and personal linkage with Li Dazhao and his followers. It was only then that Zhou embraced Marxism as a means to save China. After he left Shanghai for Europe in 1920 (with Yan Xiu's assistance), he little by little put aside his plans for study and instead became a full-time communist organizer. Specifically, he started communist movements among Chinese students in France and organized a united front between communists and Nationalists on the continent. Thus the pattern of his subsequent revolutionary activities in China was firmly set in Europe.

In addition to establishing the facts of Zhou Enlai's early years, this study places Zhou's experience in the broader historical context of challenges and opportunities facing Chinese youth of his generation, notably the host of new ideas and events such as nationalism, Marxism, the Bolshevik Revolution, the First World War, and the May Fourth Movement. This detailed study of Zhou Enlai's early years and the many influences on him will, I hope, provide a better basis for understanding his pivotal role in the unfolding of China's contemporary political history.

CHAPTER ONE

Confucian Upbringing and a Turbulent Childhood

> The man of good birth is potentially capable of "patterning his coat" with culture, and thus distinguishing himself from the common herd. But good birth alone, though essential as a basis for culture, is not enough to make a gentleman in the Confucian sense.
> —Arthur Waley, *The Analects of Confucius*

Childhood is a usual starting point for any substantial political biography because it is commonly recognized that family background and early experiences have a significant influence on personality formation, political values, and adult behavior. One does not have to subscribe to the psychoanalytic theories of Sigmund Freud or Erik Erikson to accept the validity of this general assumption. Confucian philosophy, too, is built upon the popular notion that the values and habits formed during childhood persist throughout one's life. As Arthur Waley suggests in *The Analects of Confucius*, culture is just as important as good birth, and it is the judicious combination of inborn qualities and cultural refinement that makes a Confucian gentleman. Despite the existence of a number of good biographical studies of Zhou Enlai, there has been much confusion surrounding the facts of his childhood, out of which have emerged several conflicting interpretations. Although it is still difficult to establish a complete set of definitive answers, this chapter will draw upon recent research discoveries to dispel some of the prevailing misconceptions.

Family Background

Earlier studies claimed that Zhou Enlai was born in 1896 or 1899, and gave his birthplace variably as Shaoxing, Hunan, Huaian, or Huaiyin.[1] In fact, his actual birth date was March 5, 1898 (or February 13, 1898, according to the lunar calendar; he used both dates indiscriminately during his childhood).[2] It was the Year of the Dog and the 24th year of the Guangxi Reign in the declining Qing dynasty. Enlai was born in the northwestern room of his grandfather's large and comfortable residential compound on Fuma *xiang* (street) of Shanyang county, Huaian prefecture, Jiangsu province. (Shanyang was renamed Huaian county in 1914, which accounts for some of the confusion over Zhou's birthplace.) Because his grandfather, Zhou Junlong (Zhou Panlong), was born in Shaoxing county, Zhejiang province, Zhou Enlai always regarded Shaoxing as the place of his ancestral home (*yuanji* or *jiguan*), and he considered himself a Zhejiang person. This identification, although it was a source of pride for him throughout his life, was both an asset and a liability in his career.[3]

The Zhou clan had a long and illustrious lineage in a village called Baoyuqiao in Shaoxing; its former grandeur can still be seen in the imposing Hundred-Year Hall (*baisuitang*), erected in 1798 in honor of an ancestor who lived until she was nearly one hundred years old.[4] The Zhous claimed descent from the royal family of the Zhou dynasty, but the written record remains unclear. The best-known ancestor of the Zhou household is Zhou Dunyi (1017–73), an eminent Neo-Confucian philosopher, poet, and government official of the Northern Song dynasty. Zhou Enlai often quoted from Zhou Dunyi's popular poem about the water lily: "Since the opening days of the Tang dynasty, it has been fashionable to admire the peony; but my favorite is the water lily. How stainless it rises from its slimy bed! How modestly it reposes on the clear pool—an emblem of purity and truth! Symmetrically perfect, its subtle perfume is wafted far and wide, while there it rests in spotless state, something to be regarded reverently from a distance, and not to be profaned by familiar approach."[5] Zhou Enlai was also a distant relative of Lu Xun (Zhou Shuren, b. 1881) and his two prominent younger brothers (Zhou Zuoren and Zhou Jianren), whose family also came from Shaoxing.

Shaoxing was well known for producing, during the Ming and Qing dynasties, an impressive number of government functionaries and private secretaries and clerks (*shiye*), men who were not government officials but were employed by such officials as their personal functionaries. Because of the strict law of avoidance, *shiye* did not serve as officials and subofficials in their home provinces but worked throughout China; the Shaoxing *shiye* worked in Zhili, Fujian, Jiangsu, Jiangxi, Guangdong, and other provinces.[6] In the Peking opera, the *shiye* character always has a red nose, the sign of a drunkard, and he is usually depicted as corrupt, sly, and cunning; but he is also intelligent, capable, resourceful, and flexible. Zhou Enlai's grandfather, Zhou Panlong, was a *shiye*, and with one of his older brothers, Zhou Junang (Zhou Haixiang), he went to Shanyang county in the 1870's to take up work there. Together these two Zhou brothers established an extended family system in the Fuma residential complex (see Fig. 1). In 1898, the year Zhou Enlai was born, Zhou Panlong, his grandfather, was at last promoted to the position of Shanyang county magistrate (*zhixian*), but he appears to have died soon after that, while still in his fifties.[7] It is therefore very unlikely that upon his retirement Zhou Panlong took his four sons back to Shaoxing.[8]

Zhou Enlai's father, Zhou Yineng (courtesy name Mouchen), the second son of Zhou Panlong, was born in 1877.[9] The eldest son was Zhou Yigeng (1872–1933), and there were also two younger sons, Yikui and Yigan, and a daughter (older than Zhou Yineng) named Guizhen, who married Wang Shiyu and settled in Shaoxing.[10] Zhou Yineng ranked seventh in terms of seniority among his brothers and cousins in the Zhou clan and was therefore referred to as the "Seventh Uncle" by his nephews and nieces. He seems to have had a "gentle nature," but he was overshadowed by his socially more successful brothers and cousins. Kai-yu Hsu, a leading biographer of Zhou Enlai, described him as follows:

> Since he was not strong enough to defend his lack of political ambition before his brothers, he developed a resigned and retiring personality, contenting himself with any small sinecure that could supply him with a daily ration of the celebrated Shao-hsing rice wine but spare him the pressures of life. . . . If Chou En-lai had grown up under his father's direct influence, he might not have been the En-lai of today.[11]

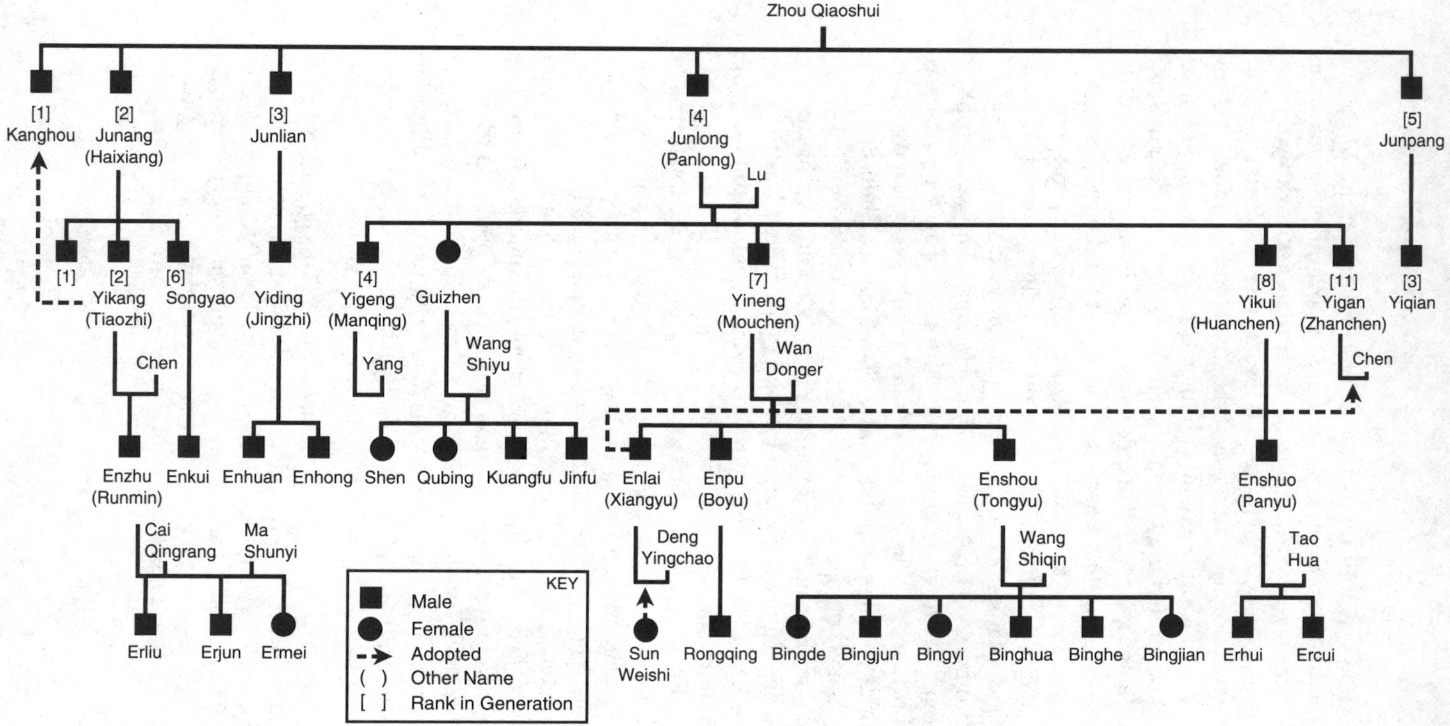

FIGURE 1. Zhou Enlai Family Tree

One of his relatives who knew him well described Zhou Yineng as a "weak, honest, and kind-hearted person," who was particularly nice and thoughtful toward his kinfolk.[12] He was well educated and intelligent, but he lacked discipline, determination, and aggressiveness, and though he passed the first level of the civil service examination, he was often unemployed and was unable to support his family.[13] He lived an uncertain and unsettled life, moving from Beijing, Shandong, and Anhui to Fengtian (Shenyang), Inner Mongolia, and, later, Sichuan. Zhou Enlai, in an extensive interview with Henry R. Lieberman of the *New York Times* at Nanjing in 1946, remembered his father as a "secretary" (*wenshu*) who was always away from home and did not earn enough money to support his family.[14] The name Yineng means literally "to bequeath ability" to posterity, and it is not unreasonable to think that Zhou inherited from his father a certain intellectual ability and gentle personality.

Zhou Enlai's natural mother, Wan Donger (lit. "the child of the winter"), was born in 1877 in Qinghe county of Huaian prefecture, about ten miles north of Shanyang. (In 1913 Qinghe was renamed Huaiyin county.) Her father, Wan Qingxuan, was also a *shiye*, who had come from Nanchang, Jiangsu province, and had served as a magistrate (*zhixian*) in several counties for more than thirty years. He was in fact a rich and prominent scholar-official in Jiangsu province and had a good knowledge of water conservancy and canal management. Zhou's maternal grandmother was a farmer's daughter (Zhou Enlai could truthfully state that he came from peasant stock), and had had little education.[15] Zhou's mother studied at her family school (academy) for five or six years. According to Kai-yu Hsu, she was "perhaps the most talented and kindest of the Wan sisters. She was well versed in classical Chinese literature, and had a disciplined hand for calligraphy and painting and fine taste for the traditional Chinese arts."[16] Ogawa Heishirō, the first postwar Japanese ambassador to China, who saw her photograph at Zhou Enlai's birthplace in 1979, describes her as having big eyes and an intelligent appearance and bearing a striking resemblance to her son.[17] Evidently she was a capable, independent-minded, and strong-willed person. As a child she was called "female chief" (*nükui*) by her older sisters and brothers. Her father often took her to social functions and exposed her to adult life.[18] Zhou

Enlai remembered her affectionately as "very beautiful, virtuous, and cheerful."[19]

The birth of Zhou Enlai brought great joy and excitement to his 21-year-old parents because he was the first male heir in the Zhou Panlong household. His parents named him Enlai (lit. "the advent of grace"; the character "en" was given to all male members of his generation in the Zhou clan). They nicknamed him Daluan, meaning "big fabulous bird," and he was called this during his infancy and early childhood. Daluan signified the arrival of a mythical and sacred bird, and it was the first of the names associated with birds that Enlai used in his self-identification. His courtesy name was Xiangyu (lit. "soaring over") and he adopted Feifei ("fly and fly") and just Fei as his pen names.

The day after Enlai was born, his maternal grandfather died in Huaiyin. Enlai's mother had been unable to go to Huaiyin and care for him because of her pregnancy and childbirth.[20] Dick Wilson suggests that her sorrow over her father's death "may have provoked her to lose interest in the boy";[21] this conjecture seems farfetched, but it is possible that she bore a sense of guilt.

Adoption and Tragedies

A number of studies say that Zhou Enlai was adopted by his "second uncle," Zhou Tiaozhi, a prominent Shanghai citizen, who had no son of his own at that time. They also say that Zhou Tiaozhi's wife, Madame Chen, was an illiterate woman with a "peppery temper" and "tyrannical manner," who imposed rigid discipline in managing her household. She was said to have given birth to a boy named Zhou Enzhu (1909–83) sometime after Enlai's adoption, but to have favored Enlai because he was the best-behaved and most intelligent child in the family. It has also been said that she hired a Western missionary to teach "new learning" to her two children at home and that Zhou Enlai developed his legendary diplomatic skills, including the tactic of frequent smiling, while dealing with this fierce "adoptive" mother.[22]

Much of this information originated from testimony by Zhou Enzhu's former wife, Ma Shunyi, who defected to Taipei before the Communist victory in Shanghai.[23] It has become clear, however, that her testimony was full of mistaken identities and factual inconsistencies. One misconception concerns Zhou Tiaozhi, who allegedly adopted Enlai and whom many referred to as Enlai's "second uncle." Zhou Tiaozhi was not one of Zhou Yineng's three brothers but was rather the second son of Zhou Junang, Zhou Enlai's great-uncle. When Zhou Tiaozhi was adopted by his father's oldest brother, he assumed the number-one status among members of his generation in the Zhou Qiaoshui clan. He passed the civil service examination in 1894, lived in Shanghai for a long time, and maintained large houses in Tianjin and Beijing. His younger brother, Zhou Songyao, passed the civil service examination in 1897. These two brothers were the most successful and influential scholar-officials in the Zhou Qiaoshui family.

Zhou Tiaozhi's only son, Enzhu (Runmin), who was born in Kaifeng, Henan province, has stated that he was ten years younger than Zhou Enlai and that they met each other for the first time at Tianjin in 1913.[24] There is no evidence that Zhou Tiaozhi and his wife formally adopted Enlai and gave him a missionary education, or that Enlai even went to Shanghai during his childhood. It is conceivable that Zhou Tiaozhi, as the number-one heir in the large Zhou Qiaoshui household, at one time planned to adopt Zhou Enlai, discussed the matter with family members, and paid keen attention to Zhou Enlai's welfare. But when his own son was born, he did not carry out this plan. The Zhou Tiaozhi family was closely associated with Enlai in Tianjin, and Madame Chen may have had some influence on Enlai's diplomatic abilities and his personable manner. Zhou Enzhu remembered that Zhou Enlai frequently stayed at the Zhou Tiaozhi house in Tianjin in the years 1913–17 and also visited Zhou Tiaozhi at Beijing in 1916 and 1917 and at Nanjing in 1920. Also, Zhou Enlai exchanged letters with both Zhou Tiaozhi and Zhou Enzhu during his stay in Europe and sought Zhou Tiaozhi's financial assistance.[25]

The correct account of Enlai's adoption is quite different, and more revealing, than what has been assumed. While he was still less than a year old, the infant Enlai was adopted by his father's youngest brother, Zhou Yigan, who was critically ill with tuberculosis. This adoption in Shanyang took place primarily because of the superstitious belief (called *chongxi*) that the arrival of a son would cure a father of illness, and secondarily because Zhou Yigan had no heir. Enlai's natural parents gave up their precious only son for the sake of an ailing younger brother. It was not a case of abandonment, as has been alleged, but rather a remarkable expression of family loyalty and brotherly love. Even though the adoption was at first merely a handing over of the infant to another room in the same Fuma household, it was, nonetheless, a sacrifice. But Zhou Yigan died within a few months, leaving his 22-year-old widow, Madame Chen (no relation to Zhou Tiaozhi's wife), who was forbidden by Confucian custom to remarry. Madame Chen dedicated herself to loving and rearing her adopted infant with the assistance of a wet nurse named Jiang Jiang. Zhou Enlai told Edgar Snow in 1936, "My aunt became my real mother when I was a baby. I did not leave her for even one day until I was ten years old—when she and my natural mother both died."[26] Enlai spent his first nine years in the affectionate, protective environment provided by the devoted young widow, and she exerted a dominant influence over him during his infancy and early childhood. In 1946 Zhou Enlai told a Chinese writer, "Even now I very much appreciate my mother's spiritual and intellectual instruction. Without her love and protection, I would not have had such educational advantages."[27]

Madame Chen was born in 1879 at Baoying, a town about 25 miles south of Shanyang along the Grand Canal. She was the youngest of three daughters of Chen Yuan, who was a distinguished scholar and a medical specialist. Chen Yuan, who had no son, gave his daughters a classical education at home. The youngest excelled in literature, Tang and Song poetry, theater, calligraphy, and painting.[28] Madame Chen's personality was quite different from that of Enlai's biological mother. She was mild mannered, introverted, reclusive, a perfectionist and a lover of learning. She imposed a strictly regulated pattern of life upon Enlai and taught him all the subjects she knew so well. Enlai's early introduction to China's best literary, theatrical, and calligraphic traditions remained a major political asset throughout his life. At the age of five he was able to recite Tang and Song poems and was thoroughly familiar with famous folklore. He said later, at Nankai Middle School, that as a child, "I loved to hear old tales all day long, but I never felt bored."[29]

Enlai's favorite old tales were *Tianyuhua* (Flowers in the Rain) and *Zaishengyuan* (The Causes of Revival). Like other Chinese children of his generation, he enjoyed reading and discussing such popular novels as *Shuihuzhuan* (Water Margin or All Men Are Brothers),

Xiyouji (The Journey to the West), *Jinghuayuan* (Flowers in the Mirror), and *Honglumeng* (Dream of the Red Chamber).[30] His folk heroes included Sun Wukong, Zhang Fei, and Yue Fei; one of his future pen names, Feifei, is consonant with Zhang Fei and Yue Fei. At Nankai Middle School in 1916 he copied one of General Yue Fei's poems, which he had seen at the Yue shrine in Shanyang. As a child he may have heard much about Shanyang's famous local authors (such as Wu Chengen of the Ming dynasty, who wrote *Xiyouji*), poets (such as Ji Zhongfu and Zhao Xia of the Tang dynasty and Zhang Wenqian of the Song dynasty), and generals (such as Guan Tianpei, a Guangdong naval commander during the Opium War). Enlai may have known that other prominent Chinese poets, such as Li Bai, Su Dongpo (one of his favorites), and Bai Juyi, visited the Shanyang area and wrote poems about its natural beauty, and that Shi Naian, the author of *Shuihuzhuan*, lived in Shanyang. Shanyang, an ancient city with a 1,600-year recorded history, was well known as a cultural, economic, and political center and as a place of great interest. It had ancient walls, pavilions, pagodas, temples, private academies. Its location at the juncture of the Grand Canal and the Huaihe River also made it an important center for transportation and commerce before the advent of railways in China. By the end of the nineteenth century, however, its economic status had begun to decline under the competition of coastal cities that were directly exposed to Western and Japanese influence.

Jiang Jiang, Enlai's wet nurse, was a woman some ten years older than Madame Chen; she was the wife of a manual laborer and had two children of her own. They were Enlai's playmates, and often Jiang Jiang took Enlai to her home in a poor, bustling market area of Shanyang. It has been suggested that this experience made it possible for Enlai, born of a feudal family, to become familiar with the day-to-day conditions of life among ordinary people. It is apparent that Enlai had a strong feeling of attachment and gratitude toward Jiang Jiang; even after becoming China's Premier, he still inquired about the welfare of her family (she died in 1942), and he recollected that "she took care of me very well and gave me a lot of knowledge. I miss her."[31]

Enlai's natural mother gave birth to two more sons, Enpu and Enshou.[32] Preoccupied with caring for Enlai's siblings, she was probably unable to express her motherly love directly to him, or perhaps was rather content to leave him to his adoptive mother's affectionate and competent rearing. Enlai may have envied his brothers, reared by his biological mother, but there was no indication of sibling rivalry; on the contrary, he was always concerned with his brothers' welfare. Jon L. Saari suggests that in China's plural mothering and extended family situations, the newborn was a member of a group that did not emphasize self-centered identity as the core element of a budding personality and that therefore "the infant internalizes a more group-oriented, group-centered world."[33] In the extended family system at the Fuma household, Enlai grew up in close daily association with three mothers—his natural mother, his adoptive mother, and his wet nurse—under the same roof. Although he had ample love, attention, and care from these three mothers, this trilateral maternal relationship, along with the aloofness of his physically distant father, created a delicate psychological milieu for the perceptive Enlai, especially since the three mothers were all such different personalities and had their own emotional demands. His wet nurse was the source of his immediate survival and his closest physical contact, but his early educational upbringing was the almost exclusive concern of his adoptive mother. His natural mother's domineering presence was inescapable in the large household.

Enlai's names for his adoptive and natural mothers seem to express his feelings: he called his adoptive mother *niang* (mother), and his natural mother *ganma* (a kind of godmother). In the interviews with Lieberman, Zhou Enlai "expressed great admiration" for the women in his early life, especially his well-educated adoptive mother.[34] He thought that his quiet and reserved personality came from his adoptive mother and his cheerful, sociable nature from his natural mother. Certainly it is likely that Madame Chen's own retiring disposition reinforced Enlai's natural shyness, gentleness, and intelligence, reminiscent of his father's.

In 1904, when Enlai was six years old, his natural mother and her brother won a substantial fortune in a lottery. His mother thereupon took her immediate family, including Enlai and his adoptive mother, to the town of Qingjiangpu, Huaiyin county, where she moved into her parents' large house. With the lottery money, she renovated the old house and subsidized the entire family for a few years. She took the family to Hankou for sightseeing and bought expensive clothing and other goods. Later in life, Zhou Enlai, remembering how his mother had squandered her fortune, was very critical of lotteries and gambling; he often told close family members that gambling served no good purpose personally or socially and that it should be avoided.[35]

Around this time Enlai was old enough to attend the Wan family school, together with his maternal cousins. He began learning *Qianziwen* (Primer of One Thousand Characters) and other Chinese literary books, and he took an interest in his maternal grandfather's large collection of old Chinese books. After one year he was sent to another family school where he received better formal training in the Confucian classics. But when the lottery money ran out and it became apparent that Zhou Yineng's meager income as a junior local bureaucrat could not support his family, Zhou Yineng moved to Hubei province hoping to earn more money. His wife was left with financial difficulties, and in the spring of 1907 she died of stomach cancer. The family was so impoverished that it could not afford an appropriate coffin and she was buried temporarily in Huaiyin.[36] (In 1933, Zhou Enlai's father moved her grave to Huaian.)

Enlai's adoptive mother was also very ill, with tuberculosis, at this time. Enlai, aged nine, went with her down the Grand Canal to Baoying, where she sought medical care from her nephew Chen Borong, who was employed in medical and social service. Chen Borong's younger brother, Chen Shizhou, twelve years older than Enlai, taught at a private family school. During the summer months spent in the Chen household in 1907, Enlai came to appreciate and respect Chen Shizhou's remarkable personality and erudition. For years after, Enlai regarded this cousin as one of his close intellectual mentors and personal confidants.[37] Madame Chen's health did not improve appreciably in Baoying, and mother and son returned to Huaiyin. One year later, in July 1908, Madame Chen died.[38] Enlai's life had been intimately linked to that of his adoptive mother, and he seems to have felt a greater sense of loss at her death than at that of his biological mother. His strong sense of emotional and intellectual indebtedness toward his adoptive mother persisted throughout his life. In 1918, on the tenth anniversary of her death, Zhou Enlai, then in Japan, wrote in his diary that he had reread her poems and essays, knelt down, and burned incense in her memory—a traditional Confucian practice.[39] He candidly revealed his lasting affection for his adoptive mother in his interviews with Edgar Snow in 1936 and Henry Lieberman in 1946.

The loss of his two mothers within such a short time severely disrupted Enlai's life. As the eldest son, he had the obligation to look after his two younger brothers, who were nine and four years old, and together they took Madame Chen's coffin to Shanyang, where she was buried in a small family graveyard. This return to Shanyang was a depressing contrast to the exuberant arrival of the Zhou family four years earlier. Now that Enlai's two mothers were gone, and with his natural father far away, and poor, in Hubei province, Enlai, at the age of ten, had to take on the heavy moral responsibility of carrying on his family's proud heritage. He was well aware of his position as the oldest male of his generation in the Zhou Panlong family. Survival amid this utter adversity was difficult.

Enlai and his brothers moved back into the Fuma house, which his father's younger brother, Zhou Yikui, managed, and Enlai resumed his elementary schooling at a private family academy located near the Eastern Gate, not far from Fuma Street. The director of the academy was Gong Yinsun, a maternal cousin of Enlai's natural mother. Gong had studied in Japan for a few years and had for a time espoused the reform measures advocated by Kang Yuwei and Liang Qichao. He then became an ardent supporter of Sun Yatsen's revolutionary movement and a member of Sun's Revolutionary Alliance (*Tongmenghui*), which was established in August 1905 at Tokyo, and made frequent trips to Shanghai, Nanjing, and other urban centers in support of the movement. Even before the Republican revolution, Gong had defiantly cut off his queue, the pigtail that was imposed by the Manchu rulers as a sign of submission. As a modernized, progressive-minded scholar, he opposed superstition, religion, and female foot binding, and he favored a program for coeducation. Enlai's schoolmates included girls—one of them was his cousin Gong Zhiru, Gong Yinsun's daughter. Gong hired another enlightened teacher named Mr. Zhou (no relation of the Zhou Enlai family), who was particularly well versed in classical calligraphy; under his close guidance Enlai perfected the calligraphic skills he had learned from his adoptive mother. Gong and Zhou taught their students both Confucian classics and Western science, and they introduced them to new social and political ideas. Gong interpreted recent events in Chinese history, such as the Opium War and the

Taiping Rebellion, from an antiforeign standpoint. China was at this time undergoing a national crisis, and this strong emphasis on nationalism and patriotism was crucial to Enlai's early education and political socialization.

Gong's mother and wife were especially supportive of Enlai, and his long days at the Gong academy were intellectually stimulating and rewarding. In a meeting with his cousin Gong Zhiru in 1952, Zhou Enlai said that her father had enlightened him politically, whereas the teacher named Zhou had enlightened him culturally.[40] He also said that although he had felt under restraint in the Zhou and Wan families, he enjoyed the atmosphere of "freedom and joy" amid the Gong family.

This comfortable and productive connection with the Gong family ended around the beginning of 1910, when Gong Yinsun and his family left Shanyang permanently and moved to Huaiyin. The Gong family academy closed its doors, and Enlai's schoolmates and cousins dispersed. In the spring of 1910, Enlai's uncle Zhou Yigeng, his father's older brother and the titular head of the Zhou Panlong family, wrote him from Fengtian (now Shenyang) inviting him to come to Manchuria. When Enlai's father's older cousin Zhou Yiqian returned from Yinzhou (now Tieling) to Shanyang for a family visit, he took Enlai to Manchuria.

Enlai, now twelve years old, left the Shanyang-Huaiyin area with mixed feelings. In spite of the series of unhappy events just a few years before, he was sad to leave the Fuma house where he was born and where he had spent most of his boyhood. And his two younger brothers were to remain in Shanyang to be cared for by others. But Enlai was eager to see the "new world" that was developing in Manchuria under the competitive influence of Japanese, Russian, and other foreign powers.

In assessing the overall life and thought of Zhou Enlai in Shanyang, Hu Hua, a prominent senior historian of the Chinese People's University (Beijing), applies a standard Marxist framework of class analysis. He argues:

> At the tender age of ten [Zhou Enlai] had frequently to run to the pawn shop with its high counter to pawn articles. When he knocked at the gates of the rich to beg for loans, he was often greeted by heartless mocking faces. The landlords and gentry who hitherto had sucked up to his family now became hostile and turned the screws. The hypocrisy and cruelty of feudal

morality and the inconsistency of human relationships in the old society made him begin to hate the heartless rich . . . he hated the dark and decadent society there, hated the feudal aristocratic families which had shown him only cruelty, hypocrisy and deceit. He was not sorry to leave them. He never returned.[41]

Hu Hua's interpretation is intended to demonstrate Enlai's precocious ideological formation and correct political orientation. It glosses over the fact that, although Enlai was bright and sensitive, he was still only a child of twelve and not intellectually sophisticated or logically coherent. If he did indeed espouse antifeudalistic views at that age, it is difficult to discern any lasting effects upon his opinions on social and political issues that emerged during his adolescence. They are certainly not evident in any of his numerous high school publications, nor are his written memories of Shanyang anything but warm, positive, and nostalgic. Moreover, he felt quite comfortable associating with the powerful and famous people in Tianjin, whose class affiliations were indeed feudalistic.

It is true that he never saw Shanyang again. But in later years, he expressed fond memories of Shanyang and Huaiyin and made many inquiries about his hometown, his family home, and the historic sites. He recognized and appreciated the people from his hometown (*tongxiang*), maintained lifelong social and personal ties with Jiangsu province, and never lost his distinct Jiangsu accent.[42] When he met with a Huaian political delegation in 1960, he spoke of how as a child he used to go in a small boat from the creek to the river gate where he would play, and of how busy and noisy it was there. He asked whether people could still use that creek to reach the river gate, and he wondered whether his old family home still had a deep well, a big fruit tree, and a high wall. "Yes, I wish I could go back there," he said. "I left Huaian when I was twelve years old; it is now 50 years ago!"[43] On one occasion in 1960 he meant to visit Huaian after attending a meeting in Shanghai, but he was obliged to cancel the trip at the last minute because he received an urgent telephone call from Mao Zedong and had to return to Beijing at once.[44]

As premier, Zhou Enlai took extraordinary steps to prevent his birthplace from becoming a popular pilgrimage center that would compete with Mao Zedong's well-publicized birthplace, Shaoshan, in Hunan province. This was part of Zhou's conscientious effort to avoid any hint of a personality cult. Unlike other leaders of the

Chinese Communist Party, he scrupulously refused to give any sort of preferential treatment to his native place, his relatives, or his childhood friends.

Scholars have offered various interpretations of the relationship between young Enlai and his natural father. One interpretation suggests that, because of rejection and "abandonment" by his biological parents during his infancy, Enlai was "consistently bitter and angry" toward his "irresponsible" father.[45] Another biographer maintains that at Chongqing and elsewhere during the war, Zhou Enlai looked upon his father as an utter nuisance because he was always asking for money.[46] The Freudian-Eriksonian psychoanalytic approach has also been drawn in, focusing on the theme of abandonment and loss in Zhou Enlai's "creative revolutionary personality."[47] This interpretation relies on what is described as a "triple abandonment," that is, Zhou's early loss of his mother, the withdrawal of his father from active participation in his upbringing, and the transfer of responsibility from one uncle to another. This "sense of abandonment" is said to have so chilled him that he developed a "deep-rooted anger" against his father and the whole adult world, which ordinarily would have been an extension of his father's personality. Moreover, according to this interpretation, because of the weak male figures represented by both his natural father and his adoptive father, Zhou is said to have suffered from ambivalence and difficulty in attaining "male identity."

Zhou Enlai certainly may have thought that his father was an ineffectual and irresponsible provider, who, by being unable to offer psychological and material security to him and his two younger brothers, failed to live up to the Confucian ideal of a powerful disciplinary father. If it is correct to assume that Mao Zedong's rebellious personality was formed in response to his highly authoritarian and repressive father, one can suggest that Zhou Enlai was constantly in search of authority figures because he was deprived of his natural mother's direct love and was neglected by his unsettled father early in his childhood.[48] His situation compelled him to strike a compromise among his conflicting conditions, to adapt himself to unpredictable human relationships, and to make himself acceptable and loved by other persons—teachers, friends, and colleagues—with whom he came into intimate contact. It may well be that a subconscious fear of loss made him hesitant to offer total loyalty or complete commitment to any one person and therefore he was always prepared to keep his choices open. It does appear that his tendencies toward compromise, conciliation, and accommodation emerged from his childhood experiences and survival instincts. Growing up in an environment of loving and kind maternal authority, Zhou Enlai may have developed a "strong sense of autonomy, initiative, and self-worth."[49] Like Gandhi, Chen Duxiu, and Hu Shih, Zhou Enlai identified himself closely with his mother(s) and showed enormous respect for women.[50] The death of his adoptive mother and the ending of direct parental love and protection compelled Zhou Enlai to be independent and resourceful.

Zhou Yineng's failure was as much attributable to the changing social and economic conditions of China as to his own personal frailties or deliberate abandonment. Enlai may have realized this, for despite his father's shortcomings, he continued to uphold the Confucian code of filial piety toward his father, and he went to Manchuria in part because his father worked there.[51] In the Confucian ethical system, the concept and practice of filial performance did not require reciprocity; rather, it was an expression of a son's unilateral and unconditional devotion to his parents. A recent study indicates that Zhou Enlai joined his father at Yinzhou (Tieling) and that they probably lived together at a house owned by a Mr. Peng.[52] In later life, on numerous occasions, Zhou Enlai communicated with his father, agreed to see him, and offered him a modest allowance for his subsistence in the 1930's.[53] In turn, his father gave Zhou Enlai love and whatever support he could in his revolutionary activities; from time to time he served as a messenger in clandestine revolutionary communications. When Zhou Yineng died in July 1942 at Hongyancun, a suburb of Chongqing, where the 18th Group Army and the Southern Bureau of the Chinese Communist Party had a military liaison office, Zhou Enlai placed an obituary in an official newspaper of the Chinese Communist Party, *Xinhua Ribao* (New China Daily News, July 15, 1942), and had him buried in a private graveyard.[54]

One advantage of the extended Confucian family system was the close-knit network of mutual support, clan solidarity, and shared responsibilities. This was essential to Enlai's survival and education amid otherwise overwhelming personal tragedies and calamities, and it does not fit with any notion of Enlai's having harbored "extreme hostility" toward his feudalistic family. On the contrary, Enlai was proud of his Confucian heritage and deeply appreciative of the love and protection he received from his uncles, aunts, and other relatives during his uncertain childhood. He made a special effort to visit his ancestral home at Shaoxing in March 1939, during his inspection tour of the New Fourth Army in Wannan, in the southern area of Anhui province.[55] Throughout his life he displayed a high degree of family loyalty—a fact that even Ma Shunyi recognized despite her biting condemnation of the Zhou family. As premier, he received and entertained a variety of family members. He reared one of his nieces (Zhou Bingjian, the youngest daughter of his brother Zhou Enshou) in his home, and he provided funds for the college education of two young nephews, Zhou Erliu (Zhou Enzhu's son), who attended Nankai University, and Zhou Erhui (Zhou Enshuo's son), who attended the Beijing Aeronautical Engineering Institute. He also took care of his great-grandfather's grave at Shaoxing. He did all this in such a way as to avoid any appearance of nepotism or favoritism, and occasionally, as he felt necessary, he was critical of some of his relatives.

On the Manchurian Frontier

The decision to have Enlai go to Manchuria was a family decision. Two of his uncles, Zhou Yigeng and Zhou Yiqian, were there, and also his father. Since Enlai was the oldest grandson and the number-one male heir in the Zhou Panlong lineage group, the family was naturally determined to raise him well and to give him the best possible education. In a way, the future glory of the clan depended upon Enlai's success or failure, and it was a common Chinese practice that an important child be educated by a successful member of his extended family.

Zhou Enlai spent the first six months in Manchuria with his uncle Zhou Yiqian in Yinzhou because he had not been admitted to an appropriate school in Fengtian, where his older uncle, Zhou Yigeng, lived. (Enlai may also have briefly lived with his father in Yinzhou.) Zhou Yiqian was a director of the Municipal Tax Bureau in Yinzhou. Enlai entered the Yingang Academy (*Yingang shuyuan*), a private school established in 1658 and very traditional in its curriculum;[56] this was the first time that Enlai had studied at anything besides a family school.

In October 1910 Enlai moved to Fengtian. He lived with his uncle

Zhou Yigeng and attended a newly founded public school called the Sixth Two-Level Primary School, meaning that it combined a four-year lower-level unit and a three-year upper-level unit. This was not a missionary school, as has sometimes been assumed, but a nonsectarian school. The two levels were housed in two different two-story wooden buildings, facing each other, and there was also an auditorium, and a sizable playground. The school was located near the Eastern Gate, not far from the old Manchu Imperial Palace. After the Republican revolution of 1911 it was renamed the Dongguan ("Eastern Pass") Model School. Zhou Enlai entered the sixth grade and finished his studies there in early 1913.

Zhou Yigeng and his wife, Madame Yang, had no children of their own, and they assumed the bulk of Enlai's living and schooling expenses in Fengtian, and also later in Tianjin. Madame Yang's family originally came from Shandong province, but she remained in Tianjin during most of the time her husband worked in Manchuria. Although it is generally accepted that Zhou Yigeng played an indispensable role in Zhou Enlai's early education and personal guidance, his exact occupation and financial situation have been subject to conflicting speculations. Some state that he was the police commissioner in Fengtian, but others suggest that he worked in the court or in the tax bureau. A number of scholars identify him as a high government official with substantial financial resources. Others call him a junior government functionary receiving a meager salary.

The recent discovery of Zhou Yigeng's bureaucratic résumé dated 1921 has clarified most of these questions. Zhou Yigeng was born at Shaoxing in 1872. In September 1908 he was appointed as a clerk (*zhengsi shuguan*) in the payroll section of the Department of Finance in Fengtian province (now Liaoning province).[57] He remained in the same section and was slowly promoted to the position of secretary (*keyuan*). In 1912, the first year of the Republic, he assumed several concurrent positions in the Appropriations Agency and the Department of Finance in Fengtian province. One can conclude that he was neither rich nor poor but belonged to the solid and stable lower middle class. Certainly he was not so poor that his wife had to become a seamstress (as has sometimes been said). His income was by no means abundant, but it was sufficient to give his nephew a good, modern education, especially because he had no other child to support. Zhou Yigeng was a much stronger person in every way than Enlai's two fathers, and he was a Confucian scholar as well as a liberal-minded government official. Enlai's direct and daily association with him made him comfortable with Confucian values and way of life, and it also made him aware of the complications of government service and financial management. This uncle may have taught Enlai the importance of economic and budgetary matters in China's governing processes.

In many ways Enlai had real problems to overcome in his new environment, physical as well as social. He had lived twelve years in the part of Jiangsu province renowned for its mild climate and gentle customs, and he had a distinctive Southern accent. In the rugged northeastern region, the winter months were windy, icy, and snowy. It was a home for many people who had come from other regions, and it was undergoing rapid political and social upheavals. Enlai stood out among his fellows because of his heavy Jiangsu accent and his unusually white face, so he was an easy object of ridicule and teasing. He recalled on one occasion that the first challenge he faced in Manchuria was that of handling the bullies in his school, who called him *xiaomanzi* (a little barbarian)—a common pejorative term for Southern boys—and beat him up almost every day. His best defense was to make friends as quickly as possible and to form a kind of "united front" against those roughnecks.[58] In the absence of protective parents, he learned to regard loyal friends as the most effective means of keeping safe, and friends became not only a source of security but also a source of happiness. His lifelong commitments to friends, regardless of political affiliations, are legendary.

In Manchuria, bitter cold continental blasts blew from Siberia and Mongolia; subzero temperatures were common. Dr. Dugald Christie, a British Presbyterian missionary at Fengtian at the time, noted that in the first two months of 1911, "We had a most exceptional amount of snow, two of the falls being over a foot, and several four or five inches. Most of the streets were often almost impassable."[59] People burned stalks of sorghum to heat up the *kangs* (the elevated sleeping place made of bricks) in their houses. All the winter months were severe:

Cold November, the wind whistling over the dreary Manchurian plain of dull, brown, hard earth, with not a blade of grass, leafless brown trees, earth-coloured houses with low earth-coloured roofs, no hills, no colour, all a dead level of monotony; only the brilliant blue arch overhead and the clear dazzling sunshine mocking the dullness and chill dreariness.[60]

To make matters worse, there was a devastating epidemic of pneumonic plague in Manchuria that winter of 1910–11, with widespread panic. Enlai and his relatives escaped infection, but they could see the public notices warning about this highly infectious disease.

In this climate, Enlai, who had been accustomed to a diet of rice and fresh vegetables, had to adjust to a new diet based on sorghum and maize. In retrospect, however, he acknowledged the benefits of his three years in Manchuria. In the interview with Lieberman in 1946 he recalled how he had "at the age of twelve" left home and gone to the Northeast. "It was a key to the transformation of my life and my thoughts," he said. "If I had not left home at that time, I might not have achieved anything at all in my life and might have faced a tragic downturn as my brothers at home did."[61] He also informed his relatives in 1964: "Going to Manchuria had two good points: first, it toughened my body. When I was in school, regardless of whether it was summer or winter, I wanted to go outside and strengthen my body, weak from studying. The other good point was eating sorghum. My living habits changed. My bones grew. My stomach toughened. It all made my body able to cope with years of struggle and intense work."[62] Zhou Enlai also mentioned this regimen and its effects in his meeting with the Liaoning University Red Guards during the Cultural Revolution in 1966. He explained that while he stayed in the Northeast during his boyhood, sorghum, severe winds, and yellow dust (loess) trained him very well.[63]

The contrast between the harsh conditions of life in Manchuria, with its regional characteristics of the strong, tough, and aggressive northern urban subculture, and the more temperate and gentle traditional southern subculture of his childhood opened Enlai's eyes to another dimension of duality or ambivalence. Although he remained proud of his southern cultural roots, he often identified himself with the peculiar historical trends and aspirations of the Northeast. Many of his close friends at Nankai Middle School came from Fengtian and Jilin provinces, and he showed a keen personal interest in leaders who came from the Northeast.

Unlike the tradition-bound Yingang Academy in Yinzhou, the Dongguan Model School in Fengtian emphasized "new knowledge" or Western learning; its curriculum included mathematics, English, history, geography, literature, and self-cultivation. Manchuria was not one of the most advanced educational centers in China, in part because many of those who came to Manchuria to seek new opportunities were not well educated, but after the old standard system of civil service examinations was abolished in 1905 and there was an increased demand for "new knowledge" throughout China, education began to improve in Manchuria. Enlightened Manchurian leaders such as Chao Er-sun, Governor-General of Fengtian, 1905–7, and Viceroy, 1911–12, gave a high priority to public educational programs, sometimes in cooperation with Western missionary organizations.

Enlai had been exposed to the elementary contents of the "new knowledge" under Gong Yinsun's tutelage in Shanyang, but it was a new intellectual challenge for him to study English and other subjects in the modern Western curriculum in a large public school. He was fortunate in having several able teachers. One of them was Gao Gewu, who taught history. Gao, from Shandong province, belonged to Sun Yat-sen's Revolutionary Party, and like Gong Yinsun he had cut his queue as a sign of anti-Manchu resistance. He introduced progressive and revolutionary ideas and books to his students, especially those published by Sun's Revolutionary Alliance (*Tongmenghui*).[64] He particularly favored the progressive literature of the noted Japanese-educated scholar Zhang Binglin (1868–1936), a Zhejiang native. Zhou Enlai later said that Zhang Binglin's writings exerted a profound influence on his patriotic and democratic ideas during his childhood.[65] The political writings that Enlai read under Gao's influence included *National Essence Journal* (*guocui xuebao*), a scholarly publication with nationalistic appeal, published in Shanghai; *The Revolutionary Army* (*gemingjun*), an extremely popular and influential tract of some 20,000 words written by Zou Rong in Japan, with an introduction by Zhang Binglin;[66] "Alarm to Arouse the Age" by Chen Tianhua, who committed suicide in Japan;[67] and *Popular Rights Journal* (*minquanbao*), edited by Dai Jitao.[68]

The Revolutionary Army was an outspoken denunciation of the Manchu regime and advocated many reforms, including the establishment of a republican form of government modeled after that of the United States, with freedom of speech, thought, and the press; it stressed China's national dignity and potential greatness. In the editorial pages of *Popular Rights Journal*, Dai Jitao sharply criticized Yuan Shikai's plan to sabotage the new republic and his *Tongmenghui* colleagues' collaboration with Yuan. Zhou Enlai said in 1946 that he began reading Dai's *Popular Rights Journal* commencing with its inaugural issue, published in Shanghai toward the end of 1911.[69] Gao discussed with his students the reasons for the failure of the revolutionary uprising led by Huang Xing at Canton on April 27, 1911, and the sacrifice of 72 revolutionary martyrs at Huanghuagang. He took his students on field trips to historical sites near Fengtian where the Russo-Japanese battles (1904–5) were fought at the cost of innocent Chinese lives.

The geography teacher, named Mao, a Manchu, introduced Enlai to the writings of Kang Youwei and Liang Qichao, whose advocacy of constitutional monarchy was in direct contradiction to the positions held by Sun Yat-sen, Zhang Binglin, Zou Rong, and Chen Tianhua. Mao was a member of the "Protect the Emperor Society" (*baohuanghui*), which was organized abroad in 1899 under the influence of Kang Youwei and Liang Qichao. Zhou Enlai recalls that whereas Zhang Binglin's works, composed in classical forms, were very difficult to understand, Liang's writings were easy to read because they were written in a modern style. Zhang was, of course, a distinguished classical scholar who staunchly defended the rigid tradition of Chinese classics and ethical codes and opposed the use of vernacular literature (*baihua*). The young Enlai was much influenced by Liang's poems, social commentaries, and political manifestos throughout the 1910's. John K. Fairbank characterized Liang as "the Chinese students' window on the world,"[70] and Liang indeed educated Zhou Enlai and his contemporaries about China's changing relations with the world.

Another teacher at Dongguan, Zhao Xiwen, apparently helped to develop Zhou's understanding of literature. According to Zhang Jingxuan, who shared a faculty apartment with Zhao at Dongguan, Zhou Enlai often came to their apartment and discussed literary subjects with Zhao.[71] Zhang remembered the young Enlai as slender, with a white face, thick eyebrows, a clear voice and a rather quiet manner. Enlai was an avid reader of a variety of extracurricular reading materials, including the revolutionary journals and tracts, and though he may not have understood the nuances of all the competing theories and arguments, he was amply exposed to the challenges and opportunities of contemporary political discourse.

Enlai's patriotic feelings were stimulated in the summer of 1911 when he and his friends visited the battlefields along the Shahe River on the southern outskirts of Fengtian. One of his classmates had invited Enlai to visit his house at Weijialou. His friend's grandfather, He Dianjia, who in his 60's taught at a private academy, took the boys to the hills where there had been fierce fighting in October 1904 during the Russo-Japanese War.[72] He Dianjia vividly described the bloody battles he had witnessed seven years earlier and pointed out battlefield relics—cannons, trenches, and bullet holes. He told them that although the Chinese government had remained neutral in that war, its innocent citizens suffered greatly at the hands of foreign soldiers. He spoke of meeting wounded villagers with tragic stories, and of seeing the damaged houses and buildings in the area. Enlai also saw the war memorial with its Russian and Japanese inscriptions. It was powerful evidence of China's national vulnerability and national humiliation, the theme of a popular song, "When Can Our Party Awake?" He Dianjia was apparently impressed by Enlai's intensely inquisitive and serious attitude and promising future, for he composed two poems for him in 1913, before Enlai left to attend school in Tianjin. The poems expressed his hope that although Liaodong (Fengtian) and Jiangbei (northern Jiangsu) were far apart, both regions would be united in the pursuit of justice and that the classmates (his grandson and Enlai) would form an alliance of close friendship.[73]

Studying China's recent history with Gao Gewu and He Dianjia, Enlai began to share the northeasterners' rising anti-Japanese sentiments. Dugald Christie observes that the Chinese in the Fengtian area were generally anti-Russian and pro-Japanese during the war, which lasted for one year and seven months, because they remembered how czarist Russia had dispatched about 150,000 troops to occupy much of Manchuria as part of the eight-nation intervention in China in 1900. However, sympathies changed rapidly after the war:

> A great nation [Russia] had been defeated, Japan was exalted and supreme, China was nothing. They [the Japanese] came not as deliverers but as victors, and treated the Chinese with contempt as a conquered people. Then with peace came crowds of the lowest and most undesirable part of the Japanese nation. The Chinese continued to suffer as before, and the disap-

pointment made their resentment the more keen. . . . Thus there grew and rankled in the popular mind an unfortunate dislike for the Japanese, and suspicion of their motives, an unwillingness to have dealings with them, which feelings are difficult to eradicate.[74]

Traveling between Fengtian and Yinzhou, Enlai himself rode the Japanese railway, a new means of transportation that symbolized Japan's expanding influence from Port Arthur to Harbin and Korea. After the Russo-Japanese War, Japan and Russia had agreed in 1907 to establish their respective spheres of influence—Russia in Outer Mongolia and Northern Manchuria, and Japan in Inner Mongolia and Southern Manchuria. In 1910 Japan had successfully annexed Korea and had accelerated its imperialistic momentum in Manchuria. In Fengtian the Japanese had their own railway station, separate from the one used by the Chinese railway. Enlai also witnessed the demonstrable presence of Japanese officials, soldiers, and merchants in the Northeast. His patriotic feelings are evident in a legendary incident that occurred at the Dongguan Model School. When the Principal Wei asked his students why they were studying, some replied that they studied to seek a good career and others said that they did so to become rich. The young Enlai declared that his study was for "the national resurrection of China."[75]

Awakened by Gong Yinsun, Gao Gewu, Zhang Binglin, Zou Rong, Chen Tianhua, and other anti-Manchu intellectuals, Enlai undoubtedly welcomed the Republican revolution of 1911–12. In Fengtian, however, the revolution progressed relatively quietly and moderately in comparison with other major cities, mainly because it was under the firm control of Viceroy Chao Er-sun and General Zhang Zuolin, who hoped to remain neutral in revolutionary conflicts and sought to maintain peace and order. Chao Er-sun headed the Peace Preservation Committee that cooperated with the revolutionaries, and Zhang Zuolin quickly arrested and summarily executed a group of local revolutionary agitators. For a few months most of China was in turmoil. In February 1912 the Emperor Hsuan-t'ung, later known as Henry Puyi and the Emperor of the Manchukuo, abdicated, and the Republic was proclaimed. When Yuan Shikai was elected Provisional President of the Republic, Zhang Zuolin, his protégé, emerged as the most powerful military commander in the Northeast.[76] In June 1912, when nearly a thousand soldiers roamed the streets and looted shops and houses in Fengtian, Zhang Zuolin ruthlessly put down this mutiny.

In spite of the political upheaval in Beijing, very little substantive change occurred among the ordinary Chinese people. The young Enlai joined the other male children in cutting their queues, thus severing a symbol of submission to the Manchu rulers, but Fengtian was the traditional seat of Manchu royalty, and many of Zhou's Manchu classmates and teachers, such as Mr. Mao, were no doubt much less enthusiastic than the liberal-minded faculty. Enlai noted that the name of his school changed and that the Dragon Flag of the Qing dynasty that had flown at the school was replaced by the new five-color flag of the Republic. The international (solar) calendar replaced the traditional lunar calendar. But his uncle kept his job in the Department of Finance, and Enlai faced no appreciable change in his daily life and educational activities. Yet it was a time of significant governmental instability and nationwide uncertainty. Enlai followed the developments of China's domestic affairs and foreign relations by discussing them with his uncle and schoolteachers and by reading a variety of publications.

Enlai's single most important accomplishment at Fengtian stemmed from his budding literary skills. Zhao Xiwen, one of his teachers at the Dongguan Model School, often praised Enlai's Chinese compositions and placed them in the exhibits of meritorious works. Of these, the earliest still surviving is an essay of some 900 characters entitled, "Some Reflections on the Occasion of the Second Anniversary of the Dongguan Model School," which Enlai wrote in October 1912, when he was fourteen.[77] The essay deals in a remarkably thoughtful fashion with Enlai's views on educational requirements and moral standards, and it gives constructive recommendations and admonitions to teachers and students alike. His advice to schoolmasters and teachers reflects a Confucian background, but it also shows a forward-thinking enthusiasm for change:

> They should voice self-criticism in order to set an example for others. They should not be superficial and extravagant to gain a favorable reception. Neither should they try to further their personal interests by throwing themselves into politics and political parties, for this will confuse their aspirations and make them perform their work perfunctorily. . . . The principle of respecting the dignity of teachers should be followed, and the habit of being arrogant and impetuous should be eliminated. Moral education,

supplemented by the very beneficial training of aesthetics, should be emphasized. Moreover, the spirits of our army, our country, and our people should be strengthened.

In an unsophisticated way, his exhortations were reminiscent of Beijing University President Cai Yuanpei's call for "education above politics . . . beyond political control" issued in the same year.[78]

Enlai's advice to his own generation was equally serious:

As to all of our schoolmates, who are we? Aren't we the citizens who will be responsible for the future of our country? What is this place? Isn't it the school that educates us to become perfect citizens? Why do we study and discuss the masters' books and various sciences? Why should we learn from our teachers' statements and illustrations, and from friends visiting our school with whom we exchange views? Isn't it for us to gain a complete education, to become great persons, and to shoulder arduous responsibilities for our country in the future? Our ability to bear such responsibilities will be based on the first several years we spend in elementary school. . . . How can we become perceptive of the minutest detail and discriminate wisely? The only way is to study, to question, and to think.

In conclusion he mentioned that the essay was written to express hope for those who were in charge of education and encouragement for his schoolmates. He implied that on this day in the following year he would look back on Dongguan Model School, especially his schoolmates. He was very pleased to learn that his teachers, including Zhao Xiwen, and fellow students praised his essay and recognized his literary competence.

In June 1913, shortly after Enlai left Fengtian for Tianjin, this essay was selected as one of the best student compositions and was displayed at the exhibition of educational materials held by the Fengtian Provincial Government. It was included as a model composition in the book entitled *The Achievements of Chinese Literature at the Fengtian Educational Exhibition*. A reviewer commented that this composition showed "sincere words and earnest wishes" and "wonderful foresight and a smooth, flowing style."[79] Another commentator wrote that unless this student's statements and recommendations were followed, one could not talk about the excellence of education, study, school, and composition. Two years later this composition was again included as a national model essay in two other books, *Chinese Achievements at Schools* and *Selections of High School Students' Achievements in Chinese*, both published in Shanghai. A comment in one of the books said, "brilliant with substance; fitting and complete."

Enlai was enormously satisfied to be recognized as an important student essayist. After his earlier unhappy times, including the teasing and the bullying, he could savor a show of public praise. He gained confidence in his own literary ability and began to recognize his potential and self-worth. It is not too much to say that this recognition was the stimulus he needed to work hard at improving his literary and journalistic skills at Nankai Middle School, and following that, during the May Fourth Movement, and in Europe. From then on, his academic and political career was intimately tied to his writing ability.

In February 1913, shortly before Enlai was graduated from the Dongguan Model School, Enlai's uncle Zhou Yigeng was transferred from Fengtian to Tianjin to become a secretary (*keyuan*) in the Office of Salt Transportation.[80] Tianjin was at that time a center of salt production along the Gulf of Bohai and it engaged in the lucrative business of selling this product to other parts of China and foreign countries, including Japan. Zhou Yigeng took Enlai with him to a small house in Tianjin, where his wife, Madame Yang, had been living for several years. One other perhaps important reason for Enlai to accompany his uncle rather than enroll in a higher school in Fengtian was that Zhou Tiaozhi, who had apparently thought of adopting Zhou Enlai, was at that time a magistrate in the Tianjin area.

Enlai's father may still have been living in the Fengtian-Yinzhou area, but for all practical purposes he had entrusted his son's upbringing and education to his successful older brother. Certainly, Enlai's uncle could hope that, given his academic promise and his status as the oldest heir in the Zhou Panlong lineage group, Enlai would study at one of China's best high schools in or near Tianjin. None of the high schools at Fengtian had yet attained national prominence.

The move meant that once again Enlai had to face the challenge of social and psychological uprootedness. During three formative years, he had grown accustomed to the northeastern region and he was not happy to leave the area and the many teachers and schoolmates whom he admired. As farewell tokens, he gave them cards with special messages neatly written in calligraphy. One that has survived reads, "Let us unite and climb up the 10,000-*li* ahead."[81] He was to return to Fengtian to see his teachers and friends several times during the next few years, and he maintained a lifelong association with the Northeast. Now, however, unlike his earlier change in locations, he had a relatively clear sense of direction for his academic and personal life, and he had developed independent judgment and personal preferences.

For a few months in Tianjin, Enlai was enrolled temporarily in a small, irregular tutorial program at a preparatory school (*Daze yingwen suanxue buxi xuexiao*), where he concentrated on English and mathematics, the two most important subjects in the entrance examinations for Westernized high schools in China. A few of the friends he made at this school joined him later at Nankai Middle School.[82] But the preparation was inadequate to get him through the entrance examinations to the Qinghua School (*Qinghua Xuexiao*) that summer. This school was a prestigious boarding school in Beijing, financed by the Boxer Indemnity Fund that President Theodore Roosevelt and the United States Congress had decided to use for educational programs in China. Qinghua students, who numbered about 500 at that time, received full government stipends, and upon graduation they were by and large admitted to colleges in the United States. After the civil service examination system was abolished in 1905, the Qinghua School administered the most competitive examinations in China, a functional equivalent to the civil service examination.[83]

For applicants in the twelve–fifteen-year age bracket, Qinghua School required examinations in Chinese, English (composition and translation), mathematics, history, science, and geography. Enlai's major academic handicap was his limited competence in English, which had been little emphasized in the Northeast because of the Japanese and Russian influence. Elsewhere, particularly in the eastern and southern coastal regions such as Jiangsu, Guangdong, Zhejiang, Fujian, and Shandong provinces, which were more under British and American influence, English was very important. Qinghua School admitted students in accordance with a provincial quota system, which was primarily determined by the proportion of the Boxer Indemnity Fund paid by each province, and therefore Enlai was required to compete against students from his ancestral province, Zhejiang, who were beneficiaries of the British and American educational influence. Many ambitious Zhejiang students attended well-established Westernized or missionary schools in Shanghai, Hangzhou, Suzhou, Nanjing, and other cities. Only about a dozen students out of 300 applicants from Zhejiang province were admitted to the Qinghua School each year. If he had been successful in his attempt to enter Qinghua, with its strong emphasis on American-style education in 1913, Zhou Enlai might have become immersed in the American educational programs at Qinghua for up to eight years, and might then have entered an American university for advanced study. If this had happened, he might well have missed altogether the opportunity to join the initial stage of the communist movement in China. He might have gone on to become a distinguished college professor or a high-level bureaucrat, as many Qinghua School graduates did, but it would have been most unlikely that he would have played such an eminent historical role in the Chinese communist movement or in the People's Republic of China. Very few of the leaders of the Chinese Communist Party were American-educated; such persons tended to be more comfortable with Chiang Kai-shek.[84] Thus Enlai's failure at Qinghua proved to be a tremendous blessing to the cause of communism in China. His case eloquently suggests that personal accidents do make a difference in the shaping of history.

Since his dream of entering a free boarding school in Beijing was shattered, Enlai settled for another boarding school also famous for "Western learning," Nankai Middle School in Tianjin. Although Nankai Middle School lacked the prestige of the Qinghua School, it was a private, nonmissionary school that ranked among the outstanding modern academic institutions in China at that time. Despite the evident misgivings of some of his uncles because of the school's "antitraditional" reputation,[85] Enlai matriculated at Nankai Middle School in 1913 after passing a rigorous three-day entrance examination in August, not long after failing the Qinghua exams. Nankai examined prospective students in arithmetic, general science, elementary English, classical Chinese literature (*guwen*), and the Four Books (*sishu*), that is, *The Analects* (*lunyu*), *Great Learning* (*daxue*), *Doctrine of the Mean* (*zhongyong*), and *Book of Mencius* (*mengzi*). This "competitive, strict, and lengthy" examination was designed to weed out candidates because there were more applicants than available spaces.[86] Again, Enlai did not do well in the English section, but this deficiency was more than compensated for by his competence in the Four Books and classical Chinese literature. Also, the fact that Nankai did not have a provincial quota system may have worked in Enlai's favor. He was ready to begin a new and exciting phase in Tianjin.

Conclusion

As his name, Daluan, suggests, Zhou Enlai, like a bird, had a high degree of residential mobility, moving from Shanyang and Huaiyin to Yinzhou, Fengtian, and Tianjin. Adoption, tragedy, uprootedness, financial fluctuations, and educational discontinuity disrupted his early childhood. But this unhappy, unstable, and uncertain period was also a strengthening. He matured precociously, learning how to overcome adversity, to survive in a crisis, and to adapt to changing circumstances. This instinct for survival, adaptation, and compromise was to serve him well in his future political activities.

Despite the Zhou clan's misfortunes, Zhou Enlai remained proud of his Confucian background and family ties, and of his early associations with Jiangsu and Zhejiang provinces. His exposure to the Confucian value system, literary tradition, and behavioral mold, and his childhood training in classics, history, and calligraphy laid a solid foundation for his educational advancement. The Confucian extended family system supported, protected, and comforted him, and provided funds for his personal well-being and intellectual development. As the oldest male heir in the Zhou Panlong household, Zhou Enlai developed a sense of his own importance and responsibility toward family members.

As he himself noted, he received contrasting personality traits from his two mothers—a cheerful and outgoing side from his natural mother and a sensitive and introverted side from his adoptive mother. This duality, coupled with a bi-regional background during his formative years, may have been responsible for his later flexibility and eclecticism; by learning how to appease both mothers and to play a subtle role of mediation between them when tensions and conflicts arose in his extended family, he acquired the ability to feel comfortable in situations with contradictory elements. One of his striking characteristics was his sense of satisfaction and genuine pleasure in solving intricate interpersonal problems and bringing about a commonality of interests and feelings.

The gentle, shy, and reserved side of Enlai's personality, as well as his intellectual curiosity and cultural awareness, may well have come from his natural father. His relationship with his father was by no means intimate or mutually supportive, but, according to Confucian prescriptions, Chinese fathers were supposed to be distant and aloof from their children. Contrary to the common view held by his major biographers, Zhou Enlai was probably more sympathetic than critical toward his father's failure to provide economic support, and he continued to practice the Confucian custom of filial piety. But his father's ineffectualness may have led Zhou Enlai to seek a strong surrogate father figure.

The turbulent changes that took place in China's national political landscape from the abortive Hundred-Day Reform movement in 1898 to the Republican revolution in 1911 do not seem to have had an adverse effect upon Zhou Enlai or his immediate family members. But even as a young boy, Zhou Enlai could hardly escape from the prevailing atmosphere of political commotion and social unrest and from the incessant debates in school and at home over China's domestic and foreign affairs. It was only natural that the children of his generation, who were subjected to the vagaries of a rapidly shifting environment, felt vulnerable and insecure and were attentive and sensitive to the unavoidable signs of China's revolutionary transformation.

Zhou Enlai appreciated and recognized his initial intellectual indebtedness to his adoptive mother, relatives (such as Gong Yinsun and Chen Shizhou), teachers (such as Gao Gewu and Zhao Xiwen), and writers (notably, Zhang Binglin). As a southern boy, he grew accustomed to the Manchurian frontier and to its modern educational programs. Compared with the vast majority of young Chinese at this time, Zhou Enlai was rather fortunate to have received a balanced training in Confucian classics and in the "new knowledge" during his childhood. This background was to help him significantly at Nankai Middle School and beyond.

CHAPTER TWO

Modern Enlightenment at Nankai Middle School

All the world's a stage,
And all the men and women merely players:
They have their exits and their entrances;
And one man in his time plays many parts,
His acts being seven ages.
—Shakespeare, *As You Like It*, ii, 7

Zhou Enlai was fifteen years old when he entered the stable and disciplined educational environment at Nankai Middle School. There were about 180 select matriculants, divided among the three freshmen classes. For the first time in his educational experience, Enlai was a board pupil, not a day pupil. He shared a room with three other boys in a one-story campus dormitory. At this time he began his 40-year association with Nankai President Zhang Boling (Chang Po-ling), a remarkable leader whose dominant personality and educational philosophy had a great influence on the intellectual and political life of many students. Here Zhou Enlai's systematic introduction to the process of modern enlightenment began.

Nankai Model

Zhang Boling's background prepared him well for his innovative tutelage at Nankai Middle School. He was born in 1876 at Tianjin, where his family, formerly of Shandong province, had been settled since the early part of the Qing dynasty. The family operated a transportation business along the Grand Canal. His father had failed the government examination but was an accomplished musician. After completing a good traditional Chinese educational program, Zhang Boling entered the Beiyang Naval School in Tianjin at the age of sixteen.[1] This was a Westernized tuition-free boarding school that was established by Li Hung-chang. It had some eminent teachers, such as Yan Fu (Yen Fu), a British-educated scholar, who translated the works of Adam Smith, Thomas Huxley, John Stuart Mill, and Herbert Spencer into Chinese.[2] The school also invited British naval officers to teach its students. China's future at that time seemed bleak, because Japan controlled Lüshun and Dalian and Germany occupied Qingdao, but under the influence of Christianity and study of the Bible, Zhang Boling's early pessimism lifted; he emphasized that his belief in Christianity was prompted by patriotic feelings.[3] In 1895, the year Zhang Boling was graduated from the Naval School, Japan destroyed the Chinese navy, and Zhang realized, with great disappointment, that the superiority of China's British-equipped naval vessels was not enough to compensate for the lack of discipline and dedication in the Chinese mercenary sailors who manned the ships. After Li Hung-chang and Ito Hirobumi signed the Treaty of Shimonoseki, in which China agreed to make huge financial and territorial concessions, including Taiwan, to Japan, Zhang Boling served as a cadet officer on the naval training ship *Tongji*.

In 1897, joint pressure by major European powers forced Japan to withdraw from the Chinese naval base Weihaiwei, on the north of the Shandong Peninsula, which Japan had occupied since 1895, but China was in turn compelled to lease the base to Great Britain. The Chinese government dispatched the *Tongji* to Weihaiwei to receive the base from Japan and then to hand it over to the British Navy the following day. Zhang Boling remembered this humiliating experience for the rest of his life:

> I took part in the transfer of Weihaiwei. I saw the flags [over Weihaiwei] change color three times in two days. I saw the Chinese Dragon Flag replace the Japanese Rising Sun; on the next day I saw the Dragon Flag replaced by the British Union Jack. Sorrow and indignation set me to thinking that this happened because our nation was weak. I arrived at the firm conviction that the only way to strengthen our nation [*ziqiang zhi dao*] depended on a new kind of education that would produce a new generation of men. And

I resolved to dedicate my own life to the task of national salvation through education.[4]

After the abortive Hundred-Day Reform movement in 1898 (the year of Zhou Enlai's birth), Zhang resigned from his naval career, fueled by a burning nationalistic commitment for modern education. One of his father's friends, Yan Xiu (Yen Hsiu; courtesy name Fansun), former Education Commissioner (*xuezheng*) of Guizhou province, invited him to the Yan Family School (Yan Guan) in Tianjin as a private tutor for Yan's five sons. As a teacher, Zhang Boling emphasized "Western learning," that is, English, mathematics, science, chemistry, and physical education. A few years later, he assumed additional teaching responsibilities at the Wang Family School (Wang Guan), set up by Wang Xiying, a member of one of the ten great families in Tianjin. Zhang taught in the morning at Yan Guan and in the afternoon at Wang Guan.

Zhang and Yan spent the months of April to August 1904 visiting Japan, attending the World Fair and observing Japanese educational facilities. They also met with Ōkuma Shigenobu, former Japanese prime minister, who was the president of Waseda University. They were most impressed by the Japanese emphasis on modern science and the use of the Confucian concept of self-cultivation (*xiushen* in Chinese or *shushin* in Japanese) to inculcate a strong sense of loyalty to the Japanese emperor. They brought scientific equipment and other educational materials back to Tianjin, and Zhang revised his teaching program along the lines of the Japanese model. This interest was in part a reflection of the conscious campaign in China during that period to emulate Japanese modernization and industrialization; the decade 1897–1907 is characterized as a "golden decade" for Chinese learning from Japan. Soon after their return from Japan, the two family schools, Yan Guan and Wang Guan, were merged to become a private middle school with four teachers and 73 students. The school was first called the Private Middle School (*sili zhongxuetang*), then, briefly (1904), the Jingye Middle School and then, in 1905, the First Private Middle School. That same year, the Qing government, under Yan Xiu's influence, abolished the civil service examination system and adopted educational regulations based on the Japanese model.

There were ten in the first class to complete the two-year senior-level program in 1906. Two years later, 33 students completed the first four-year regular program. They included Zhang Pengchun, Zhang Boling's younger brother and a future professor at Nankai University, Mei Yiqi, future president of Qinghua University and Minister of Education, and Jin Bangzheng, also a future president of Qinghua University. Meanwhile, several local notables and close friends of Yan Xiu donated land or money so that in 1908 the school could construct a set of new buildings in the area called Nankai in Tianjin; the school was then given a new name, Nankai Middle School.

In the same year Zhang Boling went on an extended visit to the United States and returned home via Europe in 1909. He was so impressed by the Phillips Academy in Andover, Massachusetts, that he shifted Nankai's educational programs from the Japanese model to the Phillips system. One of Zhang's students, Meng Chih, who attended Nankai Middle School from 1912 to 1916, explained that Zhang Boling admired the Phillips Academy "for its integrated programs which dealt with students not only in their studies, but also in their recreation and behavior, for almost twenty-four hours of the day."[5] Zhang's ideal headmaster was Endicott Peabody of Groton, a pioneer educator who in his role as parent, teacher, and confessor inspired many students.

Zhang cultivated personal and financial ties with a diverse group of high government officials, contributors, intellectuals, foreign educators, and religious leaders. One of his friends, J. Leighton Stuart, who was president of Yanjing University (1919–46) and United States ambassador to China (1946–49), lauded him as a "pioneer" in "heroic" private educational endeavors and praised "his buoyancy, vision, unfailing enthusiasm, and unstained moral integrity" and also "his tact, ingenuity, courage, and resourcefulness."[6] One of Zhang's biographers described his vitality and generosity:

> A tall northern Chinese, Chang Po-ling towered over most of his compatriots. He was fond of strenuous exercise and participated in many of the games that his students played. An eloquent and persuasive public speaker, he was a master in the art of charging simple moral truths with dynamic emotion. Always generous in spending for his schools, he nevertheless demonstrated an exemplary frugality in his personal life.[7]

John Hersey, who was born in Tianjin and whose parents, Mr. and Mrs. Roscoe M. Hersey, worked closely with Zhang Boling, recalled, "In my childhood, Dr. Zhang had been held up as one of his country's heroes, and I remembered his tall, massive figure, his dark bandit mustache, his piercing eyes."[8]

Zhang Boling in his autobiographical essay written in 1944 said, "Since the Nankai School was born out of China's national calamity, its educational objective was to reform old habits of life and to train youth for national salvation."[9] He identified the "five illnesses" (*wubing*) of the Chinese people as ignorance, weakness, poverty, disunity, and selfishness. Ignorance, influenced by conservative tendencies and educational stagnation for a thousand years, along with an emphasis on literary education, had combined to lessen both physical power and spirit, and this deterioration went along with the chronic poverty that was worsened by scientific underdevelopment, low productivity, political corruption, and economic bankruptcy. For over two thousand years the Chinese had failed to develop the ability to organize and unite themselves; they had no concept of group (*tuanti*), but rather only selfishness, which indeed was the greatest illness of the Chinese people. They pursued individual interests at the expense of public morality, and they lacked nationalistic sentiments and a strong appreciation of the state.

Zhang's program to cure the "five illnesses" was the same as the one he prescribed for his students at Nankai: physical education, scientific education, group activities, moral training, and an awareness of national salvation. Zhang urged the expanding of athletic facilities and physical training to encourage competition and the spirit of fair play and sportsmanship. Scientific education and training in modern Western science would help eradicate superstition and build up the nation: "There is no defense without science and no state without defense," he said. Zhang also urged the development of group activities such as extracurricular lectures, publications, drama, music, group sports, social organizations, and other forms of teamwork, and moral training to reform one's personality, control individualism, and emphasize patriotic commitment, nationalism, and strict discipline. Finally, he wanted young people to become aware of the need for devoting themselves to China's benefit, develop a nationalistic consciousness, engage in patriotic activities, and acquire international awareness.

Zhang adopted the two Chinese characters *gong* (public-spiritedness) and *neng* (ability) as the school's motto, and he made a systematic effort to mold his students into future national leaders who would be equipped with practical and efficient abilities and have a spirit of public-mindedness. To an extent, Zhang was a representative of the Anglo-American intellectual—moderate, pragmatic, and cosmopolitan—but he was suspicious of radicalism and political activism. His students, including Zhou Enlai, were made aware of their future role as China's saviors, and they invariably had a great deal of self-confidence. A visionary leader, Zhang combined personal integrity with total dedication. Nankai Middle School embodied his educational philosophy and his single minded quest for national salvation.

It is often said that without Yan Xiu, the Nankai system would not have been born and that without Zhang Boling, Nankai would not have been a success.[10] The symbiotic relationship forged between Yan and Zhang was crucial for Nankai's modern educational programs and outstanding national reputation. Hu Shih, who was a trustee of Nankai School and later Chiang Kai-shek's ambassador to the United States and president of Beijing University, observed:

> From the very beginning, the association and cooperation of Chang Poling and Yen Hsiu was a happy event. Mr. Yen was one of the most lovable and inspiring representatives of the best intellectual and moral tradition of old China. He was a scholar, bibliophile, poet and philosopher; a public-spirited citizen and a patriot. His faith in education, his open-mindedness to the new learnings of a new age, and his great moral prestige in the Tientsin district and in Chihli [Hopei] Province were of immense help to the youthful Chang in building up his educational enterprises.[11]

Yan's ancestors had moved from Zhejiang province to Tianjin, where they established a successful salt business. He obtained the Metropolitan Graduate (*jinshi*) degree by passing the civil service examination at the age of 23. After his first appointment as a compiler at the prestigious Hanlin Academy, he went on to hold numerous high-level provincial and central government positions in educational administration, including Commissioner of Education (*xuezheng*) in Guizhou province.[12] He established the School of Practical Learning in Guizhou and made a successful appeal to the Qing Court for a special section on economics to be instituted in the civil service examinations. He studied English, mathematics, painting, astronomy, and music.[13] He encouraged Guizhou students to go abroad. He supported the Hundred-Day Reform movement in 1898, engineered by his friends Kang Youwei and Liang Qichao. When the Dowager Empress brutally suppressed the reformers, his life was saved by his friend Yuan Shikai.

Yan was a witness to the terrible destruction and loss of life that were part of the Boxer Rebellion and the intervention of the eight-nation expeditionary forces. The experience made him determined to learn from the Japanese system of modernization. Following the Boxer Rebellion he spent fifteen months in Japan (1902–3), during which he visited a prison, courts, hospitals, newspaper publishers, museums, breweries, aquariums, telephone bureaus, and educational institutions. Yan was an avowed admirer of the Japanese educational system with its emphasis on scientific training, and his friendship with both Ōkuma Shigenobu and Matsumoto Kamejirō had considerable influence on the direction of Nankai Middle School and its many students.

Yan Xiu was Commissioner of Education in Zhili province under Governor Yuan Shikai in 1904, and then joined Zhang Zhidong, Lu Muzhai, and other reform-minded leaders in a 1905 memorial designed to abolish the archaic imperial examination system and to recruit modernized intellectuals like Yan Fu into government service.[14] In 1905 when the Qing administration set up the Ministry of Education (*xuebu*), Yan Xiu was appointed Vice Minister (*xuebu shilang*), a position that he retained until illness forced him to retire in 1910. He played a central role in establishing modern educational institutions throughout China and in expanding opportunities for Chinese students to study abroad. In cooperation with the United States he nurtured the Qinghua School programs and helped to conclude the intergovernmental educational exchange agreement with Japan. He hired several Japanese tutors to teach his own children and sent his sons to Tokyo to study in Japanese schools. In addition, he supported the activities of the YMCA, mainly because of its active involvement in educational missions. Two of his sons were baptized before 1911.[15]

After the 1911 revolution, President Yuan Shikai wanted to appoint Yan Xiu minister of finance in his first cabinet, but Yan declined this position as well as other subsequent job offers, such as that of minister of education, governor of Zhili province, and president of the National Historical Academy.[16] He felt that since he had been a high official in the Qing dynasty, he should follow the Confucian code not to serve in the succeeding government, and that instead his energy and fortune should be devoted to the development of Nankai School. For eleven months in 1913–14, Yan traveled with Yuan Shikai's three sons in Europe, going there by way of Siberia. While Yuan's sons attended school in England, Yan Xiu studied English in London and visited his anarchist friend Li Shizeng in France and traveled to Belgium, Germany, Austria, Switzerland, and the Netherlands.

Yan Xiu's home in Tianjin was about one mile from Nankai Middle School. He attended major school events and he reviewed student essays and drama programs and invited his friends as public speakers. Many of the young students at Nankai regarded Yan as a somewhat awesome figure, but he exemplified what Beijing University President Cai Yuanpei called the "noble quality" in China's moral tradition. Whereas Zhang Boling was a modernist who emphasized Western science, Christianity, and democratic values, Yan Xiu was a farsighted neotraditionalist who had the intelligence to combine his basic Confucian orientation with progressive educational programs in order to promote China's national resurgence.

Daily Life

The daily routine at Nankai Middle School was highly disciplined and was based on a strict code of moral behavior. The students—all boys according to the standard segregation of the sexes—were made aware of what was expected of them by a large mirror that hung in the entrance hall of the main building, Eastern Hall, on which a 40-character maxim was neatly inscribed in Yan Xiu's elegant classical calligraphy. All beginning students were supposed to memorize the maxim and follow its principles diligently. The maxim exhorted the students as they stood before the mirror to be sure that their face, hair, clothes, shoelaces, and buttons were clean and in good order. They were to check their posture: erect head, evenly balanced shoulders, broad chest, straight back. They should not look arrogant, violent, or lazy, but rather calm, serene, and serious. As several Nankai graduates amply testify, these admonishments had a lifelong effect upon their daily habits and self-assurance.[17] Zhou Enlai himself proudly reported in the Nankai School newspaper, *Xiaofeng* (School Wind), that an American educator, "Dr. Buttrick," admired the maxim and that "Mr. Greene" wanted to have an English translation and photograph.[18]

Nankai students were strictly forbidden to drink, smoke, gamble, marry, or attend the theater; any violations meant summary expulsion. Like Shanghai and Hong Kong, Tianjin, a major treaty port city dotted with nine foreign concessions, contained openly "sinful" enclaves that could easily attract and corrupt students. Segregated from the old Chinese section of Tianjin, the intrusive alien concessions with their modern buildings and Western entertainment facilities bustled with commerce, and were given extraterritorial privileges. There were many temptations, but the Nankai students stayed away from the off-limit areas. Meng Chih remembers: "In all my years there I never heard of any violators. In fact, we all felt proud of our responsibility to set examples for those who could not go to school—so much so that we behaved scrupulously and often self-consciously to let others see how good we were."[19] In a report in *Xiaofeng*, Zhou Enlai supported President Zhang's emphasis on stringent regulations with quotations from the Confucian classics.[20]

Every Wednesday afternoon Zhang Boling held a student and faculty assembly in the large auditorium and lectured on self-cultivation.[21] All Chinese schools at that time were mandated to offer self-cultivation (*xiushen*) courses, but instead of relying on the standard textbooks, Zhang developed his own lectures and discussions. One of Zhou Enlai's intimate friends, Wu Guozhen (K. C. Wu), who attended Nankai School from 1914 to 1917, characterized Zhang's talks as basically moralistic.[22] In addition to his sermon-like speeches on moral issues, Zhang often used the occasion to reminisce about his own experiences such as the Weihaiwei episode, to discuss a wide range of domestic and foreign issues, and to conduct question-and-answer sessions with students. He usually singled out and praised a few model students. From time to time he invited distinguished guests—Chinese statesmen, scholars, and scientists, such as Liang Qichao, Cai Yuanpei, Fan Jingsheng, Hu Shih, Wang Jingwei, Li Shizeng, and Xiong Bingsan, or foreign visi-

TABLE 1
Nankai School Students: Provincial Origins, 1917, 1919

Province	November 1917	March 1919	Province	November 1917	March 1919
Zhili	577	427	Heilongjiang	9	19
Tianjin City	346	280	Guizhou	8	11
Guangdong	58	65	Fujian	8	16
Zhejiang	55	57	Hubei	7	15
Anhui	44	64	Shanxi	6	12
Jiangsu	40	52	Hunan	3	5
Jilin	30	36	Shaanxi	2	2
Henan	24	42	Yunnan	1	3
Fengtian	22	47	Gansu	1	0
Shandong	21	45	Others	—	62
Jiangxi	13	14	TOTAL	939	1,001
Sichuan	10	7			

SOURCE: *Xiaofeng*, Nov. 29, 1916, and Mar. 25, 1919.

tors, including American YMCA secretaries and Japanese artists. American-educated Hu Shih talked about "the New State and New Literature," and W. H. Tuttle gave a lecture on "How the Chinese and Americans Can Help Each Other." Roscoe M. Hersey talked about the YMCA, and there were talks on Africa, "Tuberculosis," "The Importance of Education in China," "The Downfall of Seven Countries" (Korea, Vietnam, Poland, Burma, India, Persia, and Afghanistan), "Economics and Sociology," and "The Essence of Socialism." Some of the Americans who appeared were university professors; others were consular officials from Tianjin.

Zhang Boling's eloquent weekly speeches mesmerized Nankai students, and many remembered them for the rest of their lives. One of Zhou Enlai's classmates expressed admiration for Zhang's superb ability to grasp the psychology of young minds: his was truly an "art of charging simple moral truths with dynamic emotion."[23] In the volumes of essays written in honor of Zhang Boling, graduates invariably refer to his Wednesday lectures and the large mirror as their most vivid memories of Nankai.[24]

Nankai Middle School admitted Chinese students from all regions of China and some overseas Chinese communities as far away as San Francisco; it also had a small number of foreign students, mostly Koreans. As Table 1 shows, many students had their ancestral origins in Zhili, Guangdong, Zhejiang, Anhui, Jiangsu, Jilin, Henan, Fengtian, and Shandong provinces. Because tuition and dormitory fees were relatively high, a large number of students came from wealthy families.[25] About one-third of the students were day boys, but they were still required to buy lunch in the school dining halls. The day students were somewhat set apart in that they had two worlds—the free and gregarious life on the "democratic" and Westernized campus and the restrictive "feudalistic" life at home. Because Zhou's aunt's house in Tianjin was small and far from campus, Zhou Enlai lived in the dormitory throughout his Nankai years and apparently even during school holidays: in his unpublished essays written during his Nankai years, he lamented that he had no home to return to during vacations and said that he looked upon his school as home, and his friends as brothers.[26]

Following the Phillips Academy model, Nankai teachers were encouraged to live on campus so that they could have closer contact with students. President Zhang lived off campus, but he slept on campus a few nights a week. During his freshman year, Zhou stayed in the old dormitory, Northern Hall, which housed about 100 students. In his second year he moved into a newly built unit, Western Hall, sharing a room with three boys from Manchuria—Zhang Honggao, Chang Ceou, and, apparently, Wu Hantao.[27] Their relationship was congenial, and lasting: toward the end of the decade, Zhou Enlai relied upon Zhang Honggao's financial support in Japan, and a few years later Chang Ceou helped him while they were in England. Wu Hantao also helped Zhou Enlai financially and academically while he was in Japan.[28]

Zhou Enlai's financial status during his Nankai years is not exactly clear. Meng Chih remembers Zhou as a person wearing "fancy clothes," but Wu Guozhen says that he was neither rich nor poor.[29] Undoubtedly his uncles provided most of the funds for Zhou's schooling. His father's contribution appeared to be either nonexistent, or at best negligible. During most of Zhou's years at Nankai, his uncle Zhou Yigeng worked as a minor government official in Tianjin. He was promoted to the position of first secretary (*yideng keyuan*) in the transportation and sales section of the Tianjin Office of Salt Transportation in December 1913, and in July 1914 he also held another position as director (*juren*) of the Certification Agency. The following January he became general manager of the

Tianjin branch of a government-run bank of Jilin province.[30] These positions apparently gave him enough money to continue to bear the basic educational costs for his nephew, although there may well have been help also from Zhou's uncle Zhou Tiaozhi, who was a county magistrate in Zhili province and had a large house and a secure financial position in Tianjin.

However, Zhang Honggao, who was one of Zhou's closest Nankai classmates and roommates, describes Zhou as a poor student who had only two outfits—white and blue.[31] And when Zhou visited Chang Ceou's home in Tangshan in the winter of 1917, the Chang family made a warm cotton coat for him because he had only light clothing.[32] Other accounts say that Zhou sometimes brought vegetables and bread from his aunt's home to supplement his meager food at Nankai. In the Graduation Book of 1917, his peers noted: "Because his family was poor, his situation was so difficult that he was unable to pay tuition fees. He strove by himself amid ten thousand sufferings and a thousand difficulties. However, thanks to his various talents and capabilities, he managed to achieve much."[33]

Zhang Boling, too, assisted Zhou Enlai financially from his sophomore year on. Zhang Xilu, Zhang Boling's eldest son, who was one grade below Zhou at Nankai Middle School but was closely associated with Zhou in several extracurricular organizations, says that his father hired Zhou to cut stencils and copy school documents and teaching materials.[34] Two other contemporaries of Zhou Enlai, Duan Molan and Zheng Daoru, also seem to have had financial aid from Zhang at that time.[35]

The resident students at Nankai got up at 6:30 A.M. every day; breakfast was at 7:00. (During final examination periods, the light in the dining hall was turned on as early as 5:00 A.M. so that students could study there before breakfast.) Classes began at 8:00. All the students, both resident and day boys, ate lunch together in the dining hall, with eight boys and at least one teacher at each table as another way of promoting rapport between students and teachers. At 4:00 P.M. regular classes were over and students engaged in a host of extracurricular activities—sports, drama, music, speech, calligraphy, group meetings—for a few hours. After dinner there was homework in the rooms from 7:30 to 9:30.[36] Even after lights were turned off at ten o'clock, some zealous boys stayed in the bathrooms, where lights were kept on, for further study. Regimented student life was neither new nor unique in China's educational systems, but at Nankai it was particularly pronounced, partly because of President Zhang's navy training and also because of his conviction that Chinese needed more discipline in their life to strengthen the nation.

On Sundays Zhou Enlai went downtown with friends, visited his uncles and aunts, or spent time with the Zhang Boling and Yan Xiu families and other Nankai teachers. Zhang Xilu recalls that Zhou Enlai came to talk to Zhang Boling frequently on Sundays and stayed on to have dinner.[37] As a genuinely warm and easily accessible individual, President Zhang Boling was indeed an ideal surrogate father figure to Zhou and other favored students at Nankai; in Zhou's case, because of his absent father, this psychological bonding was, of course, especially important. One of Zhou's classmates and covaledictorians called the Nankai School a "big happy family" and a "paradise for children" where Zhang, like Endicott Peabody at Groton, was viewed as the head of the household.[38] Wu Guozhen, who was the youngest student at Nankai during Zhou's years, was tucked in by Zhang at night; at the age of 80 Wu remembered the president as the "most influential person" in his whole life.[39] Zhang Boling set himself up as a role model to be emulated by his young disciples. Meng Chih recalled that Zhang took "special pains to be our parent and coach; in the morning he washed [his] face and brushed [his] teeth with us in the common washroom, ate breakfast with us in the school dining room, took exercises with us, and coached us in hygiene and other good habits in daily living."[40] As Hu Shih pointed out, this free and democratic association between teacher and pupil in work and play was a very unusual practice that marked Zhang as one of the founders of a new philosophy of education for China.[41]

Zhang Boling's belief in the integral role of physical education in the educational process was particularly a departure for China. Zhang taught his students various exercises and outdoor sports and organized track events, gymnastics, football, bicycle riding, and basketball, and he gave lessons in whist, weight lifting, and billiards. He was active in organizing college athletic competitions and the Far Eastern Olympics, and he invited Robert Gailey and other U.S. Olympians to Nankai. His objective was to break down China's Confucian disregard for physical exercise and manual labor and to strengthen the Chinese students' physical as well as mental health. Zhou Enlai accepted this new kind of all-round education enthusiastically. According to his own report, he was proficient at high jump and group ball games; in intra-class contests his teams won basketball and volleyball championships.[42] But he won no awards in individual competition such as track, hurdles, broad jump, relays, fast walking, or discus throwing. In fact, in spite of his experience and training in Manchuria, he was not physically strong or agile. Meng Chih recalls: "He was among eight of us who trained for the five-mile run, and in the final tryout finished next to last."[43] Nonetheless, Zhou Enlai faithfully followed Zhang's model of daily physical exercise (calisthenics) throughout his youthful years. He shared his mentor's view that a healthy body was a precondition to spiritual soundness.

At Nankai, Zhou Enlai learned much about Christianity, which was one of the basic features of Zhang Boling's educational program. Zhang had been baptized in the Congregational Church in Tianjin in 1909 and since then had been actively involved in YMCA activities. He sponsored the translation and dissemination of the Bible, and in addition to inviting American YMCA secretaries and workers to lecture on religion, science, and sports to his students, he organized a branch of the YMCA at the school, with its own office in the auditorium building.[44] A few Nankai teachers were Christian converts, and some of Zhou Enlai's friends, including Zhang Xilu, Zhang Ruifeng, Zheng Daoru, and Mei Yibao, were very active in the Nankai YMCA programs. Although Nankai, unlike missionary schools, did not require its students to study the Bible or go to church but left religious study voluntary, the Christian teachers—Zhang Pengchun, Ma Qianli, and Kang Nairu—nonetheless were of some influence.

Zhou Enlai participated in this to a degree. In his essay "My Outlook on Human Dignity," published in 1916, he favorably compared Jesus Christ's "spirituality" with Confucius's "loyalty," Gautama Buddha's "universal love," and Muhammad's "ten commandments,"[45] and he participated in a Bible study group. Although it seems clear that he was not swept away by Zhang Boling's idea of using Christianity for China's salvation, he developed a degree of appreciation and sensitivity toward Christianity. It is therefore not surprising that Zhou fully cooperated with Christian friends and organizations during the May Fourth Movement. In Europe during the early 1920's he served as a special correspondent for the Catholic newspaper, *Yishibao*, published in Tianjin.

Academic Programs

By the time Zhou Enlai arrived at Nankai Middle School in 1913, its academic program had been largely established along the lines of the Phillips Academy model, which had replaced the former Meiji model, and emphasized programmatic integration of intellectual, moral, and physical development. Like Qinghua, Nankai recruited American-educated faculty, hired American teachers, including Bayard Lyon, Albert P. Ludwig, W. H. Tuttle, and Mrs. Roscoe Hersey, to teach English and sciences, and adopted English-language textbooks in almost all courses except Chinese literature and history. Meng Chih reported on the popularity of things American among Nankai students during that decade: "Our principal spoke favorably about America and Americans publicly and privately. . . . Admiration for American democracy and the American people was at its highest point among Chinese students. Our country had decided to modernize itself not in the European or Japanese styles, but in the American way. We believed American education would help us to solve our problems, personal and national."[46] Wu Guozhen adds that the American system was more popular than the British among Chinese students because in the post-1911 era they were antimonarchist.[47] Meng and Wu mention that this universal popularity of the United States at Nankai School was due in part to Sun Yat-sen's identification with Abraham Lincoln's democratic ideals. On the wall of the Nankai school library hung a large portrait of Lincoln; the opposite wall had a picture of Paul Monroe, an American educational philosopher. At Nankai Zhou Enlai himself wrote an essay in praise of Lincoln's speeches and quoted from his writings. The front page of a Tianjin student newspaper that Zhou Enlai edited during the May Fourth period quoted (not quite accurately) Lincoln's words from the Gettysburg Address as its motto.[48]

The basic Nankai curriculum consisted of seventeen subjects. English, Chinese literature, and mathematics (algebra, geometry, calculus, and trigonometry) were required of all students throughout their four-year study at Nankai. Other subjects were physics, chemistry, Chinese history, Western history, Chinese geography, Western geography, natural sciences, biology, law, accounting, music, drawing, physical education, and self-cultivation.[49] Students took examinations at least once a month in each subject, and comprehensive final examinations were held at the end of each semester.

English was of course a vital part of the curriculum and an important medium of instructions, and Zhou Enlai, like other students, took about ten hours of English lessons a week throughout his Nankai years. Zhou's severe handicap in English, as a student coming from Manchuria who had started learning English late, may have had something to do with his saying later that he did not like English—but he also disliked chemistry—but did like Chinese literature, history, and mathematics.[50] He admired those who were fluent in English or performed well in English-language dramas,[51] but he himself never obtained any award or recognition in English compositions or speaking contests, nor was he active in the English drama programs. At the time of his graduation in 1917, his peers noted that his English was not good at the beginning but that he had made steady progress through determination and hard work.[52]

In Chinese literature, however, Zhou Enlai clearly excelled. He was always grateful to his adoptive mother for his head start in Chinese literature and to his solid formal training in Fengtian. He continued to remember his literary achievements at the Dongguan School. Except for an uncertain freshman year at Nankai, he turned out to be a prominent and prolific contributor to various campus publications, writing essays, poems, short stories, and commentaries and serving as a student journalist. He edited two student publications, the newspaper, *Xiaofeng*, and the literary journal, *Jingye Review*. Even in March 1915, when he was only a sophomore, he composed one of the best Chinese essays in the entire school.

His most memorable literary performance at Nankai took place on May 6, 1916, when about 260 students of all grades participated in a three-hour contest in Chinese composition. Students were given a choice of two topics: "Sincerity Moves Things" and "Japanese Prime Minister Count Ōkuma's Thesis That the Present War in Europe is a Birth Pang of a New Civilization." Using ink and brush, Zhou Enlai composed a 100-character essay on the first topic and received the highest marks, which also boosted the overall standing of his class to highest in the school.[53] The class award, written in Yan Xiu's calligraphy, was hung on the wall of his classroom. It was quite a feat for an eighteen-year-old junior to surpass contestants from the senior class and the two postgraduate classes. At that time Nankai Middle School had an enrollment of about 1,000, as a result of Zhang's ambitious programs to expand Nankai's classes and to take over other schools in Tianjin.

Zhou Enlai's essay on "Sincerity Moves Things" states a thoughtful ecumenical philosophy:

> Nothing can be accomplished without sincerity, these are the words of Confucius. Be sincere and believe firmly, this is the principle of Jesus. No lies, no deceit, are the warnings of Buddha. Defending the true and guarding the genuine, moving people by sincerity, following the principle of the universe, and acting on the orders of reality are the common deeds of these three saints. The words and the deeds of the three saints are deeply touching because they sincerely believe in mercy. Sincerity can move things. However, this cannot come about by knowledge. It originates from inside, and is then expressed by action. This is what Confucius called mercy, Jesus and Buddha called spirit. Mercy and spirit are part of the common nature of human beings.

The essay also mentions George Washington's virtuous influence over the people, and it cites Abraham Lincoln's dictum, "You can fool some of the people all of the time, and all of the people some of the time, but you cannot fool all of the people all the time." (This was one of Zhang Boling's favorite quotations.) The essay goes on to argue that if dishonesty and cheating are eliminated and there is no desire for personal fame and gain, all people will be part of a community of great harmony, the world will be on the road to peace, and the wishes of the three saints will become reality. He regretted, however, that "everyday people calculate their own interests, do almost everything to seek gain for themselves, even by cheating. If we let things go on like this, people will be killed and states will destroy each other."

Zhou Enlai's teachers were lavish in their praise of his essay.[54] One of them commented: "The style is vigorous and the structure is compact. These are the skills that can only be found in excellent scholars. This article definitely deserves the crown." Another teacher recognized Zhou Enlai's "profound insights and lucid ideas." Zhou Enlai got rave reviews also for another essay he wrote during his junior year. In this essay, titled (presumably on an assigned subject), "Lao-tzu Emphasizes Modesty and Resignation and Huxley Emphasizes Competition, Which of the Two Is Right, Try to Discuss It," Zhou Enlai argued that even though Lao-tzu and Huxley differed in their historical perspectives and moral prescriptions, they shared a common goal: to solve the basic human problems faced during their respective times.[55] Lao-tzu lived in the violent period of "Spring and Autumn," when "Heresies filled the ears of the people, evil thinking and cunning lay in the hearts of thousands of millions of people, and courteousness and justness could not serve as a model for them. Filial piety and brotherly love could not teach them. At that time ministers murdered their kings, and sons killed their fathers." Under these conditions of anarchy, which could also apply to warlord China, Zhou Enlai argued, Lao tzu considered the teachings of Confucius ineffective and spoke against worldly things, hoping that people would awaken and understand, return to "primitive innocence," comprehend life and death, and revert back to their modest and original selves.

Huxley, Zhou argued, like Lao-tzu, "lived in an era after great wars. Life was ebbing, but courage and intelligence were growing with the ever increasing progress of science and technology." He recognized that people had given up their usual way of life, sacrificed their lives in pursuit of national honor, disregarded outmoded religious teachings, but still had to compete to share in the limited public good. Hence he taught that "life and death could be seen as a difference between strength and weakness" and that "one has to depend on oneself in order to survive." In summary, Zhou said that Europe and China continued to suffer misery because Lao-tzu's and Huxley's teachings were not put into practice. If there are any persons who can appreciate and practice Lao-tzu's and Huxley's doctrines, he declared, "I would be very happy to be in their service."

Zhou Enlai's literary achievements at Nankai sealed a lifelong personal and financial association with Yan Xiu, who reviewed the best essays in the student literary contests and had the experience to recognize literary talent and future promise. After the success of Zhou Enlai's essay "Sincerity Moves Things," Yan accepted the young student as a frequent guest in his home, called him potential material for a Chinese prime ministership, and invited him to meet the eminent scholars and statesmen who visited the Yan residence. Yan Renzeng, one of Zhou Enlai's Nankai contemporaries, who was raised by Yan Xiu, recalls that no other Nankai student was ever accorded such unusual treatment by Yan Xiu, who to most students was a rather remote figure,[56] and certainly Yan Xiu, who had seven sons and six daughters, did not lack young company. A few years later, Yan Xiu discussed with his eldest son in Tokyo the possibility of arranging a marriage between Zhou Enlai and his youngest daughter, Yan Zhian, who was three years younger than Zhou. The idea did not materialize, perhaps because she decided to remain single.[57] Others suggest that in view of his family's declining economic conditions, Zhou Enlai did not want to be dominated by the powerful Yan family.[58]

Yan Xiu's interest in his protégé was to continue, even after Zhou Enlai's communist activities were well known and it became clear that he was following a different political path from the one Yan Xiu had envisioned for him. The interest was mutual. Zhou described Yan Xiu as a "glass of clear and pure untainted water."[59] Although Zhang Boling's Westernized and scientific orientation directly influenced Zhou Enlai's educational experiences at Nankai, Zhou, because of his own Confucian background, understood and felt at home with Yan Xiu's neotraditionalist framework, as he had done with Liang Qichao's. When Yan Xiu died in March 1929, Zhou, at considerable risk because of his illegal political activities, stole into Tianjin and paid his last respects at the Yan tomb.

Closely related to Zhou Enlai's literary and journalistic activities at Nankai was his successful participation in speech contests on and off campus. Meng Chih writes: "Usually, Chou spoke in a low key, blushed when teased, and was regarded as a bashful loner. But when aroused by a discussion in the Ching Yeh [Jingye] Society, he could be quite forceful and eloquent."[60] Zhou won the fifth-highest award in the school's speech competition in October 1916 with a speech entitled "China's Present Crisis." The text was printed a month later in *Xiaofeng*.[61] It was a concise, knowledgeable, and devastating critique of China's corrupt warlord politics and of foreign imperialist powers, especially Japan.

Zhou Enlai was one of the three students who represented Nankai Middle School in the debate tournament among six Tianjin schools, and he contributed to his school's municipal championships for two years in a row. He was one of the ten speakers chosen by the Speech Club at Nankai, and he was elected its vice president in his sophomore year. Yet Wu Guozhen recalls that Zhou's "shrill voice" was a natural handicap that he was unable to overcome despite his eloquence and superior ability in composition.[62] Another rising star in the Speech Club was Ma Jun, of Hui nationality, from Jilin province; he was three years older than Zhou but two grades behind him at Nankai. Zhou was much impressed by Ma's oratorical skill and brilliant mind,[63] and their early relationship began a friendship and political alliance that continued during the May Fourth Movement, at the Tianjin prison in 1920, and during their early Communist activities until 1927, when Zhang Zuolin's troops executed Ma, who was secretary of the Chinese Communist Party's Beijing District Committee.

In addition to his literary and forensic achievements, Zhou Enlai did well in mathematics, calligraphy, and chemistry. The Tenth Graduation Book notes that his corresponding-style (*xingshu*) calligraphy was especially good and that occasionally he quickly came up with new methods of solving mathematical problems. In March 1916 he received the highest score in his class in a chemistry test. He also correctly answered 26 out of 50 questions in a calculus test in April 1916, which placed him among the top 30 out of 600 contestants.[64] On the other hand, he is not mentioned in the Nankai records as an outstanding student in history, geography, physics, biology, or music. His literary and journalistic interests prompted him to read a variety of books and periodicals during his Nankai years. He was intensely interested in recent political history—works by the early Qing nationalist scholars (Gu Yanwu and Wang Fuzhi), the late Qing reformers (Kang Youwei and Liang Qichao), the Western Han historian Sima Qiang, a Northern Song scholar named Sima Guang, and revolutionary leaders such as Zhang Binglin, Qiu Jin, and Chen Tianhua.[65] Like other Chinese students of his generation, he was an enthusiastic reader of the leading liberal journals, including *Xinqingnian* (The New Youth), *Jiayin Zazhi* (The Tiger Magazine), and *Dongfang Zazhi* (Eastern Miscellany). One of Zhou Enlai's Nankai schoolmates says that when *Qingnian Zazhi* (Youth Magazine, renamed *Xinqingnian* a year later) first appeared in 1915, many Nankai students read it because they thought it was fashionable to do so. He also mentions that Nankai School imposed no restrictions upon students' readings.

Among popular Western writings translated into Chinese, Zhou

Enlai is known to have read Jean-Jacques Rousseau's *The Social Contract*, Montesquieu's *The Spirit of the Laws*, Adam Smith's *Wealth of Nations*, Charles Darwin's *On the Origin of Species*, Herbert Spencer's *The Study of Sociology*, and Thomas H. Huxley's *Evolution and Ethics*.[66] Whether or not Zhou read all the works cited by his friends and biographers is impossible to say; some of them may have been used in his Nankai classes. His essays and reports written at Nankai clearly show his familiarity with the major works of Liang Qichao, for whom he expressed the greatest admiration and whose words he once praised as "gold and jewels."[67] He also favored some of Liang's poems.

Zhou discussed Yan Fu's translation of *Evolution and Ethics* in one of his school essays.[68] It should be noted here that the British-educated Yan Fu had taught Zhang Boling at the Beiyang Naval School and that Lu Muzhai (a Nankai trustee) had published Yan Fu's translation of *Evolution and Ethics* as *Tianyanlun* (On Evolution) in Tianjin. This work had had a pervasive intellectual influence in China, as Benjamin Schwartz points out:

> Not only did it cause a stir among Yen Fu's contemporaries in the ranks of the literati, but a whole literature of memoirs and reminiscences testifies to its resounding impact on the youth of the dawning twentieth century. As the first serious attempt since the Jesuits to present contemporary Western thought to the literati, and to demonstrate the high seriousness of this thought, it was bound to create a sensation.[69]

However, Liang Qichao pointed out that Yan's translation was rendered in extremely difficult, though elegant, classical Chinese, which made it hard for young Chinese students to fully comprehend Huxley's thesis. Zhou Enlai did seem to grasp the main thrust of Huxley's powerful arguments, and he felt that Huxley's analytical approach was helpful in understanding the dynamics of international power struggles with respect to China.

Although Zhou Enlai, like his natural father and adoptive mother, was by nature rather shy and reserved, he was at the same time warm and sensitive, and in the atmosphere of the boarding school he had the chance to cultivate deep-rooted relations with his Nankai teachers. In his Nankai publications, he frequently mentioned Ma Qianli, Kang Nairu, Shi Zizhou (or Shi Zuoxin), Meng Jinrang, Hua Wuqing, Zhang Shiling, Zhang Gaoru, Han Zhifu, and Zhang Pengchun. Shi, Meng, and Han had been in the first graduating class of Nankai's two-year program in 1906. Both Shi and Han took part in the drama programs with Zhou Enlai; Shi, of Hui nationality, was the chairman of the New Drama Club. Han and Meng served as faculty advisers for *Xiaofeng*, which Zhou worked on and edited in his senior year. In one play, Shi and Zhou were cast in roles of father and daughter. Later, in 1920, they joined the street demonstrations and they were prison inmates together for six months.[70]

Another future prison inmate was Ma Qianli (b. 1882), a 1911 graduate of Nankai Middle School.[71] Both Ma and Zhou had their ancestral homes in Zhejiang province. Ma, who was married to Zhang Boling's younger sister and was converted to Christianity in 1911 under Zhang Boling's influence, held strong anti-Confucian views and advocated women's liberation. At Nankai he taught English, mathematics, and law. He started *Xiaofeng*, founded the Speech Club and acted in school plays, and served as a judge at Zhou's speech contests. The teacher whom Zhou Enlai liked most at the personal level was his chemistry teacher, Kang Nairu. Kang was a graduate of the Zhili Higher Engineering School and apparently brilliant; he served as Zhang Boling's chief secretary and brain trust. He was not a popular teacher among the students, but he and Zhou had a friendly rapport and they worked well together. Zhou, as a student assistant to the president, worked closely with Kang's office, and they shared an interest in drama-related activities. They were like brothers.[72]

Zhou Enlai was very much indebted to Zhang Shiling (who died in early 1917) for training in literary and speech skills, and to Zhang Gaoru for assistance in refining Zhou's knowledge of classical Chinese poetry. Both Zhang Shiling and Zhang Gaoru were editorial advisers to *Xiaofeng*.[73] In response to Zhang Gaoru's inspiring poem, "Grieving Over Current Events," which said of the conspiracy of post–Yuan Shikai warlord politics, "the life of the nation is cut short by the hands of a few," Zhou composed his own poem in the five-legged classical form and published it in the fifth issue of *Jingye Review* in October 1916.[74] The poem reads:

> Whirls the Wind-and-Cloud
> The dusty continent over.
> All throughout the land
> Sinks in a hushed gloom.
> To top off the heartbreak,

Autumn is here again.
Chirp, chirp the crickets—
O, too much for the ear!

Zhou's first poem published at Nankai was called "Notes on a Spring Day"; he wrote it in the spring of his freshman year (1914) and published it with twenty other poems in the inaugural issue of *Jingye Review*, which he edited and produced the following autumn.[75] He published another of his poems, "Thoughts on Seeing Pengxian Off Home," in early 1916; this was occasioned by the departure of one of his Nankai classmates and roommates, Zhang Ruifeng, who was leaving for his home at Changchun in Jilin province on his way to Japan, supported by a government stipend.[76] The poem read in part:

There seemed a fated affinity
Though duckweed-like we met.
Nor was it accident that we
Bore the satchels both in Tianjin.
Constant in weal and woe,
We mean to drink the gall.
The first to fight for our cause,
Dare we shun responsibilities?
Promise, I pray, that some day
When task done, we go back farming,
We'll surely rent a plot of ground
And as pairing neighbors let's live.

The translator, Nancy T. Lin, notes: "These poems . . . demonstrate Chou's full mastery of the classical prosody. The noble resolve and the delicate sense of personal friendship as expressed here are traits Chou faithfully retained through the rest of his life."[77] Another commentator, Hu Hua, says that Zhou's "skilled use of words, fine prosodical qualities and bold creative style all combine to make a fine poem indeed."[78]

Organizational Activities

The high priority Zhang Boling placed on group activities and teamwork resulted in a proliferation of extracurricular organizations for students and teachers alike at Nankai. Zhou Enlai quite agreed with Zhang's conviction that Chinese youth should transcend their tradition of selfish individualism and pursue collective interests. Zhou thrived in small groups, in which he could use his organizational initiative and leadership; these experiences increased his self-confidence in organized activities and human relations, later to become major assets in his revolutionary and administrative responsibilities. One organization to which he devoted a great deal of time and energy at Nankai was the Jingye Recreational Society (*Jingye lequnhui*), which literally meant a society to "respect work (or study) and enjoy group life." A brief history of this organization, written by Zhou Enlai and Chang Ceou under the pen names Feifei and Guzhu yaren, recorded its origin, objectives, organizational framework, and leaders.[79] The authors humbly apologized for all the mistakes committed in managing the Jingye Society because of their limited ability and experience, but declared optimistically, "Our road ahead is broad like the ocean and our future is very long." They expressed their determination and courage to forge ahead and to reap benefits in the end.

During Zhou Enlai's first winter vacation at Nankai in early 1914, he and about ten Nankai "comrades" (*tongzhi*) talked about launching a new student organization to "study and support all kinds of knowledge" outside the regular classes. Although some students were skeptical, and others expressed reservations because of the practical difficulties of getting approval and soon, they finally agreed to make an attempt. As soon as the spring semester started in February 1914, Zhou approached two other classmates, Zhang Ruifeng, who was a leader of the Nankai YMCA, and Chang Ceou, and obtained their ready support. They began meeting every Wednesday and Friday to discuss specific methods for implementing their idea. On March 4, a group of 25 interested students met in a "formal" organizing session. Li Mingxun presided over the session, which included Zhou Enlai, Zhang Ruifeng, Chang Ceou, Zhang Honggao, and Wu Hantao.[80] At this meeting participants agreed to concentrate on two major areas, antiquity and speech, and they adopted the name Jingye Society—from an earlier name of the school—for the new organization. The four-member committee appointed to draft a charter included Zhou, Zhang, Chang, and Wu Jialu.

The same evening Zhou joined Zhang and Chang in drafting a charter and went to see President Zhang Boling and one of their teachers, Meng Jinrang. Although Meng was at first reluctant to endorse an additional student group, they successfully persuaded the president to approve the new organization. They also negotiated with a leader of another potentially competitive organization and obtained his commitment to disband it and to transfer its funds and books to the Jingye Society. Once this groundwork was laid, the plenary session was held on March 7 to discuss and adopt the new charter. Afterward they held a "tea and talk" celebration in a small restaurant.

The society was organized into two broad branches, Study and Management. Under Study were four departments with specific concentrations: Antiquity, subgroups Bible study and Buddhist study; Speech, subgroups propaganda and debate; Intellectual Development, subgroups poetry and military study; and Recreation, subgroups drama and music. Management included the two departments of Budget and Publication. At a meeting on March 10, the charter members elected Zhang Ruifeng as president and Chang Ceou as vice president and also elected chairmen of the various departments and several management officers. Zhou Enlai was chairman of the department of Intellectual Development. As Huai En and Wang Jingru suggest, Zhou Enlai, despite his pivotal role in the conception and organization of the new society, gracefully conceded the two top leadership positions to his friends and patiently waited for his turn to lead.[81] In his subsequent political career, Zhou Enlai continued to exhibit this ability to attribute credit and leadership positions to others and to refrain from seeking the top position.

The Jingye Society was only a campus club, not a political association, but its charter demonstrated the extreme care and precision with which Zhou Enlai and his friends handled the most crucial issues of any good voluntary organization—membership, leadership, finances, and decision-making procedures.[82] The charter consisted of ten articles and one addendum, all of which outlined in logical order the name, objectives, organizational structure, times of meetings, dues, details of membership, and procedures for amendments. The principal goal was to promote intellectual development, and they also sought to uphold morality, foster harmony among schoolmates, and supplement areas not covered in classes. Meetings were to be held once each month, and every two weeks there would be a "tea and talk" party. The first meeting was held on March 14, amid great fanfare. The auditorium was decorated with the national flag and a big placard that read, "The Inaugural Convention of the

Jingye Society." About 200 members, teachers, guests, and other students attended. The school band played, and Zhang Ruifeng delivered the opening speech, followed by Zhang Boling's congratulatory remarks. The finale of this three-hour program was a new drama called *Five O'Clock* (*wugengzhong*), which depicted "social corruption" and a certain boy's "patriotic spirit."

Under the harmonious and effective leadership of the trio, Zhang Ruifeng, Chang Ceou, and Zhou Enlai, the membership of the society grew rapidly from about 20 charter members to 285 in two years, thus embracing about one-fourth of the entire student body at Nankai.[83] It emerged as one of the three most influential student organizations on campus, together with the Self-Government Promotion Society (*zizhilixuehui*) and the YMCA. Whereas the Self-Government Promotion Society, one of the oldest campus groups, was dominated by upper-class students, the Jingye Society was especially popular among lower-class students. In the summer of 1915 Zhou Enlai was put in charge of the Children's Group (*tongzibu*), which accepted students who were under the age of fifteen. Zhou treated them like brothers and coached them in soccer, table tennis, and other sports; many young boys regarded him as their leader.

One of Zhou's most loyal followers in the Children's Group was Wu Guozhen. In 1984, Wu, then 80 years old, recalled that he was a "sincere admirer" of Zhou Enlai at Nankai and that the young Zhou was a "kind, thoughtful, and considerate person," who possessed "all the qualities of a leader."[84] In answer to the question whether Zhou exhibited any personal weaknesses, Wu maintained that he found "no fault at all" in Zhou's personality or behavior at that time. Wu vividly described his first encounter with Zhou and their special relationship during and after their Nankai years. Once, in 1914, Nankai School arranged a game of riddles called *dengmi*. In response to a riddle about "beasts running wild"—a quotation from Mencius—Zhou wrote anonymously that the "beasts" meant student athletes. Angered by this negative characterization, several student athletes asked President Zhang Boling to reveal the respondent's name, but the president insisted that the principle of anonymity should be upheld in the traditional game of riddles. However, on a campus wall poster, Zhou Enlai voluntarily identified himself as the respondent and admitted his mistakes to the student athletes, whom he called "good people." He then visited each athlete's dormitory room to offer a personal apology. When he came to see Wu Guozhen's athletic older brother, Wu Guobing, Wu Guozhen was seated at his desk, writing in his diary. Zhou looked over the diary and asked if he could publish it in the *Jingye Review*. Zhou also invited Wu to serve on the editorial board of the journal. This was the beginning of the close personal association between Zhou and Wu.

As an extension of their friendship, Zhou and Wu joined their mutual friend Li Fujing in an agreement to become sworn brothers. Li had to back out because his parents objected to such a ceremony for their only son. Wu remembered this episode: "Because Li Fujing changed his mind, Zhou and I never went through with the formal pledging ceremony. We meant to do so after we persuaded Li's parents to rid themselves of the old superstition. While we were in Beijing, Zhou took me to have our photograph taken together as a token of the bond, and later introduced me to his uncle and aunt to signify that he had opened up his family to me."[85] The pledging ceremony was to be performed in accordance with procedures described in the popular novel *Three Kingdoms*. Wu carefully preserved that picture in which he and Zhou are holding hands. Zhou, in a white gown, is seated on a garden bench and Wu is standing, wearing a hat and dark winter clothing, which Wu described as a kind of "boy scout uniform." On the back of this picture Wu recently wrote a moving poem that spoke of their promise to be sworn brothers and of the "emptiness of human life" (*rensheng wuchang*). When another old Nankai photograph of the Jingye Society was presented to him, Wu was extremely happy to recognize Zhou Enlai and himself and other members of the society. The two childhood friends sustained their "brotherhood" throughout their subsequent political contests and confrontations.[86]

Zhou Enlai's special section in the Jingye Society, the department of intellectual development, held study sessions after regular classes were over on Mondays, Wednesdays, Thursdays, and Fridays. The military study group, also under Zhou's chairmanship, organized discussions and speeches on China's national defense and invited specialists to talk about aspects of military technology, such as naval vessels, artillery, and logistics.[87] On one occasion Zhou and his friends arranged a guided tour of an American naval ship that was docked at the Tianjin harbor. The Jingye Society also had an ambitious library project that included holdings of several hundred books and other reading materials contributed by its members. The collection was kept in the Jingye Society office and four students took turns as librarians in charge.[88] The collection contained some of the most liberal journals published in China, such as *Xinqingnian*.

Like other student organizations at Nankai, the Jingye Society sponsored picnics, special excursions, and field trips to broaden its members' appreciation of the real world. On such occasions they wore military uniforms, sang school songs, and marched with the student band. One of Zhou's articles in *Xiaofeng* described his experiences while serving as general commander of the Children's Group that visited experimental farms, botanical gardens, a fishery school, and experimental industrial plants.[89] Zhou Enlai also reported on visits cosponsored by the Jingye Society and other student organizations of prominent persons such as Beijing University President Cai Yuanpei, Beijing University Professors Li Shizeng and Hu Shih, and Wu Yuzhang, a Japanese-trained educator and member of the Revolutionary Alliance.[90] While Zhou served as chairman of the department of antiquity for the first eight months of 1915, it was part of his duty to supervise the Bible study group and the Buddhist study group; he probably attended both groups regularly and gave much thought to religious issues. (When he went to Japan in 1917, he confessed his belief in the Buddhist doctrine of human emptiness.)[91] In September 1915 Zhou was elected vice president of the society, and in December he became president.

Zhou's particular interest, however, was editing and publishing the *Jingye Review*, a semiannual journal. The first issue, of about 200 pages, appeared in October 1914 and sold at two jiao per copy. It was in so much demand that 1,200 copies were printed of the third issue one year later. The fourth issue, in April 1916, was about 50 percent larger than earlier issues. The sixth, and last, issue, was published in June 1917 during Zhou's senior year. After Zhou was graduated, the journal became defunct, presumably because its founder and publisher-editor, as well as contributor, could not be replaced. Poems, essays, short stories, reminiscences, notes, and drama critiques by Zhou under the pen name Feifei or Fei appeared in all six issues, and Zhou also wrote a column of miscellaneous articles for the fourth, fifth, and sixth issues.[92] He devoted much of his spare time at Nankai to this publication, which always appeared on the announced date and was meticulously edited.

The school's weekly newspaper, *Xiaofeng*, was not Zhou's private domain.[93] He worked his way up, from reporting and administrative duties, to chief of the literary and cultural department (January 1916), and then the news department, which covered school events and group activities and also published communications, announcements, and English-language notices. After winning the top award in the Chinese literary contest, Zhou was made editorial chief and general manager of *Xiaofeng* for the first half of his senior year. It was one of the most coveted positions among Nankai students, and, as usual, he carried out his responsibilities with utmost seriousness and the careful attention of a perfectionist. In May and June 1917, just before Zhou's graduation, *Xiaofeng* published, in six consecutive issues, Zhou's five-part report entitled "Views on This Newspaper's Responsibilities."[94]

Zhou's interest in drama at Nankai was no doubt inspired by the very active group of teachers and students, led by Yan Xiu and Zhang Boling, who promoted "new drama" (*xinju*), a Westernized popular dramatic movement begun by Chinese students in Tokyo in 1907.[95] Both Yan Xiu and Zhang Boling looked upon this movement as a useful educational group activity that would arouse student patriotic and social consciousness and expose a large audience, both on and off campus, to the new message of social responsibility. Yan Xiu enthusiastically read scripts, attended rehearsals, and signed letters of invitation to guests.[96] In 1909, Zhang Boling conceived, wrote, and directed a play on campus, and even acted a principal role, along with Yan Xiu's two sons and a teacher (Shi Zizhou). The new drama programs enjoyed rising popularity in Tianjin where a famous actor named Wang Xiaoyi set up a Drama Reform Company. All this drama activity attracted Zhou's attention during his first year at Nankai, particularly a popular play entitled *New Boys* that depicted two good, courageous, and helpful boys, and at the beginning of his sophomore year, in November 1914, Zhou joined the New Drama Club headed by Shi Zizhou. During the next three years he was involved in about ten different plays, sometimes as an actor, usually taking a female role, sometimes as a set designer—a section he came to head—and occasionally as director.[97]

Zhou's most highly acclaimed role at Nankai was that of the

heroine, Sun Huijuan (lit. "clever and beautiful"), in the play *One Dollar* (*Yiyuanqian*),[98] which was presented during the celebration of Nankai's eleventh anniversary in October 1915. Zhou was especially suited for the role because of his unusually fair skin (he was sometimes teased as *xiaobailian*, gigolo: lit. "little white face") and his slender body and clear voice.[99] *One Dollar* was a modern adaptation, in seven acts, of a traditional theme. There were 26 in the cast. The play is melodramatic but has moralistic intentions. In the play, a rich man, Sun Shefu (played by Shi Zizhou), arranges an engagement between his little daughter, Sun Huijuan, and the young son, Zhao An (played by Li Fujing), of another rich family and agrees to pay a dowry of 100 yuan. Ten years later, when the Zhao family is impoverished, Sun Shefu refuses to help and breaks the engagement by giving Zhao An one yuan. Heartbroken by her father's unjust and greedy action, Huijuan, in consultation with her mother, writes Zhao An a letter in which she reaffirms her determination to honor the engagement and dowry. Soon thereafter, Zhao An's older brother, who has been away making a large fortune in business ventures, returns to save his family. Now the situation is reversed, because the Sun family is suffering financial difficulties. Answering Huijuan's plea, Zhao An gracefully comes to the rescue of the Sun family. Sun Shefu repents his misdeeds and praises his daughter's purity and wisdom, and Huijuan and Zhao An are happily married. Other members of the cast of *One Dollar* included two of Zhou's teachers, Ma Qianli and Kang Nairu, and his friends Wu Guozhen, Zhang Ruifeng, and Mei Yilin.

The moralistic message to uphold the virtues of justice (*yi*), loyalty (*ren*), and true love appealed to the audience, and two additional performances had to be added to the originally planned three. At all the performances the audience numbered over one thousand.[100] The play was in fact so successful that the school took the cast to Beijing for another performance at the Beijing Youth Center, which was attended by Mei Lanfang, a famous female impersonator in Peking Opera.[101] *One Dollar* remained as an important segment of Nankai's new drama repertoire for many years to come; the English Literature Club performed a translated version in 1916 on campus.

The Nankai Graduation Book took note of Zhou Enlai's dramatic ability: "He distinguished himself in the new drama; he disguised himself, wore cosmetics, and surprised the audience. All those in Tianjin who have attended Nankai's new drama performances have heard of him. He also made a contribution by assisting with the direction and set design for the New Drama Club." One Nankai student, Zhang Lunyuan, who saw *One Dollar* at that time, remembers being fascinated by the actors and by the colorful set design, so different from that of classical Chinese drama.[102] Zhang Lunyuan also recalls that Zhang Boling used to say that Nankai students should not limit their productions to campus but must take them to the world stage. In fact, the president was proud of Zhou Enlai's excellent dramatic performances, and some of his schoolmates, who later disagreed with him politically, made favorable comments on his memorable appearances. Mei Yibao, for example, who attended Nankai between 1914 and 1915 and later became president of Yanjing University, says, "I might not have heard of Zhou Enlai at all, except for the fact that he played a female role in a performance of the play *One Dollar*. That fact immediately made him a popular figure in the school."[103]

When Zhang Boling's younger brother, Zhang Pengchun, returned to Nankai from Clark University in 1916, Zhou Enlai assisted him in directing both Chinese and Western plays, and he also audited Zhang's classes.[104] Obviously influenced by Zhang Pengchun's introduction of realism from the Western theater, Zhou, in a report in *Xiaofeng*, used the English term "realism" in alerting his fellow students to what they could expect to see in Nankai's future dramatic programs.[105] Soon thereafter Zhang directed a Western play called *Wake Up*, which he had written in the United States. It served as a prelude to the many Western plays, including Ibsen's *A Doll's House* and *An Enemy of the People*, Galsworthy's *Strife*, and Wilde's *Lady Windermere's Fan*, that Zhang Pengchun presented at Nankai. In *Xinqingnian*, Hu Shih, an old friend of Zhang Pengchun, commented that Nankai's new drama presentations such as *One Dollar*, which had evolved over seven or eight years, could be considered the most outstanding performances in China's present world of new drama.[106]

Zhou's article on the new drama activities at Nankai showed an acquaintance with a broad span of Western drama. He quoted Shakespeare's "All the world's a stage, / And all the men and women merely players,"[107] and used such English terms as tragedy, comedy, opera, pathetic drama, musical comedy, comic opera, farce, melodrama, classicism, romanticism, and realism. He gave brief introductions to many Western playwrights and poets, from Aeschylus and Euripides to Corneille, Racine, Molière, Maffei, Alfieri, Shakespeare, Cervantes, Calderón, Lessing, Goethe, and Schiller. After reviewing the two major contemporary trends, idealism and realism, in the development of Western plays, Zhou argued that Nankai should not automatically accept all types of Western trends but rather should adopt a selective approach—*qushe quliu* (lit. "to accept some and reject some"). This moderate and eclectic view was typical of his philosophy and temperament and it became a hallmark of his political career, but it was at the time a significant departure from his earlier concentration on classical Chinese drama. He was always curious about new ideas and the unknown world, but he was extremely cautious in embracing them as his own. Just how well the young Zhou read, or understood, the works of the Western dramatists he discussed is a question, but at least his writings, along with his new association with Zhang Pengchun, indicate a willingness to move beyond his comfortable competence in Chinese classics and traditional poetry into a wider exploration of world drama, both old and new.

The patterns of Zhou Enlai's organizational and personal networks at Nankai suggest an ambivalent regional identity and loyalty. He was proud of the location of his ancestral home, Shaoxing county in Zhejiang province, which had over the centuries produced many illustrious persons. He felt a personal affinity toward those who shared the same regional origin, such as Yan Xiu, Cai Yuanpei, and Ma Qianli. At Nankai he belonged to the Association of Jiangsu and Zhejiang provinces (*jiangzhe tongxuehui*), which was organized in May 1916 with 71 participants; he was elected vice president at the time of its inauguration and president in March 1917.[108] The association held tea parties, exchanged news and information, published a directory, and organized picnics and other social events. Zhou continued to pay keen attention to the Huaian-Huaiyin area of Jiangsu province, where he was born and raised. He wrote an essay about Huaiyin in the *Jingye Review*, and his column in the same journal introduced the poems that appeared in the magazine *Student*, published by the Huaian Middle School.[109] Yet, as Meng Chih remembers, although Zhou Enlai had a distinct southern accent, he preferred to be associated with students from Manchuria.[110] Almost all his closest schoolmates—Zhang Ruifeng, Chang Ceou, Zhang Honggao, Wang Pushan, Ma Jun, and Wu Hantao—came from that region. Zhou was able to strike a reasonable balance between southern gentility, sensitivity, and flexibility and northern toughness, patience, and courage.

Political Orientations

At Nankai Middle School Zhou Enlai, for the most part, did not participate actively in politics during China's turbulent years (1913–17), especially not as they had to do with the First World War and China's ongoing internal power struggles. Both Yan Xiu and Zhang Boling maintained personal associations with China's top-level leaders in Tianjin and also in Beijing, and they discouraged Nankai students from demonstrating against national and local political establishments. The only major political campaign in which Zhou Enlai played a conspicuous role was a mass rally held in Tianjin's Hebei Park (now Zhongshan Park) on June 6, 1915, to protest China's submission to a portion of the recent Twenty-One Demands that Japan had made on China and to raise "national salvation funds" to help strengthen China's national power against foreign imperialists. Zhou was one of 22 Nankai students who spoke at the rally with President Zhang Boling's explicit blessing.

In his speech, Zhou argued that a fundamental cause of China's declining international status was its financial weakness, which kept it from developing industries and building up a defense and expanding its military power.[111] He warned that if China relied upon foreign loans as a way of solving its economic difficulties, it might lose its sovereignty, in the same way that Poland and Egypt had lost theirs. He urged every Chinese citizen to contribute one yuan to this national salvation fund so that a total of 400 million yuan could be raised. He refrained from criticizing President Yuan Shikai specifically. Soon thereafter, Zhou prepared a propaganda handbill in which he proposed that Chinese citizens set aside one-tenth of their income for national economic development. He also joined his Nankai friends in visiting Jinan City in Shandong province to see how much headway Japanese military forces had made in that area and how Chinese officials had responded to the military situation.[112]

When Yuan Shikai, a friend of Yan Xiu and Zhang Boling and a trustee of Nankai Middle School, died in June 1916, Zhou Enlai respectfully reported his death in *Xiaofeng* and noted that Nankai Middle School lowered the flag to half-mast in his memory.[113] The same issue of the newspaper reported that the school had a two-day vacation to celebrate the inauguration of the new president, Li Yuanhong, another longtime associate of Yan Xiu. Zhou did not say anything about Yuan's complicated relationship with Japan. Like many of his contemporaries, Zhou Enlai had mixed feelings about Japan—a nationalistic resentment of its imperialist policy and an envy of its modernized education, economic development, and military power. But Zhou's strong anti-Japanese sentiment was largely the result of firsthand experiences during his three years in Manchuria, where Japanese military and economic influence was inescapable. One of Zhou's Nankai schoolmates vividly recalls that Zhou "reacted emotionally against the Japanese as the worst of all the foreign powers that threatened our nation's existence."[114] Tianjin, too, however, was noticeably under the influence of Japanese imperialism; it had a sprawling Japanese concession area, with extraterritoriality rights, expanding trade, and military and consular establishments. Supported by its growing international status, the Japanese concession was the most active and conspicuous among all foreign-dominated sections of Tianjin. Between 1913 and 1917, the number of Japanese residents in Tianjin increased from 2,832 to 3,533.[115] In 1916 Japan shared 32.5 percent of Tianjin's total foreign trade, and 45.3 percent of all foreign ships entering Tianjin were Japanese. The Japanese army barracks were near the Nankai School compound, and Japanese soldiers watched Nankai students display anti-Japanese placards during athletic events. Even though Zhang Boling invited Japanese consuls-general (such as Yoshida Shigeru) to campus and used Japanese scientific equipment in laboratories and classes, Nankai's anti-Japanese position was unmistakably evident in its curriculum, history textbooks, and school songs. It was no accident that the Nankai complex was the first target of Japanese bombing attacks in Tianjin at the start of the Second Sino-Japanese War (1937–45).

In a Chinese composition written in the winter of 1915, Zhou Enlai lamented that just as England, France, and Russia had insulted the Chinese, "the Japanese people, too, insulted us" (*riren lingwo*) during the "War of Shimonoseki" (the First Sino-Japanese War). He warned against the dangers of Japanese aggression.[116] In a speech contest at the school in October 1916, Zhou discussed "China's Present Crisis" and pointed out that even if Japan was a small country and was not yet strong enough, it would eventually pose a grave threat to China.[117]

On the other hand, Zhou was persuaded by Yan Xiu and his reform-minded friends, such as Liang Qichao, Cai Yuanpei, Xiong Bingsan, Fan Jingsheng, and Lu Muzhai, that China had much to learn from Japan. Among all the talks given by distinguished guests invited to Nankai, Zhou Enlai seemed particularly struck by a speech by Xiong, the Japanese-educated former prime minister, who praised the Japanese people for their "vibrant spirit" and "self-governing ability."[118] In *Xiaofeng*, Zhou himself compared Japan favorably with England, the United States, and Germany in terms of standard of living and argued that the progress or decline of a country's civilization was closely related to this crucial economic indicator.[119] Although he acknowledged the pitifully low standard of living among those who had "lost" their countries—Koreans, Vietnamese, Indians, and Egyptians—he deplored the Chinese situation in which after 40 years of open-door policy, the majority of the people in China were no better off than those whose countries had been colonized. In contrast, he appreciated the Japanese people's "diligence, frugality, simplicity, and sincerity" (*qinjian pushi*) and their national "wealth and power" (*fuqiang*).

In his essays and speeches at Nankai Middle School, Zhou Enlai painted a relatively gloomy and pessimistic picture of the changing international situation. In an essay entitled, "My Outlook on Human Dignity," published in the fifth number of *Jingye Review* in October 1916, he spoke of the war in Europe:

> The war in Europe is intense, countries are hostile to each other, hundreds of thousands of people are being killed, countless resources are being expended, but all these events are taking place to gratify the desires of a few emperors. Human habitations are destroyed with shellfire, huge ships are demolished by the hit of a torpedo. At the center of the world is a hail of bullets. Workers stop their labors, businessmen cease running enterprises, scholars discontinue writing, and farmers abandon agriculture. People sacrifice their precious lives in order to kill each other. Is this in accordance with the creeds of religions, or the teachings of the saints? Do these people

have a clear conscience? If human dignity is lost, there is no way to talk about general principles.[120]

Zhou recognized the adverse effects of the First World War on China's declining international position, but he directed his harshest criticism against China itself, with its power struggles, bureaucratic corruption, "social darkness" (*shehui heian*), educational stagnation, moral decay, and rampant extravagance. In an article in *Xiaofeng* in 1916, during the height of the war in Europe, he wrote:

Though we want to keep pace with the major powers of the world, our society is backward, the living standard is low, the whole nation is ignorant and stubborn, just as in a nightmare. These are extravagances. Treasures are hidden, goods are abandoned, all the essential elements of the country are seized by foreigners. Poor people are homeless, desolation is seen everywhere, and the situation is deteriorating. Still, the amount of money wasted in our country is much greater than that of those civilized countries. If this is not extravagance, then there is no extravagance in this world.[121]

"Is everything all right in China?" he asked. His answer was emphatically negative; conflicts among high-ranking officials were endless, parliamentary delegates merely sought high salaries, and military commanders thought only of their own interests. "Our citizens' morality has degenerated to a very low point," he said; "education is not reformed, industry and commerce are not developed, the farmland and the forest are not cultivated." "China is now in a more dangerous and difficult situation than ever before," he concluded; and once again the only remedy lay in the rejuvenation of the nationalist spirit and national power in China.

In his final year at Nankai, Zhou paid increasing attention to the issues of democratic principles and egalitarian values. He believed that the Chinese lacked the "spirit of democracy," and in an article in May 1917 he said, "Without eliminating classes, there is no hope for equality; without popular unity, there is no rationale for patriotism":

In order to love the country, all people must unite and allow neither territorial division, nor class differentiation. Orphans and widows should be viewed sympathetically, poor and sick people should be rescued, superior people should be encouraged, and inferior people should be educated. Uniting all people can make a good society, and nurturing a good society can create a strong country.[122]

Earlier in his writings at Nankai, Zhou seldom referred specifically to such concepts as "class" (*jieji*) and "equality" (*pingdeng*). Certainly there is no indication that he espoused anything even remotely resembling Marxist class analysis at this time. His political vocabulary seemed still to be derived from the popular notions of patriotism and nationalism as preached by Zhang Boling, and from a classic Western framework of democratic ideals as advanced by Rousseau, Montesquieu, and Abraham Lincoln. And his Nankai education reinforced his moderate, patriotic, and generally liberal orientation toward domestic politics and foreign affairs.

Conclusion

The four years 1913–17 that Zhou Enlai spent at Nankai Middle School perhaps constituted the best time in his complicated and uprooted childhood. After his earlier experiences in Jiangsu province and Manchuria, he found a peaceful, stable, and satisfactory pattern of life and study in Nankai's well-structured and highly disciplined "big family." It was a warm, cooperative, and protective environment and there was a strong sense of camaraderie and community among his friends and teachers. Like other Nankai graduates, he acquired a broad range of knowledge and ability from Nankai's Westernized, innovative, and advanced academic programs. In this setting he was able to harmonize the dualistic nature of his personality traits and regional orientations and achieve personal growth and intellectual enlightenment.

At Nankai he respected and emulated President Zhang Boling as a surrogate father figure. For the first time he was closely identified with a dynamic mentor who combined Western learning with constructive nationalism, and cultural sophistication with assertive leadership. Zhang Boling's influence and inspiration were indeed enormous and ubiquitous at Nankai. From Zhang Boling Zhou Enlai learned the importance of moral integrity, public-mindedness, and nationalist commitments as a foundation for China's resurgence. In his future career Zhou Enlai attempted to follow Zhang Boling's principles of *gong*—the commitment to sacrifice oneself for public interests—and *neng*—the ability to fulfill this commitment. Zhou Enlai also appreciated Zhang Boling's pragmatism, frugality, and flexibility. At the same time, he found a perfect model of the

Confucian gentleman and scholar-official in the personality and behavior of Yan Xiu. As a person thoroughly trained in the Confucian cultural milieu, Zhou Enlai greatly appreciated and admired Yan Xiu. His lifelong associations with Yan Xiu and Zhang Boling were a direct product of his Nankai years.

In addition to his substantive modern education at Nankai, Zhou Enlai developed an interest in a number of extracurricular programs. His extraordinary performances in the literary, journalistic, organizational, and dramatic fields gave him a renewed sense of confidence in his own ability; these activities were a healthy extension of his learning from his adoptive mother and his other teachers in Jiangsu province and Manchuria. He now reaffirmed his superior skill in Chinese composition and editorial work, abilities first demonstrated at the Dongguan School in Fengtian. As a result of his participation in Nankai's dramatic and debating activities, he discovered an effective way to overcome aspects of his introverted passivity and to influence and inspire other people. Even though he was not inclined to seek a high profile in his personal and school activities, he apparently enjoyed the outpouring of applause and praise accorded him by his audience. And his experience and leadership in student organizations were a good training ground for his future political and governing responsibilities.

During the Nankai years Zhou Enlai continued to cultivate close relations with his friends. His modesty and charm easily disarmed his potential rivals and gained the confidence of his friends, whom he relied on for emotional strength and mutual help. He did not seek to exploit his friendships for personal gain or political purposes, and his friends returned his graciousness and loyalty wholeheartedly. This pattern of friendship was to be demonstrated during his difficult times in Japan and Europe and later during his revolutionary struggles, and even when he became premier of the People's Republic of China. In spite of his busy schedule, Zhou Enlai often entertained his Nankai friends in Beijing, sought them out during his local trips, consoled them when they were ill, and attended their funeral ceremonies when they died. But there is no evidence to indicate that he used his official position to offer preferential treatment to his old personal friends.

Nankai Middle School provided Zhou Enlai with an emotional and intellectual basis for his growth and resiliency. When he declared simply, "I love Nankai," in 1957, he expressed his genuine appreciation of the lasting benefits and influence he received from Nankai Middle School. Zhou Enlai's four-year education at Nankai ended in June 1917 at the tenth commencement exercise. After the Alumni Association held a welcoming ceremony and banquet, the graduates entered the auditorium and sat in the middle seats. Female and male guests were seated separately on the left and right sides, in accord with the Confucian custom of segregation by gender. All other students filled the back seats. The distinguished guests on the front podium included Xu Shichang (Nankai trustee and future President of the Republic), and the two commencement speakers, Chen Duxiu and Zhang Shizhao. A graduate of the Tokyo Higher Normal School, Chen was dean of the School of Letters at Beijing University and the editor of Xinqingnian. Zhang, a graduate of the University of Edinburgh, was a popular lawyer and published *Jiayin Zazhi* (Tiger Magazine).[123]

Xu presented diplomas to the five top graduates, and certificates to other worthy students.[124] The five honored graduates included Zhou Enlai, who was recognized for achieving the most outstanding record in Chinese literature in one of the two graduation classes. His classmate Xue Zhuodong was lauded for attaining the most outstanding record in English literature. Zhou Enlai was one of the two valedictorians. (It has been suggested that at the last minute he replaced his friend Chang Ceou, who was suddenly taken ill.)[125] The text of Zhou's speech has been lost, but one can assume that he reflected upon his four years at Nankai and expressed deep appreciation to his teachers, trustees, and invited guests. Whatever his words were, the honor was a fitting finale to his outstanding activities and rich experiences at Nankai Middle School. After the ceremony, all the students attended a farewell party and saw a student play, *Yiniancha*, a play that Zhou had helped produce in 1916.

Zhou Enlai in Shanyang (Huaian), Jiangsu province, circa 1910. He wears a traditional jacket and a cap commonly used by children of literati families in the late Qing period. (Zhou Enlai Memorial Museum)

Zhou Enlai in Fengtian (Shenyang), circa 1912; although he wears traditional formal attire, he had cut off his pigtail after the Republican Revolution of 1911. (Zhou Enlai Memorial Museum)

The main building of Nankai Middle School in Tianjin, one of China's Westernized institutions, which Zhou Enlai attended for four years (1913–17). (Zhou Enlai Memorial Museum)

Zhang Boling, a pioneering modern educator who as president of Nankai Middle School and Nankai University exerted a profound influence on Zhou Enlai's thought and behavior. (Zheng Zhiguang, ed., *Zhang Boling zhuan*, Tianjin: Tianjin renmin chubanshe, 1989)

Yan Xiu, an eminent Confucian scholar-official and a founder of the Nankai school system, with whom Zhou Enlai was closely associated in Tianjin. (Zhou Enlai Memorial Museum)

Zhou Enlai at Nankai Middle School in 1914. (Zhou Enlai Memorial Museum)

Zhou Enlai and Wu Guozhen in 1915, Beijing. They agreed to become sworn brothers; Wu was a member of the Children's Group of the Jingye Society at Nankai Middle School. (Zhou Enlai Memorial Museum)

Zhou Enlai (left front) in a biology class taught by Albert P. Ludwig at Nankai in 1916. On the wall hangs a four-character award (in Yan Xiu's calligraphy) that was given to the class largely because of Zhou Enlai's winning essay in Chinese Composition. (Zhou Enlai Memorial Museum)

Zhou Enlai (far right) was highly acclaimed as the beautiful and righteous heroine in a school play, *One Dollar*, in 1915. (Zhou Enlai Memorial Museum)

Zhou Enlai (second from left) was well known as the heroine in a school play, *Choudaniang*, in 1915. The photograph also shows his teachers, Ma Qianli (third from left) and Kang Nairu (fourth from left). (Zhou Enlai Memorial Museum)

CHAPTER THREE

The Growth of Progressive Consciousness in Japan

> We studied Western culture through Japan. . . . At the same time that the study of Japan broke the feudalistic conventions of the past, it served to further China's progress toward modernity. —Guo Moruo

After four years of American-oriented education at Nankai Middle School, Zhou Enlai would probably have preferred to continue his education in the United States, but for lack of money his choices were very limited. The American-endowed Qinghua School in Beijing sent its students to U.S. colleges, but Zhou's earlier attempt to enter its middle school in 1913 had been unsuccessful. Deficiencies in English and physics, two subjects emphasized in the extremely competitive entrance examinations to the senior division of Qinghua School, also handicapped him. And since the war in Europe still continued in June 1917, study at a European school was equally difficult and expensive. That left study in Japan.

Study in Japan was quite fashionable among young Chinese at the time, since Japan's growing national power, demonstrated in the Sino-Japanese and Russo-Japanese wars, had made it clear that China, too, should modernize. Zhang Zhidong had emphasized the point in his celebrated piece *Quanxuepian* (Exhortation to Learn), published in 1898 during the Hundred-Day Reform edicts of Emperor Kuang-hsu. This farsighted viceroy of Hunan and Hubei provinces listed four reasons for studying in Japan rather than in Europe: its inexpensiveness and ease of travel, which also made it possible for Chinese officials to be sent to Japan to inspect and supervise the students; similarity of languages, and the fact that the Japanese had

TABLE 2
Chinese Students in Japan, 1896–1923

Year	Students	Graduates	Year	Students	Graduates
1896	13	—	1909	4,000	536
1897	9	—	1912	1,400	260
1898	18	—	1913	2,000	416
1899	202	—	1914	5,000	366
1901	280	40	1916	4,000	400
1902	300	30	1918	3,000	314
1903	1,000	6	1919	2,500	405
1904	1,300	109	1920	1,500	415
1905	8,000	15	1921	2,000	465
1906	8,000	42	1922	2,246	505
1907	7,000	57	1923	1,000	413
1908	4,000	623			

SOURCE: Sanetō Keishū, *Chūgokujin Nihon ryūgaku shi* [History of Chinese Students in Japan] (1960), pp. 138–39, 544.

already distilled the essentials of complicated Western scholarship and discarded its worthless parts.[1] Also, because Japan was so close to China, Chinese students in Japan would not readily forget their motherland.

Even one of Zhang's ardent political enemies, Liang Qichao, argued that Eastern learning should provide the main educational foundation, and Western learning could then supplement this body of knowledge.[2] In 1899 he added that, whereas it might take from five to six years for a Chinese to master English, the Japanese language could be learned in a year and Japanese sentences could be composed in half a year because 70 to 80 percent of the Japanese vocabulary was written with Chinese characters. In 1896 there were thirteen Chinese students in Japan: the number reached a peak of about 8,000 in 1905, then tapered off to about 4,000 in 1916 and 2,500 in 1919 (see Table 2). This number far exceeded that of Chinese students in the United States or Europe.[3]

Zhang Zhidong's arguments for studying in Japan applied particularly in Zhou Enlai's situation—that is, the cheapness of travel and the probability of learning the Japanese language more easily than perfecting his English. Zhou went to Japan to learn the Japanese language. That was to be his sole concentration, and he hoped that with less than a year of language training in Tokyo, he would be able to pass the Chinese government scholarship (*guanfei*) examinations. An overwhelming portion of government scholarships—78 percent in 1917 (see Table 3)—were allocated to Chinese students in Japan rather than to those in Europe or the United States, and none of the scholarships available for study in the United States or in European countries was earmarked for a normal school or a teacher's college, the type of institution that Zhou planned to attend. Also, Zhou was confident that in the event of a temporary financial exigency he could rely upon a number of his friends already in Japan who were either wealthy or received comfortable government stipends. He had maintained correspondence with them while still a student at Nankai.[4]

In July 1917, shortly after graduation, Zhou, along with his close friend Li Fujing, went to Beijing to make preparations for his trip to Japan. Zhou stayed at the house of his father's cousin Zhou Tiaozhi. Zhou Tiaozhi's son, Zhou Enzhu, who was nine years old at the time, remembers that Zhou did not smoke or drink liquor and rose early in the morning and did calisthenics for about twenty minutes.[5] He quizzed his young cousin about the characters in a popular novel, *The Water Margin*, and urged him to read a new book entitled *The Scenery of Lake Xihu*. In mid-August, Zhou returned to Tianjin and bade farewell to his aunt, Zhou Yigeng's wife, and Nankai acquaintances. Zhang Boling was away in the United States, but Zhou visited Yan Xiu and may have been given some money for the time abroad.

En route to Japan Zhou took a twenty-hour train ride to Fengtian to see his primary school teachers and classmates. While there,

TABLE 3

Distribution of Chinese Government Scholarships Abroad, 1913–1917

Location of Students	1913	1914	1915	1916	1917
Japan	1,824	1,107	1,200	1,084	1,250
Europe	242	218	184	182[a]	173
U.S.A.	—	510	130	131	176
TOTAL	2,066	1,835	1,514	1,397	1,599

SOURCES: Lin Zexun, *Zhonguo liuxue jiaoyushi* [History of Chinese Students Abroad] (1976), p. 441, and Shu Xincheng, *Jindai zhongguo liuxueshi* [Contemporary History of Chinese Students Abroad] (1927), pp. 233–34.

[a]This number was divided as follows: 72 in France, 67 in England, 24 in Germany, 12 in Belgium, 6 in Switzerland, 1 in another country.

he gave one of his childhood friends a memento neatly written in classical Chinese that spoke of Zhou's high ambitions: "I hope that China will fly aloft all over the world when I see you again."[6] This calligraphy, dated August 30, reflected a willingness to link his determined academic pursuits in Japan with the nationalistic promise of China's resurgence. He expressed similar sentiments in an eight-character memento that he gave to another close friend from Nankai (Wang Pushan).[7] At about the same time he composed a poem on the theme of departure and resolve:

> Song of the Grand River sung,
> I head resolute for the east,
> Having vainly delved in all schools
> For clues to a better world.
> Ten years face to wall,
> I shall make a breakthrough,
> Or die an avowed rebel
> Daring to tread the sea.[8]

Beside allusions in its language to two of China's greatest poets, Su Dongpo of the Northern Song dynasty and Du Fu of the Tang dynasty, the poem also alludes to legends associated with the Shaolin Temple and Lu Chung-lien, a rebel against Chin hegemony in the period of the Warring States. In the same way that this legendary Buddhist monk at the Shaolin Temple in Henan province who after meditating in front of the wall for ten years was able to pierce through the wall, Zhou intends to concentrate on his studies in Japan so that a way can be found to save China. If he fails to do so, he promises to follow Lu Chung-lien, who declared that he would rather die by treading the East Sea than submit to the Chin invaders. Zhou's determination was reminiscent of Guo Moruo's resolution that if he did not pass the examination for a government stipend in Japan, he would jump into the East Sea.[9] A contemporary Chinese scholar asserts that Zhou's poem is "heroic, vigorous, and profound" and that it manifests the "high spiritual and moral qualities of [a] young idealist."[10]

After spending a few days in Fengtian, Zhou made a brief trip to Harbin to see a Nankai friend, Deng Jiemin, who had returned from Japan to set up a new middle school (Donghua School),[11] and to visit his uncle Zhou Yigeng, who had just been appointed new section chief in the finance department of Heilongjiang province.[12] This uncle continued to provide educational expenses for Zhou Enlai, and they shared a strong sense of mutual affection and loyalty. It is conceivable that Zhou Enlai also met his father in Harbin.

Sometime in late September Zhou arrived at Andong (now Dandong), a border city near Korea. The train crossed the Yalu River and took a whole day to reach Pusan.[13] No record indicates how Zhou Enlai felt about his limited but direct exposure to Korea, the first foreign country he had ever been in. Zhou had heard much about Korea, especially through Zhang Boling, and had discussed its problems in his Nankai School publications, so he must have been intensely interested in the scenery and conditions of life he could observe from the train. Other young Chinese travelers who saw Korea about this time tended to exhibit a mixture of curiosity, sympathy, and condescension toward their Korean neighbors, who had been annexed by Japan in 1910. A group of Tianjin teachers who visited Korea and Japan in the fall of 1917 reported that when their train entered Korea after crossing the Yalu River, many Koreans wearing white summer clothes, straw shoes, and all sorts of strange hats boarded the train, talking and laughing loudly. The Chinese visitors wondered whether or not these boisterous Koreans were aware of the loss of their country.[14] One Chinese student who took the train through Korea on his way to Japan in December 1917 was so moved by the tragic downfall of Korea that he wrote a poem on the subject, in which he said that he regretted that China as a suzerain state (*zongguo*) was unable to rescue Korea.[15] One of the first short stories by Guo Moruo, who traveled from Beijing to Fengtian and through Korea in 1913—"*Muyang aihua*" (The Sad Tale of a Shepherdess) written in March 1919—is set in northeastern Korea.[16]

Zhou Enlai took the same route as Guo Moruo and other young Chinese students, beginning with the eleven-hour ferry ride from Pusan to Shimonoseki across the Tsushima Straits. Zhou knew something about this historic port city where Itō Hirobumi had forcibly extracted enormous financial and territorial concessions from Li Hung-chang after what Zhou called the "War of Shimonoseki." It was another 27 hours by train from Shimonoseki to Tokyo via Kobe, Osaka, and Yokohama.

At the Kyobashi railway station in Tokyo, Zhou Enlai was welcomed by his old Nankai friends. For the first few months he lived with Zhang Ruifeng in his room near Waseda University, where he was a student; toward the end of the year he joined his Nankai friend Xue Zhuodong in rooms at a Japanese-run boardinghouse called Tamatsukan in the central Kanda district.[17] Although Zhou had never traveled abroad, he suffered less than his compatriots from cultural shock because of having spent his entire adolescence in two Chinese cities, Fengtian and Tianjin, that were strongly influenced by the Japanese presence. In a letter written in December 1917 to a Nankai schoolmate, Chen Songyan, at Tianjin, he said, "My daily life [*yinshi qiju*, lit. "drink, eat, move, and live"] is not too difficult"; in a letter to another Nankai classmate, Feng Liuqi, who was at Grinnell College in Iowa, Zhou spoke of his "satisfactory" conditions in Japan.[18]

Nonetheless, he had some difficulty at first in getting used to Japanese culture and customs, especially Japanese food and accommodations. He wrote Chen Songyan:

> When I first came, I felt quite uncomfortable about sitting on the floor to drink, eat, read, and sleep, but now I have already become accustomed to it. . . . There is a lot of fish in Japanese food. The Chinese here are not used to it, but this is similar to the way of eating fish in my hometown and therefore suits me. However, most Japanese food is broiled over a fire without much seasoning. Many Chinese live in Chinese-run inns because they want Chinese food.

He explained that he preferred to stay in a Japanese inn because in comparison with Chinese inns it was quieter and more conducive to studying. He added: "Japanese customs are not so favorable. But it is still acceptable to stay here if we behave and speak carefully. Japan [*woguo*] is a small country, but if you know your proper place there will not be much trouble." Far away from Nankai's warm and familiar environment for the first time in four years, he briefly espoused the Buddhist belief in self-denial. He often thought of his deceased adoptive mother, Madame Chen. At this time he also expressed interest in the idea of celibacy. In his diary he stated that love should be a foundation for true matrimony, thus rejecting the traditional Chinese method of arranged marriage.[19]

Like other Chinese students in Japan during the late 1910's, Zhou dressed in the black, high-collared tunic-type Japanese student uniform and wore high-heeled wooden clogs (*geta*). Only on special occasions did he wear the long Chinese white or black gowns. Because he was not enrolled in a college or higher school he did not wear the formal college hat but instead fancied the black artist's cap popularized by Natsume Sōseki, a Westernized liberal novelist whom Japanese and Chinese youths idolized.[20] His thick black hair was always well groomed, in the Nankai tradition. His mode of attire and his physical appearance in general were Japanese enough to reduce the likelihood of his being stared at or teased by Japanese, an experience that had greatly annoyed and humiliated the early Chinese students in Japan.[21] However, the heavy concentration of Chinese students made the Kanda district, where Zhou lived, a virtual Chinatown. There were several hundred small and large inns and rental rooms, and rental notices and other commercial advertisements were often written in Chinese. In addition to several preparatory schools for Chinese students, there were restaurants, department stores, tea and milk houses, printing shops, photography studios, ticket offices, and shipping agencies for Chinese students in Japan.

Japan, an inward-looking and highly structured society, was not especially hospitable to Chinese and Korean students, and particularly during their successful military campaigns abroad, the Japanese displayed a great deal of antiforeign feeling and a sense of racial superiority. A number of concerned Japanese educators, such as Matsumoto Kamejirō, principal of the East Asian Higher Preparatory School, as well as politicians, were very critical of the Japanese merchants, landlords, and private college administrators who reaped huge profits from unsuspecting foreign visitors, and they launched a campaign to make Japan less discriminatory and more cooperative toward Chinese students.[22] At the Imperial Diet in early 1918 Dietman Takahashi Motokichi made an impassioned plea that, for the sake of peace in Asia, Japan should learn from the enlightened, humanitarian, and unselfish educational policies toward Chinese students that prevailed in the United States and England.

Because Zhou Enlai was studying only the Japanese language in a school for Chinese students, he had no opportunity to cultivate close personal contacts with his Japanese peers or with teachers, and he could not meet Japanese in their homes. Other Chinese students attending Japanese colleges and universities in a Japanese milieu were perhaps more fortunate in this respect. But Zhou was very serious. He told his friends that at the East Asian Higher Preparatory School he was learning Japanese so that he could take the examination in the summer of 1918 to compete for a Chinese government scholarship. He referred to his study as a "last-ditch battle" (*beicheng zhi zhan*); the phrase is reminiscent of the poem Zhou composed just before he left China. To reinforce his determination, he wrote in his diary that unless you enter the lion's den, you cannot capture a lion. But he also admitted, perhaps with exaggeration, that although a person who has studied for one year in Japan should have no problem with the examination, he would almost definitely fail because he had been "idling about and doing no decent work."[23] Whether or not the statement was true, it is conceivable that he was so fascinated with a host of new experiences in Japan that he was unable to concentrate on language study.

One important nonacademic activity was attending the political meetings of the Chinese students in Tokyo. Zhou wrote about his own political feelings in his letter to Chen Songyan in December 1917:

> Unexpectedly, the first time I attended the meeting, the [Chinese] Legation [in Tokyo] was being besieged. I witnessed violent behavior. A crowd of [Chinese] people without any economic resources were angrily shouting invectives. Although their spirit was admirable, their behavior was reprehensible. I was heartbroken. If I had not witnessed it myself, I would not have known the truth; when I saw it with my own eyes, I understood a lot. Even though it rained heavily that day, I forgot about my clothes being soaked several times. If you had been present, you would also have felt that we can hardly bear to look at our nation's misery and political predicament! Gazing into the Divine Land [China], whose miserable condition has already reached an extreme! But some people are still bent on fighting for political power and their own interests, regardless of their own life or death. Alas! The ordinary people have to suffer the consequences of power struggles. What can they do at all![24]

Zhou's journalistic instincts prompted him to categorize Chinese students in Japan into three groups. One group, he observed, "bury themselves in their studies and do not care much about their society." He said it was a "common sight" in Tokyo to see another group of students who wanted to be in the limelight and deliberately sought publicity: "They are stupid, and will know nothing eventually." The third group wanted to be useful to society by seeking knowledge: "They study hard, concern themselves with society, and act wisely and purposefully." These students were at the top, but they were very few. One can infer from his appreciation of the third group that they were his model.

The diverse groups of Chinese students in Japan, from all parts of China, might have broadened Zhou's horizons, but his social life was largely confined to a small, intimate network of Nankai alumni in Tokyo; in this sense Tokyo was a psychological and social extension of Tianjin. Zhou also kept up a steady correspondence with Nankai friends in China and in the United States—his diary notes that he sometimes received as many as seven or eight letters a day—and he continued to read the Nankai school paper, *Xiaofeng*, and a new journal, *Nankai Sichao* (Nankai Thoughts), both of which were regularly sent to him in Tokyo. Thus Zhou's world consisted of highly personalized and particularistic relationships reflecting the traditional cultural ideal of *guanxi* (connections), which in Zhou's case was reinforced by a fierce loyalty to his alma mater and by the relatively weak and ambivalent influence of his familial and regional ties. Other Chinese students devoted a greater degree of loyalty and affection to their family network and regional affiliations. Zhou did not neglect his correspondence with his uncle Zhou Yigeng in Harbin, nor with his aunt in Tianjin and other relatives including Zhou Yikui, his father's younger brother, until his death in 1918. But because his family clan had disintegrated and his regional background was mixed, he was inclined to attach a higher priority to personal and institutional ties than to those of family and region. He may have belonged to the Zhejiang Student Association in Tokyo, which was one of the largest and most powerful provincial organizations in Japan with more than 200 members, but in any event he lacked shared experiences, a regional accent, or direct personal acquaintance with its members.

At a meeting of the Nankai Middle School Alumni Association in Japan held at a Kanda restaurant in early December 1917, Zhou Enlai was elected to its governing council. The association had been started in January 1917 by Yan Zhikai (Yan Xiu's youngest son) and Zhang Ruifeng, who were the founding president and vice president, respectively.[25] Many of the members were, like Zhou, attending the East Asian Higher Preparatory School; others were enrolled in Waseda University: two were attending the School of Fine Arts (see Table 4). The association met regularly on the last Sunday of each month. Zhou wrote Chen Songyan:

We have about 30 Nankai schoolmates here. We often get together and this gives us a sort of special feeling. "Living in a foreign land as a stranger, I very much miss my friends and relatives every time a festival occurs." Now that the New Year is approaching, we will have another big party to wipe out our loneliness. We usually live and study separately, and seldom call on others. It is not different from the life in Nankai. Whenever I read *Xiaofeng*, I cannot forget our merry life in the past, which will never return in our lives. Don't you agree with me?

Zhou's participation in Nankai circles continued throughout his stay in Japan. At a meeting of the Alumni Association on Janu-

TABLE 4
Nankai Alumni Association in Japan, March 1918

Name	Age	School
Sun Liuceng	25	EAHPS[a]
Chen Gang	25	EAHPS
Gao Renshan	24	Waseda University
Tong Qiyan	24	Waseda University
Wu Hantao	24	First Higher School
Yan Zhikai	24	School of Fine Arts
Wang Lixiang	24	Kenshū Gakkan
Zhang Ruifeng	23	Waseda University
Wang Pushan	23	EAHPS
Zhang Puen	23	EAHPS
Xiong Huairuo	23	EAHPS
Zhang Kuien	23	EAHPS
Li Xiangmo	23	Nikka Gakkō
Guo Wanyu	22	Seijō Gakkō
Sun Duogao	22	EAHPS
Xu Zepu	22	—
Zhang Honggao	21	Kenshū Gakkan
Liu Dongmei	21	EAHPS
Zhang Zaofei	21	EAHPS
Yang Boan	21	EAHPS
Fu Enling	20	EAHPS
Jiang Mian	20	Seisoku English School
Zhou Enlai	19	EAHPS
Lu Kaishu	19	EAHPS
Xia Shu	19	School of Fine Arts
Chen Tianchi	19	EAHPS
Wang Ziyu	19	EAHPS
Sun Rirong	18	Nikka Gakkō
Dong Kaijin	17	EAHPS
Chen Xinde	17	Nikka Gakkō

SOURCE: *Xiaofeng*, Mar. 17, 1918.
[a]East Asian Higher Preparatory School (*Tōa Kōtō Yobigakkō*).

ary 4, 1918, members discussed the contents of *Nankai Sichao*, with Zhou taking an active part.[26] At the March meeting Zhou gave a talk on "The Ways of Our Academic Pursuits" and Wu Hantao discussed "The Methods of Study in Japan."[27] The association also celebrated Zhang Honggao's successful entrance examination for the Tokyo Higher Normal School. In April 1918 Zhou Enlai joined a few other Nankai friends, including Wu Hantao and Tong Qiyan, in welcoming Yan Xiu to Tokyo. Yan, together with Fan Jingsheng and Sun Ziwen, who was president of the Zhili Fishery School, was just beginning an eight-month trip to the United States. Zhou Enlai accompanied Yan to Ueno Park and Asakusa Park to see the cherry blossoms and spent at least one evening with Yan at the Imperial Hotel. He even cooked Yan a meal at his communal living quarters. On April 17 the Nankai alumni held a dinner meeting in Yan's honor at a Kanda restaurant. Yan read them two poems he had composed and made a contribution of 50 yen to the association.[28] Zhou went to the Tokyo railway station to see Yan and his party off. Yan's diary makes it clear that he met Zhou Enlai at least six times during his ten-day visit to Japan.

In the spring of 1918 Zhou Enlai wrote in his diary that to be successful and prepared for the future, one should satisfy three principles: think about "new thought," do the "new thing," and study the "most recent knowledge."[29] He added that "thought requires freedom, doing things demands realism, and learning needs clarity." The main purpose for study abroad, he wrote, was to train oneself "to be iron-hearted and steel-willed" and not "to seek money or submit to force." He was generous in his correspondence with his friends, relatives, and teachers (most of the letters presumably are lost), and he also sent them books.[30]

In early 1918 his Nankai friends introduced him to another organization in Tokyo, the New China Study Society (*Xinzhongxuehui*), which Tianjin students, mostly from Nankai School and the Beiyang School of Law and Politics, had established in July 1917. Unlike the Nankai Alumni Association, this society had a clear political purpose—the reforming of China. It met every Sunday and issued a newsletter and directory. Zhou Enlai took part in its meetings and lived in its communal living quarters in the Ushigomeku district for a while in 1918. At one of its meetings he gave a talk on the importance of political action: so long as the members "have sound philosophical thought and scientific ability and positively participate in patriotic movements," he said, China still had hope.[31] At another meeting Zhou argued that Nankai Middle School should use *baihua* (vernacular Chinese) in its publications such as *Xiaofeng*, and he supported the *baihua* movement launched by Chen Duxiu, Hu Shih, and other modernized Chinese intellectuals to make the archaic Chinese language and literature more accessible to persons with a limited educational background.[32]

The Nankai connections did more than serve Zhou's psychological needs and give him the opportunity for intellectual discourse; they also were vital to his financial existence in Japan. Zhou told Henry Lieberman in 1946 that his friends had provided his living expenses in Japan.[33] According to Kai-yu Hsu's research, five of Zhou's friends in Japan pledged ten Chinese yuan each per month for Zhou's support.[34] Yan Xiu's eldest son, Yan Zhichong, who was a secretary in the Chinese Legation in Tokyo, may also have helped Zhou Enlai. Even so, Zhou still had money worries in 1918. Zhou Yikui, his father's younger brother, who had taken care of Zhou family matters in Huaian and, though he could hardly afford to, had probably given Zhou some money, died early that year. Zhou wrote in his diary on January 8 and 9, 1918, that Zhou Yikui had been very poor and had had to pawn practically everything he owned and also sell his property. "I have been unable to sleep at night for the past three days," Zhou wrote; "the more I think about the matter, the more pained I feel."[35] He was very worried about the deteriorating financial status of his family. Moreover, the economic situation both in Japan and in China was in disarray toward the end of the First World War. Japan experienced an unprecedented increase in commodity prices, which rose 130 percent between 1914 and 1918, while the real income for wage earners fell by 32 percent during the same period.[36]

In the spring of 1918 many of the Chinese students in Japan failed to receive their government stipends because of the political and economic paralysis of the Beijing government that had allowed the warlords to divert educational funds to the military budget. Privately financed students also suffered because the transmission of funds from their families was suspended. Angry Chinese students held protest meetings at their schools, demonstrated in front of the Chinese Legation, and even attacked its officials. The Japanese police arrested student leaders, and tension and frustration escalated among the Chinese student communities.[37] Under these circumstances, Zhou and his friends were equally unable to assist each other. In a letter he wrote to Feng Liuqi in April 1918, Zhou describes his diet: "Every day I do my own cooking and I'm still skipping breakfast and having vegetarian meals. I eat one bean curd a day."[38]

This letter makes it clear that as of April 1918 Zhou was no longer staying at the Japanese boardinghouse in the Kanda district but had had to find cheaper lodgings. He seems to have moved rather frequently; several places and addresses are cited as his residence in Tokyo during this time,[39] but we do not know exactly why he moved so often, or how long and with whom he stayed in each place. In any event, Zhou did not spend the entire year of 1918 in Kyoto with his friend named "Han" as has been suggested.[40]

Nagashima Masao, whose mother once arranged Zhou's housing accommodations near Waseda University, recalls that, except for his brilliant eyes, Zhou Enlai was not particularly distinguishable from other Chinese students in Japan, but says that although he was young, he was quiet, discreet, and agreeable. He remembers Zhou's competence in Japanese as being limited but sufficient for him to shop in Japanese stores.[41] Zhou assured his friends that all was going well: "I am just fine here," he wrote Feng Liuqi, his friend at Grinnell College. Nor is there any indication that his frugal existence interfered with his search for intellectual advancement and new knowledge. He wrote Feng Liuqi, "You must have gained a lot through your study in America. I sincerely wish that you could share with me what you have learned, especially the new trends of thought [*xinsichao*]."[42]

Educational Experience

As reported to his friends in China and the United States, Zhou's principal goals in Japan were to learn the Japanese language at the East Asian Higher Preparatory School (*Tōa Kōtō Yobigakkō*) and to wage a successful "last-ditch" battle to obtain a Chinese government scholarship. The East Asian Higher Preparatory School in the Kanda district was only three years old in 1917, but it was already attracting nearly 900 college-bound Chinese students in Japan, far more than the enrollments of several other well-established preparatory schools for Chinese students.[43] The school's phenomenal expansion was attributable to its energetic, dedicated, and innovative principal, Matsumoto Kamejirō (1866–1945), and his Japanese sponsors. Matsumoto had taught the Japanese language to Chinese students at *Kōbun Gakuin* (his students included Lu Xun and Qiu Jin), and when it became evident that the preparatory schools that had survived the dramatic decline of Chinese students in the immediate aftermath of the 1911 revolution were unable to accommodate the sudden influx of new Chinese students in 1914, he decided to open his own school.[44] He raised substantial contributions from Mitsubishi, Mitsui, South Manchurian Railway, the Bank of Taiwan, and other large Japanese companies that had business interests in China, and in 1918 the school had several new three-story classroom buildings and a sound teaching staff. In addition to his administrative work, Matsumoto himself taught eight hours a day.

Unlike the tightly structured educational programs offered by other preparatory schools, Matsumoto's curriculum was flexible and adjustable to the individual needs of Chinese students, whose pre-Japan backgrounds and scholastic aptitudes were often widely different. The standard one-year program was designed to train Chinese students at the levels of the fourth and fifth years of Japanese middle schools, and it usually included courses in the Japanese language, English, physics, chemistry, and graphic design. Students could enroll for less than the one-year program, since classes were not based on a semester system but instead were modular courses; a student could complete a course, taught two hours a day, in two to three months. Matsumoto's instruction in the Japanese language was based on the theory that if a Chinese student at his school attended Japanese classes regularly and studied diligently for six months, he would be able to carry on daily conversation, read books and reference materials, understand lectures given in the Japanese language, and express his ideas in Japanese composition. The real problem, he said, was the high rate of absenteeism among Chinese students.[45]

As were about half of his Nankai friends in Tokyo, Zhou Enlai was apparently enrolled in the standard one-year program, but he concentrated on Japanese-language courses at the cost of other substantive subjects. One of his closest friends in Japan, Zhang Honggao, remembers that in half a year Zhou was able to read Japanese books and newspapers. A Japanese schoolteacher, Motoki Shōgo, who conversed with him in Japanese toward the end of July 1918 reported that Zhou spoke Japanese "very well," but that he could not understand a few points made by Zhou in Japanese.[46]

For whatever reasons, however, Zhou Enlai failed the entrance examinations for the Tokyo Higher Normal School (*Tōkyō Kōtō Shihan Gakkō*) in March 1918 and for the First Higher School (*Daiichi Kōtō Gakkō*) in July 1918. And Zhang Honggao testifies that in March 1919 Zhou again failed another entrance examination to the Tokyo Higher Normal School.[47] Both schools had excellent academic reputations, and Chinese government scholarships were readily available to students who passed the highly competitive entrance examinations. In 1907, the Chinese Ministry of Education (with Yan Xiu as its vice minister) and the Japanese Ministry of Education had concluded a fifteen-year agreement under which Chinese students would attend five Japanese public schools; it was the first intergovernmental contract for long-term educational exchange between the two countries. The main objectives were to enhance the quality of educational programs that Chinese students would receive in Japan and to ensure the stable and orderly administration of Chinese government scholarships and Chinese regulations. The agreement specified the following points:

1. During the designated period (1908–22) Japan agreed to admit 165 "special contractual students" (*teyuesheng* or *tokuyakusei*) each year to five public schools: 65 to the First Higher School, 25 to the Tokyo Higher Normal School, 40 to the Tokyo Higher Engineering School, 25 to the Yamaguchi Higher Commercial School, and 25 to the Chiba Medical College.

2. China consented to pay each school an educational fee (200–250 yen) per person and to provide an annual government stipend (650 yen) to each student admitted to one of the five schools.

3. It was expected that Chinese students admitted to the four professional schools would graduate in four years, but those admitted to the First Higher School were to complete their studies in four years and then to go on to four-year imperial university programs.[48]

The contract for Yamaguchi Commercial School was suspended in 1913. In 1919 the Japanese government decided to bear the costs for special educational and administrative fees in the remaining four public schools participating in the program. Upon graduation, Chinese students were obligated to return to their home provinces for public service and to reimburse the total amount of their scholarship stipends to their provincial treasuries.

Since Zhou Enlai was not interested in the Chiba Medical College or the Tokyo Higher Engineering School, he set his sights on the Tokyo Higher Normal School and the First Higher School. In early March 1918 written examinations for the Tokyo Higher Normal School were given in eight subjects (Japanese literature, mathematics, geography, history, physics, chemistry, natural history, and English), plus a physical fitness test and oral examination.[49] Zhou Enlai was favorably disposed toward the Tokyo Higher Normal School because he had heard much about it from Zhang Honggao and knew that it had produced eminent Chinese intellectual leaders whom he respected, such as Chen Duxiu of Beijing University, who spoke at the Nankai commencement exercise, and Tao Menghe of the Beijing Higher Normal School, who was one of Nankai School's first ten graduates. Zhou may have aspired to become a teacher, perhaps along the model set by Zhang Boling. Certainly he believed that teaching was a beneficial profession, and he urged others to become teachers. He may very well have thought of studying political economy at the Tokyo Higher Normal School, for he had since early adolescence recognized that understanding economics and politics was important for China's future and he believed that the economy was the foundation of any society; his emphasis on economic matters persuaded one of his friends in Japan to change his major from medicine to economics at Kyoto Imperial University.[50]

The First Higher School enjoyed the most prestigious precollegiate academic status in Japan and had the largest number of Chinese government scholarships. Altogether at least eight years were required for graduation, combining study at this school with study at one of the four imperial universities—Tokyo, Kyoto, Kyushu, or Tohoku. This well-known school had demanding entrance requirements. Over the period of three days in July 1918, written examinations were given in five subjects (mathematics, physics, chemistry, Japanese composition, and English-Japanese translations), and there were in addition a physical fitness test and an oral examination. According to Zhou Fohai, who passed the entrance examinations in July 1918, there were about 600 Chinese applicants to the First Higher School, many of whom had already studied for three or four years at preparatory schools in Japan.[51] Zhang Honggao had entered the Tokyo Higher Normal School in March 1918 but decided to withdraw and take the examination at the First Higher School in July 1918. Zhang, who passed the examination, recalled having a long discussion with Zhou Enlai about this examination in the spring of 1918.

The competition in these examinations was stiff. To pass, Zhou had to place among the top 25 applicants at the Tokyo Higher Normal School and the top 65 Chinese applicants at the First Higher School. Because Chinese government scholarships were portioned out to the various provinces, Zhou faced an additional handicap because Zhejiang province, where his ancestral home was located and under whose jurisdiction he had to qualify, had far more students in Japan than there were scholarships. In 1918 there were 154 students from Zhejiang without government stipends, the second highest number in all Chinese provinces. Zhou sought to be one of the top nine applicants among a huge number of Zhejiang students competing to enter the four Japanese public schools under contract with China. Here again, Zhou's Zhejiang family roots proved to be a liability for his academic advancement. "How can I save the nation or love my family" without passing the examination, Zhou asked himself, and he told himself that the only way to wash away his humiliation was to succeed in the next scholarship examination.[52]

As before, Zhou's lack of competence in foreign languages was a liability. Contrary to Zhang Honggao's and Motoki Shōgo's testimony, his six months of study at the East Asian Higher Preparatory School did not give him a firm grasp of the Japanese language. Some of his competitors, especially those from Zhejiang province, had learned Japanese in China and had a distinct advantage. Guo Moruo said that it usually took at least a year and a half for Chinese students in Japan to learn enough Japanese to pass the entrance examinations for the government stipends.[53] It was clear, too, that foreign languages were no more Zhou's favorite subjects than they were his academic forte.[54] Half a century later he admitted to Japanese trade union leaders, "When I went to your country, it did not work out well for me."[55] Because the October revolution had just occurred in Russia, he explained, it was difficult for him to concentrate on learning Japanese. He added, "I understood Japanese newspapers, but my speaking was bad." Though he wanted to read Japanese, as well as Chinese, newspapers and magazines so that he could follow the important events of the Bolshevik Revolution, the First World War, Japan's Taisho democracy, and China's national humiliation, he had little enthusiasm for the tedious study of language textbooks.

Sometime in 1918 Zhou Enlai gave serious consideration to applying to Kyoto Imperial University where Kawakami Hajime taught economics. In his own calligraphy, he wrote asking for permission to take the examination for admission to the nonregular program. His curriculum vitae attached to the application form indicated that he graduated from the Tianjin Nankai Middle School and that his occupation was a student. The two documents were written almost exclusively in Chinese characters (except for one connective term used three times), which may indicate a lack of self-confidence in using Japanese. His interest in nonregular admission was necessary because he had not followed the normal academic advancement from one of the eight numbered higher schools to one of the imperial universities. This was a special way of admitting foreign students who had academic deficiencies. The number of such students was rather small; in 1916, only four out of 89 Chinese students in Japan who attended imperial universities with government stipends fell into this category.[56]

The exact date on which Zhou Enlai prepared his Kyoto University application form remains unclear. He might have prepared it in September 1918, after a brief visit to China following his failed examination at the First Higher School in July. His friend Wu Hantao was a student at the Third Higher School in Kyoto, and Zhou could have visited him there and left the form with him and then changed his mind about submitting it.[57] The fact of its discovery by a farmer in a suburb of Kyoto would indicate that the form was in Kyoto at some time or other.[58] Kyoto University did not have government scholarships allocated for Chinese students, and this may explain why Zhou did not submit his application and why, apparently, he did not apply to any other Japanese school that did not have the promise of financial support. If Zhou had had a private source of funds, he could easily have entered Waseda University or another private Japanese college at that time. It is somewhat curious, however, that Zhou apparently turned down a scholarship to Saint John's University in the United States that was arranged for by a friend who attended the missionary-funded Jinling University in Nanjing.[59] Even though he seemed to envy his friends in the United States, such as Feng Liuqi, who were learning about new trends of thought, Zhou reportedly rejected this arrangement on the grounds that missionary schools did not do "anything good for China, in reality."

Hence Zhou's goal to pursue higher education in Japan remained unfulfilled throughout 1918 and 1919. If Zhou had entered the First Higher School or the Tokyo Higher Normal School, he might have remained in a comfortable, elitist, and formal educational program until the summer of 1923 or even 1926, and consequently would very likely have missed the opportunity to participate in the May Fourth Movement or in European communist activities, which, of course, led to his subsequent revolutionary career.

Political Activities

If Zhou Enlai failed in his hopes of a college-level education in Japan, he succeeded in learning informally a great deal about political affairs. The political world of Chinese students in Japan, with its proliferation of organizations and numerous publications, was characterized by intense regional and ideological cleavages, passionate outbursts, and violent demonstrations. As one of his letters written in 1917 indicated, he did not approve of unruly Chinese student political activism, but in due course he found himself involved with his Chinese peers in circumstances related to political debates and protest movements. Freed from the protective environment of Nankai Middle School, he was ready to tackle Japanese and Chinese publications that presented a wide range of ideological orientations, including Marxism, anarchism, Christian socialism, and liberalism. He went often to the Chinese Christian Youth Center in the Kanda district to read the varied collections, and he spent many hours browsing through the district's famed bookstores.[60] His Japan diary indicates that he spent at least one or two hours a day reading Japanese and Chinese newspapers and magazines, including *Xinqingnian*, which he often borrowed from Yan Zhikai.[61] One of his roommates in Japan remembers that Zhou had an insatiable hobby of reading and that whenever they went out for a walk after dinner, he never wandered around but always rushed into bookstores.[62]

There is confusion over the extent to which Zhou Enlai was directly involved in Chinese student political organizations and activities, especially in May 1918. At that time Chinese students in Japan were very disturbed by reports that Chinese warlords, led by Premier Duan Qirui, a leader of the powerful Anfu clique, and the Terauchi Masatake government were secretly negotiating a military cooperation agreement that would allow Japan to operate military intelligence and logistical installations in north and northeastern China against the new Bolshevik government in return for loans of up to $80 million.[63] The students planned to organize massive demonstrations in Tokyo to protest this agreement, which they regarded as an extension of the Twenty-One Demands and as a convenient vehicle for Japanese military interference in China. This sounded like proof of Chen Tianhua's widely read warning of the danger of a Sino-Japanese military alliance: "If real power is not equal, there can be an alliance only in name; in reality, a protectorate. Hence wanting alliance with Japan at this point is to want to become a Korea."[64]

On May 4, 1918, about 300 members of the Fengtian and Jilin provincial student associations held a protest meeting at the Chinese Christian Youth Center in Kanda; similar meetings were convened at various schools and in large inns. A rally was organized at the East Asian Higher Preparatory School and Zhou Enlai probably attended it.[65] Following these meetings, the students issued proclamations and manifestos containing highly inflammatory political slogans and urging their countrymen in Japan to return home and rescue "our Great China" and smash the "little Japanese devils' ambitions." Immediately a host of clandestine student action groups with patriotic, militant titles, such as National Salvation Corps, Die-for-the Nation Group, Iron and Blood Club, and National Salvation Vanguards, sprang up.

Two days later, on the eve of National Humiliation Day (May 7, 1918), more than 700 Chinese students—nearly one-third of all the Chinese students in Tokyo—gathered at the Chinese Christian Youth Center. They passionately denounced Japan's aggressive schemes in China and distributed political statements. That same day a group of 46 student leaders representing provincial organizations and campus groups met at a Chinese restaurant (*Ishingō*) in the Kanda district to plan the details of their upcoming demonstration activities. Japanese police broke up the meeting and forcibly arrested the participants.[66] The students were interrogated overnight in the Western Kanda police station and were released the following morning. This incident further incensed the Chinese students. Tokyo University Professor Yoshino Sakuzō (1878–1933), whose students were among those involved in the incident, criticized the arrest and warned against the Japanese government's excessive suppression of legitimate patriotic expressions by Chinese students. Another statement also sympathetic to the Chinese students was issued by Dr. Terao Tōru, a former Tokyo University professor of international law, who had served as legal adviser to the Republican government in China.[67] The pro-Chinese sentiments expressed by Yoshino, Terao, and other Japanese intellectuals failed to have a moderating effect upon many of the Chinese students. Many boycotted their schools; many others left for China, thinking that was the most tangible way of showing their disillusionment with Japan's China policy and their determination to stop China's military collusion with Japan and protect China's sovereign independence.

Zhou Enlai joined his fellow students in boycotting classes at the East Asian Higher Preparatory School on May 6. Other preparatory schools such as *Nikka Gakkō* and *Dōbun Shoin* were also closed down completely. As Table 5 indicates, the initial student boycott was less dramatic at Tokyo Imperial University, Meiji University, Chuo University, Higher Engineering School, and Tokyo Higher Normal School, but by May 16 the boycott had almost uniformly engulfed Chinese students in all the schools in Tokyo. Groups of angry Chinese students rushed home in a flurry of patriotic rhetoric: Japanese government agencies at Kobe, Yokohama, Shimonoseki, Osaka, Nagasaki, and other ports carefully recorded information about the departing Chinese students. Just as they had done on other such occasions in the past, the Chinese viewed their return home as the ultimate demonstration of patriotic commitments. In this emotionally charged atmosphere, many Chinese students in Japan were faced with the dilemma of reconciling their desire to return to China with the heavy financial burden they would incur by spending the equivalent of one month's living expenses for travel. Zhou Fohai, for example, described his mental anguish, and Guo

TABLE 5

Chinese Student Strikes in Tokyo, May 1918

School	Total number of Chinese students	Chinese student absentees						
		May 6	May 7	May 8	May 9	May 13	May 16	May 19
Tokyo Imperial University	52	26	26	25	25	44	48	49
First Higher School	85	81	81	81	79	81	78	78
Meiji University	270	170	195	200	258	243	270	270
EAHPS[a]	900	900	900	900	900	900	900	900
Higher Engineering School	252	152	150	120	145	252	252	252
Tokyo Higher Normal School	117	—[b]	45	68	64	84	117	117
Waseda University	123	90	90	48	102	105	123	112
Hosei University	130	130	130	130	130	128	130	130
Chuo University	60	13	13	13	14	19	54	57
Nikka Gakkō	170	170	170	170	170	170	170	170
Dobun Shoin	39	39	39	39	39	39	39	39

SOURCE: Japanese Foreign Ministry Archives.
[a]East Asian Higher Preparatory School.
[b]No classes were held on May 6 at this school.

Moruo lamented that those who did not have money to return to China lost the opportunity to be patriots and were instead reviled as *hanjian* (traitors).[68]

Stunned by the effective Chinese student boycotts and growing exodus, Matsumoto, Terao, and other concerned educators quickly formed an association of eleven schools in Tokyo and, in cooperation with the Japanese ministries of Education, Foreign Affairs, and Home Affairs, attempted to find a solution. In mid-May they were successful in obtaining an explanatory memorandum from Foreign Minister Gotō Shimpei, a strong advocate of Japanese military intervention in Siberia. He stated that the only purpose of the Sino-Japanese defense agreement, still under negotiation, was to promote military cooperation between the two East Asian nations against their German enemies; the memorandum's principal message was that Chinese students were deliberately misinformed about the mutually beneficial intentions of such negotiations.[69] Equipped with this memorandum, Japanese educators posted a special conciliatory notice at their schools in an attempt to persuade the protesting Chinese students to return to their classes.

This attempt proved fruitless. As the students had anticipated, the governments of Japan and China on May 16 and 19 signed agreements for military and naval cooperation, laying the groundwork for Japan's military intervention in Siberia against the Bolshevik government in August. Matsumoto estimated that by the end of May about 1,000 Chinese students had already returned to China and about 2,000 students remained in Japan; Chinese sources indicate that only about 400 students had returned home.[70]

The Chinese returnees sent a petition to the Ministry of Education in Beijing and organized a campaign in major cities to alert the public to Japan's imperialistic designs on China. On May 21 they marched with about 2,000 Beijing University students to the office of Acting President Feng Guozhang and appealed to him not to ratify the defense agreements with Japan. In a series of policy proclamations, Education Minister Fu Zengxiang defended the defense agreements as essential to China's war efforts and expressed appreciation for the students' patriotic sentiments but urged them to return to Japan and resume their studies by June 10, 1918, for the sake of aiding China's national construction.[71] He warned them that if they did not do so, the government might revoke their student status. Since their summer vacation was approaching, most of the students did not go back to Japan for quite some time. In August, the Chinese Ministry of Education finally declared that students who did not report to their schools in Japan by September 10 would have their government stipends suspended.

Zhou Enlai's activities during the demonstrations, commotion, and exodus in Japan have been variously reported. One claim is that he asked his friend Gong Debai to read a declaration of protest, which he had drafted on May 6, at the Ishingō meeting of 46 student representatives; it has also been claimed that he delivered "anti-Japanese and anti-warlord speeches" to a rally at the Chinese Christian Youth Center and also printed and distributed protest literature; he is also said to have drafted an organizational charter for the National Salvation Corps, and to have led the student demonstrators to the Chinese Legation to denounce Minister Zhang Zongxiang's criminal acts.[72] One Japanese source says that three Chinese student representatives—Zhou Enlai, Gong Debai, and Wang Dazhen—convened a protest meeting at the Chinese Christian Youth Center and denounced a Japanese police chief who had made disparaging remarks about China and furthermore that Zhou, on behalf of Chinese students who attended private schools, drafted the statement that Gong read at the meeting. This same source also claims that the police chief was afraid that this protest might jeopardize his expected promotion to the Imperial Household Ministry and went to the Chinese Christian Youth Center to apologize to the Chinese students.[73]

In view of Zhou Enlai's deep-seated nationalistic sentiments and growing political interests, all these points are plausible, but they still remain unsubstantiated, without reliable documentary evidence or eyewitness accounts. Zhou's name does not appear anywhere in the Japanese Foreign Ministry archives that contain the names of several hundred Chinese students who were politically active in May 1918.[74] It is very unlikely that he was one of the recognized frontline leaders in the volatile world of Chinese student politics in Japan. At the age of twenty he was still a political novice and too young to claim any sort of leadership, roles that were usually held by older Chinese students with seniority and experience. Also, he was intellectually and temperamentally disinclined to jump into the vortex of political activism. Because he was not enrolled in a prestigious higher school or university, he had no particular status among the Chinese students in Tokyo, and though provincial student associations were a key organizational framework for political activism and leadership, he had no claim to such a regional power base because he was not actively involved in the Zhejiang Provincial Student Association and was largely unknown to them. And there is no indication that the organization with which he was associated, the relatively small Nankai alumni organization, was an influential political group or that any of its members became student political leaders in Japan.

It is therefore unlikely that during May 1918 Zhou Enlai was in a position to organize or lead other Chinese students in the political arena. Given his literary and journalistic abilities and dramatic and oratorical skills, he may have written some statements and essays of a political nature, assisted his more active friends (such as Gong Debai), and expressed his views and propositions at student meetings. His Japan diary contains detailed reports on the progress of Chinese student activities, including the texts of the Sino-Japanese agreements; this painstaking accounting was indicative of his journalistic preoccupation. On May 19 he attended the New China Study Society meeting and presented a report to a small circle of intimate friends from Tianjin.[75] In this report he argued that China was weak because its people had been unable to strive for a new ideology, to undertake reforms, and to understand the advantages of Western culture. Zhou's emphasis on the important role that "philosophical ideas and scientific ability" must play for China's ultimate salvation was consistent with the main theme of the new culture movement in China. After less than a year in Tokyo, Zhou was becoming increasingly critical of Japan's military policy toward China. He wrote in his diary (February 19, 1918):

> Japan is also a country where militarism [*junguo zhuyi*] is dominant. Belief in the motto "Power means justice" is a requisite principle of militarism. When militarist countries confront each other, they inevitably compete for superiority. Furthermore, militarism considers expansion abroad as an overriding priority. . . . In my opinion, militarism in the 20th century will be doomed to absolute death. Before coming to Japan, I had thought that either "militarism" or "elitism" [*xianren zhengce*] might have saved China. Now I have discovered that my earlier idea was terribly wrong.[76]

However, Zhou, though he seemed strongly opposed to Japanese militarism in China, preferred to remain anonymous in the Chinese student movement in Japan. In this instance particularly, he was a cautious, concerned, rational, and analytic observer rather than a flamboyant and fiery activist. Instead of joining the patriotic exodus to China, he stayed in Japan and took the examination for the First Higher School in July. For this examination it was necessary for him to have a statement from the Chinese Legation certifying his "good behavior." In late July, when the results of the examinations were announced and when the East Asian Higher Preparatory School still remained closed, Zhou Enlai quietly embarked on a lonely, belated journey back to China. By then, much of the student activism had subsided and he looked forward to seeing his friends, teachers, and relatives again for the first time in ten months.

On the Tokyo-Shimonoseki train that he took on July 29, 1918, he sat in front of a literature teacher at the Hakodate Commercial School in Hokkaido, Motoki Shōgo, who was on his way to a summer training program at Marugame, Kagawa prefecture, on Kyushu Island. The two strangers struck up a conversation that covered a wide range of subjects for over twenty hours. Motoki was evidently so impressed by this young Chinese student that he wrote of this encounter in his diary:

> I discussed a variety of issues concerning Japanese and Chinese literature with a foreign student from China, Zhou Enlai, who sat in front of me. He indicated that he had come to Japan last year. He spoke Japanese fairly well, but I did not understand a few points he made in Japanese. He asked me whether we could converse in English. Assuming that this might be a good opportunity to test how well I could speak English, I agreed to do so. However, I was surprised to realize that I had forgotten even the basic vocabulary of daily usage and I spoke a really broken English. Afterward we continued to communicate by writing Chinese characters on paper; in this way our discussion progressed very well. He said that he was from Zhejiang province and that he was returning to Tianjin for a vacation. Our conversation covered such subjects as Chinese prose and poetry, Chinese dictionaries, and Sino-Japanese friendship. When I praised China, he appeared to be quite pleased. At last he gave me his calling card and asked me to write letters to him from time to time. I, too, gave him my calling card, and got off at Okayama to transfer to the Uno line.[77]

The printed calling card inserted in the diary listed Zhou's name as both "Zhou Enlai" and "Xiangyu"; "Tokyo Kanda Higher Preparatory School" was written on it in pencil.

Zhou was on his way to Shimonoseki so that he could go back

to China via Pusan.[78] He arrived in Tianjin on August 1 and visited his teachers and friends at Nankai Middle School. He also spent about two weeks in Beijing and met his father.[79] He returned to Tokyo on September 4, 1918, probably via Kyoto, about a week before the September 10 date of school openings. Evidently he resumed his study at the East Asian Higher Preparatory School, and he returned to his familiar Nankai enclave in Tokyo. In October he was elected deputy secretary of the Nankai Alumni Association in Japan.[80] In December the Nankai group, together with other Chinese students from Tianjin, held a large gathering in honor of Yan Xiu and Zhang Boling, who stopped in Tokyo on their way back from the United States. The Chinese minister to Japan, Zhang Zongxiang, was also present. This was the first time Zhou Enlai had seen President Zhang in seventeen months. The group picture taken on that occasion shows Zhou Enlai sitting in front of both Yan and Zhang, with Zhang's left hand resting lightly on Zhou's left shoulder.

Introduction to Marxism

As Zhou Enlai's subsequent reminiscences indicate, the international issue that most captivated him throughout his stay in Japan was the unfolding drama of the Bolshevik revolution, which broke out about a month after he arrived in Tokyo. Japanese newspapers and books were flooded with reports and commentaries on this earth-shaking political development. Wang Yongxiang and Liu Pinqing suggest that Zhou "followed the development of the Soviet revolution with great enthusiasm and devoted all his attention every day to reading, analyzing, and comparing newspaper reports and progressive publications about it. As a result, he was deeply encouraged by the laws and measures adopted by the Soviet government."[81]

Zhou's Japan diary is known to contain many pages summarizing Japanese newspaper reports and his own occasional commentaries on the Soviet Union. He bought and perused a new Japanese-language journal, *Russian Studies*, and apparently read John Reed's sympathetic eyewitness account of the Bolshevik revolution, *Ten Days That Shook the World*.[82] The revolution was his favorite topic for discussions with other Chinese students at that time. His Nankai classmate Zhang Honggao reports that Zhou read many books on the October revolution, and Xu Kuijiu remembers his roommate's intense study of the events in the Soviet Union.[83] Zhou wrote in his diary that in February 1917 the Czar had been overthrown in Russia but that the revolutionaries were so divided that there was no unified political outlook; political views ranged from constitutional monarchy to democracy and socialism.[84] Consequently, he said, the unstable political situation presented an inevitable stage for revolution. He added that there was a cleavage among social democrats between the "moderates" (*wenhepai*) and the "extremists" (*guojipai*) led by Lenin. The moderates, he said, advocated "democracy" and "alliance between constitutional monarchy and capitalist class," but the extremists advocated "complete democracy," "destruction of the capitalist class system," and "violent resolution of all issues." About the extremists, meaning the Bolsheviks, he said: "Since their principles are most suitable to the minds of the workers and the peasants, their power must grow day by day, and they have completely destroyed the capitalist class system and religious promises. The Soviet Union will be a testing ground for the realization of socialist countries throughout the world."

In view of his limited ideological maturity at that time, Zhou Enlai probably failed to comprehend the extremists' policy orientations at the initial stage of the October revolution. Even the most experienced Japanese and Chinese socialists had difficulty understanding the true nature of the Soviet Union. Japanese newspapers, including the liberal *Osaka Asahi Shimbun*, were very critical of the Bolsheviks, whom they characterized as "German puppets" and "mad utopians."[85] Just as Li Dazhao's support for the Bolshevik revolution was "almost completely outside of the framework of Marxist categories of thought," so was Zhou Enlai's.[86] As a person who was acquainted with the history of the Russo-Japanese War and had often passed by the monument glorifying the Japanese military victory against Russia in Fengtian, Zhou Enlai espoused solidarity and sympathy with the victimized Russians and wished them well in their new revolutionary efforts.

His preoccupation with the Bolshevik revolution heightened his awareness of the growing problems of worker strikes and peasant riots in Japan, as exemplified in the rice riots (*komesōdō*) of 1918. Zhou Enlai was not an eyewitness to the rice riots, as some writers have said, but he did follow the news and analyses of this extraordinary social movement with great interest. The riot began on July 23, 1918, in a small village of Toyama prefecture, when approximately 40 poor peasant wives, gravely concerned about dramatically rising rice prices (which more than doubled in a year and a half), tried to prevent the shipment of local rice to other areas. Similar events immediately followed in neighboring villages but were not reported in national newspapers at that time.[87] By August this grass roots protest had spread throughout Japan, culminating in massive riots directed against rice merchants, policemen, government officials, and the rich. Altogether, about 700,000 persons rioted.

To control the spreading insurrection, the Japanese government declared martial law and mobilized the armed forces. In the process 8,185 persons were arrested. The main riots occurred during Zhou Enlai's absence from Japan, but the sensational court proceedings still continued after his return. This was an opportunity for Zhou, with his urban upbringing, to learn the power as well as the limits of peasants and mass movements; it was instructional because he lacked a rural background (unlike a majority of other future Chinese communist leaders). And he came to understand the weakness of the Japanese economic system, which he had praised and envied during his Nankai days. As an avid reader of Japanese newspapers, he may have read a series of critical essays on "The Problems of Rice Prices," which Kawakami Hajime wrote in *Tokyo Asahi Shimbun*. Perhaps influenced by Kawakami's critique, Zhou Enlai observed a year later, "The rice riots in Japan and the independence movement in Korea resulted from new international trends of thought and signified the achievement of an increasing national self-consciousness in the history of East Asia."[88]

Inspired by the Bolshevik revolution and the rice riots, Zhou paid close attention to the many hotly debated radical ideas and movements in Japan during the relatively free and competitive first decade of the Taishō democracy. Like many other Chinese (and Japanese) youth of his generation, he looked eagerly to socialist doctrines, particularly Marxism, as a possible solution to China's national shortcomings. While he was in Japan, he is known to have read the works of Kōtoku Shūsui (1871–1911), a noted anarcho-syndicalist, and progressive magazines such as *Kaihō* (Liberation), *Kaizō* (Reconstruction), *Shinshakai* (New Society), and *Chūō Kōron* (Central Review).[89]

The writings by Kōtoku in the Meiji era, which were popularized by Zhang Binglin and other well-known Chinese publicists, appealed to politically astute Chinese students like Zhou Enlai not only because of the author's radical doctrines and legendary martyrdom but also because he had criticized Japanese imperialism and the Japanese contempt for the Chinese in the aftermath of the Sino-Japanese War.[90] In 1899 he lamented that the Japanese, from those in the Imperial Diet to those at Keio University, held an illogical and immoral view of the Chinese. He also accused his countrymen, old and young, of despising the Chinese, scorning them as effeminate, and being "full of bloodthirsty intentions toward the four hundred million."[91] His anarchist teachings evidently attracted quite a few Chinese adherents in Japan.[92]

No other Japanese exerted more influence upon Zhou Enlai's introduction to Marxism than did Kawakami Hajime (1879–1946), professor of economics at Kyoto Imperial University. Although Zhou wished to study political economy at Kyoto primarily because of the 39-year-old Kawakami's reputation, it is most unlikely that he met Kawakami or audited his classes. As one of Zhou's friends, Xu Kuijiu, who entered the department of economics at Kyoto Imperial University in 1919, testifies, auditing privileges at this university were granted only to those who had graduated from one of the eight higher schools.[93] In his conversation with Sumiya Etsuji (former president of Doshisha University in Kyoto and one of Kawakami's disciples) in 1964 at Beijing, Zhou Enlai recalled that during his youthful years he was much impressed by Kawakami's works.[94] This statement is not at all surprising, because a whole generation of early Chinese communist leaders, including Mao Zedong, Li Dazhao, Chen Duxiu, Yu Shude, Zhou Fohai, and Guo Moruo, were also strongly influenced by Kawakami's books, many of which were translated into Chinese during the 1920's.[95] Uchiyama Kanzō, who had a Japanese bookstore in Shanghai, remembers that a number of future Chinese communist leaders, including Li Dazhao and Chen Duxiu, frequently came to buy Japanese books; Kawakami's *The Tale of Poverty* sold as well as popular novels, and *Social Organization and Social Revolution* sold out quickly, despite its high price.[96] He stated that books on socialism, and any books entitled *shakai* (social), sold well in China.

The Tale of Poverty was first serialized in *Osaka Asahi Shimbun* in 1916 (appearing in 53 issues between September 11 and December 26) and was then published as a book in March 1917. This extremely popular and influential best-seller went through 30 reprintings in just two years, until May 1919 when Kawakami decided to suspend further printings.[97] One can suppose that Zhou Enlai, like his Japanese and Chinese contemporaries, read, and probably owned, a copy of *The Tale of Poverty* and understood its contents, since it was written in a relatively easy and lucid journalistic style with many concrete examples. Zhou's roommate in Tokyo, Xu Kuijiu, recalls Zhou's constant references to this book in early 1919.[98] Zhou may also have read the Chinese-language edition that was published in China in 1920.

The Tale of Poverty contained a number of important analyses and messages that may have appealed to Zhou Enlai and other Chinese youth because they were based on modern scientific discourse and Confucian moral prescriptions. In his preface to the book Kawakami criticized economists who took the progress of material civilization—namely, the growth of wealth—as the only yardstick by which to measure civilization, and argued that because economic conditions were a means of fulfilling the moral goals of human life, the issues of wealth and poverty should be considered in the Confucian context of many people "hearing the way" (*michi o kiku*). This methodology challenged Zhou Enlai's earlier simplistic notion that the progress of a country's civilization depended upon its standard of living. Citing statistics, graphs, the Lorenz curve, and survey data from various sources, Kawakami irrefutably demonstrated that even though the civilized Western nations, especially Great Britain, the United States, France, and Germany, were wealthy, a great number of people in those nations were still in a state of poverty. This argument, too, was a revelation for Zhou, who had admired the tremendous national wealth of the West and had deplored China's economic backwardness. Although Kawakami did not utter a single word on China's contemporary affairs in this book, his message was loud and clear: the problems of poverty existed universally, not only in the East but also in the West. Kawakami severely criticized capitalism as a cause of economic poverty and social misery and charged that Adam Smith's classical economic theory was based on immoral individualism. "The greatest damage done by individualism under modern economic organizations is the impoverishment of many people," he declared.[99]

Kawakami concluded that it was hopeless to try to eradicate poverty as long as the present organizations persisted, the extreme gaps between the rich and poor remained, and the rich continued to buy and consume luxury items. In order to uproot poverty, he saw no other alternative but to adopt three measures: (1) to effect moral constraints and philosophical changes among the rich so that they would voluntarily give up hedonistic life styles and luxurious consumption; (2) to enact social policies that would correct the wide economic gap between the rich and poor; and (3) to transfer private industry to state management, as in the case of education and armaments.[100] He praised Lloyd George's sponsorship of social welfare legislation in Britain, such as the school lunch program and the old-age pension program, and Germany's nationalization of key industries. Yet he attached highest priority to a moralistic solution; for this purpose he emphasized the social virtues of frugality and altruism, and quoted liberally from the teachings of Confucius and Mencius. As Sumiya Etsuji puts it, *The Tale of Poverty* was built upon the "spirit of Confucian humanism" and the "sermon on ethics."[101] All three "correct" methods proposed by Kawakami were not completely alien to Zhou Enlai, who had studied Confucian ethical systems and had learned from Zhang Boling's anti-individualistic admonitions and Liang Qichao's social and institutional reforms.

Gail Bernstein points out that *The Tale of Poverty* helped to instill a "new sense of social responsibility" in Japanese students in the late 1910's and early 1920's and stimulated an interest in the study of economics.[102] Many students flocked to Kyoto Imperial University to study under Kawakami. One notes that the same effects were evident in Zhou Enlai's case, as shown by his interest in political economy and in Kyoto Imperial University. There was a special attraction, too, one can suggest, in the fact that both Kawakami and Zhou came from upper-class families that were colored by the Confucian cultural heritage. This background made it easy for them to assume a sense of moral obligation toward society, especially its poor populations.

Beyond that, however, it is difficult to accept the assertion that Zhou Enlai learned Marxism from *The Tale of Poverty*. Aside from a cursory account of some aspects of Marxism, the work is devoid of Marxist thought. It contains a brief segment in which Kawakami calls Karl Marx one of the greatest thinkers of the nineteenth century, quotes sympathetically from Marx's letter to his future wife and from *The Critique of Political Economy* (1858), and explains Marx's concept of economic substructure and its determination of the superstructure.[103] It describes the First World War as being a result of economic conflicts among nations, and in one place Kawakami notes that Marx had led him to believe that economy exerted a significant influence over the human mind. Kawakami rejected any extreme form of materialism as well as individualism, and he maintained that Marx's economic and social views were not much different from those preached by Confucius, but Kawakami himself was not prepared to embrace Marxism until 1919. It was then that he decided to stop the reprinting of *The Tale of Poverty*, and in *The Second Tale of Poverty* (*Daini bimbō monogatari*) published in 1930, he criticized his own "stupidity" and "utopianism" at having written *The Tale of Poverty* in 1916.[104]

Kawakami's serious search for Marxist economic doctrines was recorded in *Research in Social Problems* (*Shakai mondai kenkyū*), a private monthly journal that he started in January 1919. He expected to sell two to three thousand copies of each issue, but his writings were so popular that the first issue required an eighth printing within three months, and total sales amounted to 20,000 copies.[105] The first four issues were published while Zhou was in Japan (January 20, February 15, March 15, and April 4). The fourth issue was available in Kyoto during his final visit there. The four issues, totaling altogether 146 pages, included Kawakami's personal reflections, brief essays, bibliographical commentaries, and introductory articles on Marxism. In his editorial preface to the journal he continued to emphasize that the moral fulfillment of mankind should be the ultimate standard by which all social policies were judged; it was important to cure social illness, but the spirit should never be sacrificed in this process. He expressed support for gradual social reforms, and at that time disavowed any advocacy of "dangerous thought."

The comments most relevant to the Marxist exposition were those in his seven-part series, "The Theoretical System of Marx's Socialism," the first three parts of which appeared in the first three issues.[106] The fourth issue, in April, was devoted exclusively to Kawakami's introduction to and selected translations from Marx's *Lehnarbeit und Kapital* (Wage Labor and Capital), which had first appeared in *Neue Rheinische Zeitung* in April 1849. Kawakami said that his series on Marx's socialism was prompted by the Bolshevik revolution, but he declared that Marxism had nothing to do with the reported execution of the deposed Russian czar—news that shocked and embarrassed Japanese socialists. At the outset he emphasized Marx's "extremely important position" in solving present social problems and compared the principal elements of socialist economics with those of "individualistic economics" and "humanitarian or moralistic economics." He explained that Marxism consisted of three principles: a materialistic or economic view of history, a theory of capital, and social democracy. The theory of class struggle, he said, was like a "string of golden thread" that held all three principles together. On the basis of *Communist Manifesto* (1848) and *A Contribution to the Critique of Political Economy* (1859), Kawakami succinctly summarized Marx's materialistic view of history in the first three issues of his journal.

Kawakami introduced Marx's writings on class struggle, *The Poverty of Philosophy* (1847), surplus labor, the capitalist system, and social change in the subsequent issues of his journal, which Zhou Enlai did not see in Japan. Conspicuously absent in this entire series was any comment on Marx's dialectical materialism—an indication that Kawakami did not yet fully comprehend Marx's Hegelian philosophical foundations. Another series Kawakami included in *Research in Social Problems* was a three-part selected translation of Boudin's *Socialism and War* (1916), which analyzed the First World War within the Marxist framework. If Zhou Enlai indeed had an opportunity to read the first four issues of Kawakami's journal in the spring of 1919, he may have grasped an overall outline of Marx's historical and economic theory. However, owing to his limited competence in the Japanese language, he would probably have found it rather difficult to follow Kawakami's complex and subtle scholarly and theoretical expositions. Unlike the easily readable prose of *The Tale of Poverty*, Kawakami's *Research in Social Problems* was not readily comprehensible, even to native speakers with a high school–level education. It is conceivable, too, that, compared with *The Tale of Poverty*, Zhou would have found Kawakami's comments in *Research in Social Problems* less compatible with his Confucian and nationalistic point of view and also less relevant in his view to the precapitalistic social problems of China. Zhou Enlai could very well have continued to read Kawakami's writings after he returned to China because *Xinqingnian* published Li Dazhao's translations and summaries of *Research in Social Problems*.[107]

All this is speculative, however. What one can say with some certainty is that by the time Zhou Enlai decided to leave Japan early in 1919, he had been exposed to some of Kawakami's non-Marxist as well as Marxist writings, both of which he found potentially useful for his analysis of China's domestic and foreign affairs. They also helped him to understand the Bolshevik revolution and its broad international implications. He gained a rudimentary introduction to Marxism through Kawakami's writings, but it is, I think, incorrect to conclude that he became a Marxist in Japan under the direct influence of Kawakami, whose own understanding of Marxism was not fully matured in the spring of 1919.

Return to China

The exact circumstances of Zhou Enlai's personal and social life, academic programs, and political activities during the last few months of his residence in Japan remain unclear; there are conflicting stories even as to where he stayed during this period. There is no scholarly agreement on his reasons for leaving Japan, or when, exactly, he left, except that it was sometime in the spring of 1919. Kai-yu Hsu, on the basis of extensive interviews with Zhou's friends, concluded that while Zhou lived with "Han" (probably Wu Hantao) and his wife in Kyoto from the winter of 1918 until his departure for China in 1919, he sensed the gathering storm of the May Fourth Movement in China.[108] He adds:

> At this juncture, a letter from Ma Chun [Ma Jun, one of Zhou's Nankai schoolmates] reached Chou. It contained a brief message, "If even our country is about to disappear, what is the use of studying? . . ." Chou determined to return to China immediately. Packing for him was simple. Next morning, Mrs. Han went to town to sell an expensive ring to raise travel money for him, and in the same afternoon she put him on a train to Tokyo.

One of Zhou Enlai's chief biographers in China, Hu Hua, asserts that Zhou, faced with China's stirring historic movements, "boldly abandoned his studies and returned to China in order to devote himself to the revolution."[109] He believes that Zhou Enlai went back to Tianjin in June 1919. An even more specific statement was made by Jonathan D. Spence, who argued that after the May Fourth demonstrations were held in Beijing and a political coalition of student organizations was formed in Tianjin, "the political excitement was so great that Zhou Enlai broke off his studies in Japan and returned to Tianjin to head the journal of the expanded student union there."[110]

Contrary to some of the above-mentioned statements, there is enough direct and circumstantial evidence to suggest that political and revolutionary considerations were not the main reason for Zhou's return to China and that he made the decision before May 4, 1919. It appears that he was in Tokyo during the early spring of 1919 and visited Kyoto for three to four weeks in April on his less than "immediate" way back to China, and that he left Kobe for China toward the end of April. It seems likely that he did receive a letter from Ma Jun at about this time and borrowed travel money from Wu Hantao. His growing interest in radical political works such as those of Kawakami may have made him less interested in studying the Japanese language and in preparing for school entrance examinations. As indicated earlier, he seems to have taken another entrance examination for the Tokyo Higher Normal School in March 1919, and again failed. The decision to break off his studies in Japan was therefore not a precipitate one, although a letter from Ma Jun could have been persuasive.

China had suffered diplomatic setbacks at the Paris Peace Conference, which had convened in January 1919, and Japan's expansionist policy toward China was more and more evident. Zhou was a witness to the great national jubilation in Tokyo after the Japanese military success in the war that had just ended. They erected a colorful victory arch in the Ginza district, and very quickly they used their military strength to press another series of demands on China, a further extension of the Twenty-One Demands and defense agreements. Zhou also witnessed the Korean student demonstrations at the Korean YMCA building in Kanda in December 1918 and February 1919 and heard about the March First Independence Movement in Korea. Those, too, would have been strong persuasion to return to China to help Ma Jun and other patriotic student leaders.[111] According to Xu Kuijiu, who spent about a month in March 1919 with Zhou Enlai at Wang Pushan's two-story wooden house in the Kanda district, Zhou frequently brought up the question of China's future and the course of the Bolshevik revolution. Xu Kuijiu noted his serious and thoughtful attitude "without jokes" and his "good memory and logical clarity."[112]

There were also compelling financial considerations for his return home, which affected his academic plans. Xu Kuijiu speaks of Zhou's economic hardships and his reliance on Wang Pushan's assistance. His family's fortunes had not improved, and he was becoming a growing financial burden to his friends in Japan. His failures in the entrance examinations for the Tokyo Higher Normal School and the First Higher School had made it quite certain that he would have to continue to depend upon his friends, and they were themselves probably going to be in straitened circumstances because the Chinese Ministry of Education was in the process of tightening its regulations concerning privately funded students abroad and limiting government subsidies to them.[113]

The prospect of passing any entrance examination was less and less promising. With all the distractions from his study of the Japanese language and other subjects of examination, Zhou's goals in Japan became more realistic. Since he could no longer hope to enter a Japanese school with a government scholarship, he chose to satisfy his intellectual and political interests in world affairs, current events, and radical theories. He gave up aspirations of attending a Japanese institution and decided to enter Qinghua School or Beijing University.[114] He had learned from Zhang Boling and Yan Xiu in December 1918 that they were planning to open a new Nankai University in the fall of 1919 and to admit Nankai Middle School graduates without entrance examinations. This was therefore a last resort that he could fall back on in Tianjin.

After Zhou announced in March 1919 his plans to return home, Zhang Honggao, who was a student of the First Higher School, invited a few Nankai friends to his place in Tokyo for a farewell party for Zhou.[115] After dinner Zhang brought out a piece of rice paper, ink, and brush, and requested a written memento from Zhou, whose calligraphy and literary skills were well known among his friends. He obliged them with the poem that he had composed in 1917, before his Japan journey. His calligraphy is clearly dated "March of the Eighth Year of the Republic of China," that is, March 1919. He added a few lines of postscript explaining that he was writing this poem again to bid farewell to his friends and to admonish and encourage himself, and that "after years of my drifting and wasteful life [*langdang nianyu*] and my failure in examinations [*luodi*] I am glad to return to my country."[116] This postscript was a typical gesture, acknowledging his failure to live up to his resolve of two years earlier, regretting the failure, but showing no bitterness or frustration. As always, he could reprove himself for his prodigal ways and at the same time renew his determination to do better in the future.

Zhou's memento to Wang Pushan, for whom he had written a phrase in 1917, reflects the same spirit. This memento, in Zhou's calligraphy, reproduced a famous poem by Liang Qichao, written in 1901 during Liang's exile in Japan after the failure of the Hundred-Day Reform movement.[117] In the poem, Liang reaffirms his dedication to China's future no matter what others might say and promises to seek new knowledge and to reform China's outmoded social customs by upholding popular rights (*minquan*); ten years hence, he says, others will understand and support his position. The poem expresses a state of mind that was much like Zhou's in the spring of 1919, and in choosing it as a parting gift, Zhou seemed to be saying something about his persistent attachment to China's traditional literary values despite the socialistic perspective and new knowledge he had acquired in Japan. His Japan diary contains frequent references to Liang's writings.

In addition to receiving financial assistance from his friends, Zhou Enlai apparently borrowed travel funds (worth about 400 yuan in Chinese currency) from the Nankai Alumni Association in Japan and the New China Study Society.[118] On April 1, 1919, he paid his last visit to Kyoto and stayed at the home of Wu Hantao. Admiring the serene natural beauty of this ancient dynastic capital, he walked leisurely through the gardens and hills and had some time for self-reflection. Faced with his forthcoming departure to China, he composed at least four poems.[119] These poems, unlike his pre-Japanese poetry, which was written strictly in the classical Chinese form of five- or seven-character stanzas, were composed in *baihua*—an indication that he now fully accepted the rationale for its usage.

All four of the poems show a romantic and subtle appreciation of the enchanting beauty of Kyoto in the springtime, combined with thoughts of both a philosophical and a political nature. One poem has the title, "Arashiyama After the Rain":

> Rain over,
> The hill darkens with the clouds.
> Dusk is approaching.
> A backdrop of multitudinous green
> Offers up a nimbus of cherry blossoms—
> Delicately pink, tenderly sweet.
> All soul-enchanting!
> Beauty of nature, untouched by artfulness,
> Unconstrained by man.
> O, the plaster ornaments of religion, feudal
> ethics and outworn arts and letters,
> The frustrating doctrines that are still
> being bandied about on so-called belief,
> sentiment and aesthetics!
>
> A look in the distance
> From heights ascended:
> Hills met in grey.
> White clouds, part shaded,
> Narrow down to a stripe.
> A dozen electric lights glare from the dark
> formless metropolis.
> For a moment, a cry from the island people's
> hearts seems to break through the scene:
> Elder statesmen, warlords, party bosses,
> capitalists, what from this, are you going
> to fall back on? [120]

Later in the poem he says that "bloom and decay/triumph and defeat/are the objective givens in this world of men," but he also cheerfully sings of discovering "a chance glimpse of a spark in the haze."

According to Zhou's recollections shared with Japanese visitors in the early 1970's, including Prime Minister Tanaka Kakuei and Ambassador Ogawa Heishirō, Zhou Enlai spent about a month in Kyoto just before his return to China and departed from Kobe, where he found the cherry blossoms in full bloom.[121] He also said that "soon after my return to China, the May Fourth Movement occurred." [122] This timing is important in determining his residence and activities during the May Fourth Movement in China.

Conclusion

The young Zhou Enlai was one of several tens of thousands of ambitious Chinese students who flocked to Japan to receive a modern education in the first quarter of the twentieth century, but he failed to enter a prestigious institution of higher learning. He did not pass the competitive examinations at the Tokyo Higher Normal School and the First Higher School, nor did he pursue regular studies at Kyoto, Waseda, Hosei, or Nihon universities. His study at the East Asian Higher Preparatory School in Tokyo was mostly limited to elementary instruction in the Japanese language, which he absorbed bit by bit without any degree of sure mastery. His absence of college-level formal education in Japan, however, was amply compensated for by his diligent and enthusiastic reading of Japanese and Chinese materials that covered a broad range of contemporary affairs and "new thoughts."

In particular, his early exposure to the Bolshevik revolution, the rice riots, the Taishō democracy, and Kawakami Hajime's works had a lasting effect on his subsequent intellectual and political growth. He had no personal association with Kawakami, but developed a generally favorable orientation toward Marx, due in part to the October revolution in Russia. Admittedly he had no profound immersion in Marxist literature, but his head start in learning the elementary principles and promises of Marxism in Japan gave him a huge advantage over his peers back in Tianjin. In early 1919 Zhou Enlai was no more a full-fledged Marxist believer than were Li Dazhao, Chen Duxiu, Mao Zedong, and other future Chinese communist leaders.[123] By 1920, this uncertainty had already begun to change, and Chinese intellectuals especially were in the process of rapid ideological radicalization. But by the time Li Dazhao declared himself a Marxist and devoted his *Xinqingnian* to discussions of Marxist doctrines in September 1919, Zhou Enlai had already been aware of the general tenets of Marxism and its relationship with the Bolshevik revolution. His obtaining even a modicum of advance knowledge about Marxism before it became fashionable in China made him an authority of sorts, to the extent of his giving lectures on Marxism to fellow prison inmates in early 1920. This was a distinct asset that accrued from his informal educational experiences in Japan.

Added to this intellectual advancement was his direct contact with the political dynamics of Chinese student communities in Japan: it was his first exposure to the real world of violent political struggles, a sharp contrast to the rhetoric of passionate nationalism that he had encountered during his Nankai years. Although he was initially "heartbroken" at witnessing the unruly Chinese student demonstrations and was disillusioned with the uninformed political activists, he gradually came to recognize the nationalistic justification for Chinese student political organizations and activities in Japan and also to assume a role within them. He was never a fiery frontline political activist, however, one who sought the limelight or publicity; rather, he was a low-profile strategist and publicist who took a cautiously calculated political stand. For all his experience in the theater at Nankai, he was by nature uncomfortable in large anonymous crowds and noisy environments and preferred to work behind the scenes helping activists such as Gong Debai. It was a way of keeping his options open. This personal and political modus operandi recurred during his pre-communist period. In the Chinese student protests in May 1918, his contributions were probably journalistic and organizational rather than actively demonstrative. His taste of the real political campaigns in Japan rendered him a little less constrained and more susceptible to student political activism than before.

Zhou's Nankai friends liked and respected him for his personal warmth and future promise. His self-effacing modesty made him welcome among both potential competitors and rivals. He felt comfortable and productive in small parochial groups. In Japan, the Nankai Alumni Association and the New China Study Society gave him the financial support that he needed, and he was always grateful for that, even when, in later years, his political position was far to the left of theirs. But his experiences in Japan, unlike those in Europe a few years later, did not result in any lasting network of political or ideological alliances. In great part this was due to his own uncertain ideological and political point of view at the time, and to his undefined institutional and regional alliances. It is interesting that none of those who were close to him in Japan stayed in contact with him during his future leadership in the Chinese Communist Party; indeed, a few, including Wu Hantao, Tong Qiyan, Gong Debai, and Yan Zhikai, assumed important positions in the Guomindang-dominated systems.

Despite his earlier literary and dramatic achievements at Nankai

Middle School, Zhou did not show much interest or involvement in the modern drama movement among Chinese students in Japan, or in the popular poetry of Walt Whitman, Goethe, or Tagore, whom Lu Xun, Guo Moruo, and other Chinese literary aspirants in Japan admired and emulated. Zhou Enlai's poetry, devoid of Western or Japanese influence, combined the classical Confucian mode, youthful romanticism, and social criticism. The influence of Japanese journalism was evident in Zhou Enlai's subsequent writings, in which his intellectual maturity and forceful arguments clearly indicated a departure from the constrained and sophomoric style of his Nankai publications. Although he cared little about the Japanese language as such, he learned a great deal from Japanese newspapers and magazines, and his acquaintance with the style of the informative, investigative, and critical Japanese press of the Taishō era helped him greatly in carrying out his political responsibilities during the May Fourth era and in Europe.

Zhou's two years in Japan were in many ways very limited. He had almost no opportunity to become acquainted with Japanese leaders, teachers, students, girlfriends, or families. Yet his observant eye and analytic mind enabled him to understand many aspects of Japanese society and politics and to achieve a degree of understanding of Japanese life. In his Japan diary he expressed a determination to watch and study "every act and movement [*yiju yidong*] of the Japanese people."[124] Certainly he could have learned more, and met more people, if he had been more fluent in the Japanese language, but he did learn something, and after he returned to China he was able to translate a few Japanese writings into Chinese, and his easy access to Japanese newspapers helped his journalistic activities during the May Fourth Movement.

Zhou Enlai apparently cherished fond and somewhat romantic memories of his life in Japan. In 1954 he told Japanese Dietmen in Beijing that although his Japanese was inadequate during his youthful experience in Japan, he had a "profound impression" of Japan's beautiful national culture.[125] He liked especially to recall the Kanda bookstores, Kawakami, and Kyoto with its cherry blossoms—and bean curd.

When Zhou Enlai returned to China in 1919, he was in transition from adolescence to personal maturity. He was no longer a somewhat carefree teenager but was more sophisticated and sensitive, and his nationalistic and progressive fervor was substantially refined. The experience of living in a powerful foreign country had broadened his horizons in regard to world affairs, political activism, Marxist writings, and modern journalistic practices, and this new awareness, coupled with his enduring Nankai ties, made him better prepared to assume a position of political and intellectual leadership at the historic juncture of the May Fourth Movement in Tianjin. His Japanese experience also showed that he still had the resilience, as he had had as a child, to transform failure and adversity into new opportunities for positive self-renewal.

CHAPTER FOUR

Political Activism During the May Fourth Era

> Hope cannot be said to exist, nor can it be said not to exist. It is just like roads across the earth. For actually the earth had no roads to begin with, but when many men pass one way, a road is made.
> —Lu Xun, "My Old Home"

Chinese youth during and after the May Fourth Movement faced China's escalating social injustice and political problems with a mixture of realistic assessment and optimistic idealism. Lu Xun, the famous Japanese-educated writer, lamented that the Chinese people were burdened with "many children, famines, taxes, soldiers, bandits, officials, and landed gentry," but he still hoped that China would somehow have a "new life," a life never before experienced in that country.[1] In search of such a new life, an increasing number of Chinese intellectuals, whose political and social consciousness was stirred by the May Fourth Movement, followed Beijing University Professors Li Dazhao and Chen Duxiu in pursuing the road toward Marxism. Upon his return from Japan at the age of 21, Zhou Enlai, like many of his generational cohorts, found himself in the tumultuous but enlivening era from the May Fourth Movement to the Marxist revolution, when China underwent rapid political development.

The May Fourth Movement in Tianjin

Although Zhou Enlai's return to China coincided with the beginning of the May Fourth Movement, there is no evidence to corroborate the assertions that the movement prompted his return or that he immediately plunged into the movement's political activities. Zhou apparently returned to China (either at Dalian or at Tianjin) via ship in the latter half of April 1919 and spent time in Tianjin during late April and May. A report in the Nankai Middle School's newspaper, *Xiaofeng*, on April 30, 1919, said, "Our alumnus, Mr. Zhou Enlai, returned to Tianjin from Japan the other day, and we heard that he intended to take the entrance examinations to Qinghua or Beijing University."[2] *Xiaofeng* also reported (May 19) that Zhou Enlai attended a tea party given by the Jingye Society at the school on May 17. Zhou, who had been one of the principal organizers and leaders of the society, was welcomed back to his comfortable niche in the old Nankai network. At the tea party he gave a brief speech, and three of his former teachers, Zhang Pengchun, Kang Nairu, and Hua Wuqing, performed a sword dance and dramatic sketch. In mid-May, Zhou wrote in a letter to the Nankai Alumni Association in Japan, "I go to Nankai every day."[3] At this time he lived with his aunt in her small house in Tianjin. However, Zhou, though he was on the scene, was not a leader or even a participant in the initial stages of the May Fourth Movement.

The movement began on May 4 in Beijing, when about 3,000 college students held demonstrations in Tiananmen Square to protest the announcement that the Peace Conference in Paris had acceded to Japan's acquisition of Chinese territories (especially, Qingdao) previously controlled by Germany. Physical attacks were directed against several Chinese officials, notably Cao Rulin, minister of communications, Lu Zongyu, director of the Currency Bureau, and Zhang Zongxiang, minister to Japan on home leave, who were known to be pro-Japanese. The Chinese government, headed by President Xu Shichang, brutally suppressed the demonstrators and arrested 32 leaders.[4] This was a historic turning point for the massive nationwide campaign, which was later called the May Fourth Movement.

News of the Beijing incident reached Tianjin the next day via *Yishibao*, *Dagongbao*, and other newspapers. The account in *Yishibao*, a paper that Father Vincent Lebbe, a Belgian Catholic priest, had founded in 1915, was particularly sympathetic to the students.[5] Tianjin, with its geographical proximity and close political connection with Beijing, was especially sensitive to political unrest in the capital, and in the ensuing weeks an increasing number of students, intellectuals, merchants, religious groups, and civic leaders in Tianjin (as elsewhere throughout China) held mass rallies, street demonstrations, petition campaigns, and general strikes urging the Chinese government to release student leaders from prison, to dismiss the Chinese "traitors," and to reject the Paris Peace Treaty. They also organized a popular movement to boycott Japanese goods. The Tianjin government authorities, led by Zhili Provincial Governor Cao Rui, Police Commissioner Yang Yide, and Education Commissioner Wang Zhanggu, attempted without success to prevent the escalating student agitation.

On May 5 officials at the Beiyang School of Law and Politics in Tianjin cabled Beijing University in support of the student demonstrations; they urged President Xu to release arrested students and asked the Chinese delegation in Paris not to submit to the Japanese demands. Student leaders at the First Zhili Women's Normal School, including Guo Longzhen and Deng Yingchao, met and decided to organize a patriotic association for women in Tianjin.[6] On May 6, a group of 29 student representatives from ten middle schools and colleges in Tianjin adopted specific demands to be made on the Chinese government and began making plans to organize mass rallies and to dispatch a delegation to Beijing. On May 7 (National Humiliation Day), Nankai Middle School held a campus meeting to discuss China's national crisis.[7] In an attempt to forestall demonstrations, the Tianjin authorities proclaimed martial law. A meeting of student representatives chose temporary leaders for the Tianjin Student Union (*Tianjin xuesheng lianhehui*); Ma Jun, one of Zhou Enlai's close Nankai friends and an active political leader, was named vice chairman. On May 12 about 1,000 students gathered at Hebei Park in memory of Guo Qinguang, a Beijing University student who had died as a result of the May Fourth demonstrations.

On May 14 the Tianjin Student Union was formally inaugurated at the Zhili Fishery School; Chen Zhidu (a student at the Hebei Higher Technical School) and Ma Jun were elected chairman and vice chairman, respectively. This union quickly organized a general strike, which was staged by about 10,000 students in fifteen middle schools and colleges on May 23, following a similar strike that had taken place in Beijing on May 19 and had spread to some 200 cities all over China. On May 25 the Tianjin Association of Patriotic Women Comrades was set up under Chairman Liu Qingyang (a Moslem and a graduate of the First Zhili Women's Normal School); its council members included Zhang Ruoming, Guo Longzhen, and Deng Yingchao. On June 5 the Tianjin Student Union sponsored a patriotic rally of several thousand students at Nankai Middle School. At this rally six resolutions were adopted, and demands were made that the Chinese government release imprisoned student leaders, nullify the Twenty-One Demands, and recover Qingdao from Japanese control.[8] On June 9 about 20,000 citizens of Tianjin protested at Hebei Park; this city-wide general strike shut down all businesses the following day. On June 27 ten student and civic leaders, including Liu Qingyang and Zhang Ruoming, went to Beijing and joined representatives of other areas in petitioning President Xu not to accept the Peace Treaty at Paris. When President Xu not only accepted the resignation of the three "traitors" but also refused to sign the Peace Treaty on June 28, the intensity and scope of the May Fourth Movement subsided in Tianjin, especially during the summer vacation of 1919.

In all the accounts of the tumultuous student activities in Tianjin in May and June, Zhou Enlai is conspicuously absent. His name does not appear in the extensive written records of the May Fourth Movement, nor did any of the Tianjin student leaders who were active in the early stage of the May Fourth Movement recall his presence in the mass rallies and demonstrations. Liu Qingyang, one of the most active female leaders of the May Fourth Movement in Tianjin, even believes that Zhou did not return from Japan to Tianjin until June.[9] After being absent from Tianjin for two years, Zhou Enlai only gradually and deliberately reentered and readjusted to the changing local conditions; hence he first participated in the Jingye Society, with which he was thoroughly familiar and comfortable. Since he was not a student at that time (until August 25 when he was admitted to Nankai University), he had no institutional basis that would have permitted his immediate participation in the Tianjin Student Union, which was a coalition of student organizations from various schools and colleges. More importantly, Zhou's whole manner had always been one of caution and discretion. It was not characteristic of him to rush into unfamiliar, uncertain, and violent mass activities or to seek the limelight position of top leadership without adequate preparation. Even though he had overcome his shyness by his extensive dramatic and forensic activities at Nankai, he still felt uneasy in large gatherings of unfamiliar people and preferred to work in small groups or behind the scenes.

And so, evidently, Zhou remained in the background during May and June. But he was a keen observer, and it was again characteristic of him to express his observations and patriotic feelings in writing. In mid-May he sent a report to the Nankai Alumni Association in Japan. The subject was not specifically the May Fourth Movement or any of the recent demonstrations, but he alluded very clearly to the root problem:

> I do not want to be so presumptuous as to talk about or get involved in the affairs of Nankai. Examining the situation from all angles, I must frankly say that it is very dangerous. The President may have his own ideas, but I cannot tell what he is thinking about. Not only I, but all those who know the President think that way. . . . I love Nankai, but it seems to me that Nankai is alienating itself from society. If a person becomes intolerable to society and yet what he does still paves the way for society, this person is still not too bad. But, if he goes back to and reaffirms the ideology of the 17th or 18th century, or even that of the 13th or 14th century, I should say that this person is devoid of all merit, and the same assessment would hold true for an institution such as Nankai. What an institution should do is work for new issues. If the institution befriends traitors and allows them to rob the government and the people, it would be most shameful for this institution, not to mention that it would not work for society. All the students of Nankai are educable. Besides, they all have great enthusiasm and willpower. And yet the school does not cultivate real abilities and encourage learning, so students lack genuine knowledge. Furthermore, the President has changed drastically. He is now using political methods in the Chinese style to administer a school. The only new hope now lies in the students. The President talks about "democracy" every day, but actually he is merely an arbitrary ruler, and thus everybody is at odds with his leadership.[10]

This unusual and very strong criticism of President Zhang Boling was prompted by Zhang's decision to accept financial contributions from Communications Minister Cao Rulin and to appoint him as a member of the new Board of Trustees for Nankai University. In view of Zhou's long and intimate ties with President Zhang, the letter demonstrated how deeply he was disillusioned by Zhang's association with the "traitor." He did not like President Zhang's "arbitrary" style that appeared to suggest that the ends justified the means: in order to promote education and to build Nankai University, Zhang did not hesitate to ask for contributions from persons like Cao, one of the main targets of student demonstrations. In part, Zhou's candid remarks reflected the prevailing atmosphere of the May Fourth era, which subjected the established authorities to scrutiny and criticism, but they also indicate a certain maturity of thought that impelled him to focus on principles rather than on personal loyalty. Zhou expressed his opinions frankly to Yan Xiu; Yan Xiu defended Nankai's acceptance of a 10,000-yuan contribution from Cao with the adage, "You may not drink water stolen from another person's well, but you can certainly use it to wash your legs."[11]

Even though he was not a recognizable leader of the May Fourth Movement in Tianjin during May and June, it is entirely possible that, just as he had been in Tokyo the year before, Zhou was in some way a behind-the-scenes adviser to Ma Jun and other frontline student leaders; he may have drafted their statements and petitions. Ma Jun was a prominent and ubiquitous student leader and he represented the Tianjin Student Union at an organizational meeting of the All-China Student Union in Shanghai in mid-June. A letter he wrote Zhou from Shanghai clearly indicates that he was in close consultation with Zhou Enlai in regard to the student movement.[12]

There is good reason to believe that Zhou Enlai was away from Tianjin shortly after he returned to China, perhaps in late April or early May, on a trip to visit Fengtian and Harbin.[13] His uncle Zhou Yigeng had worked in the Heilongjiang Provincial Office of Finance since October 1917, and apparently his father was still working near there. According to eyewitness accounts, Zhou Enlai visited the Donghua School at Harbin (which his Nankai friends had set up in April 1918) at about this time and delivered some lectures there. He was apparently offered a teaching position at Donghua, which he declined.[14] He had visited Harbin on his way to Japan in 1917. However, if he did go to the northeastern region in April or May, he was certainly in Tianjin on May 17 for the tea party given by the Jingye Society, and he was in Tianjin on July 7, attending another tea party, as reported by the Nankai School *Daily*. The tea party was given in honor of the Chinese students who returned home from Japan to take part in the May Fourth Movement. Zhou, a returned student himself, made a welcoming speech in which he noted the lack of freedom in Imperial Japan and showed his appreciation and encouragement for the patriotic sentiments of the returning students.[15]

Political Activism

The evolution of Zhou Enlai's gradual involvement in the May Fourth Movement was intimately tied in with the Tianjin Student Union. The union's platform exhorted patriotism, patience, and self-sacrifice in carrying out its organized activities. As a coordinating body of fifteen middle schools and colleges in Tianjin, the union emerged as the principal voice and vehicle for directing student operations, and it cooperated with other associations in the city, including the Tianjin Alliance of All Circles for National Salvation and the Tianjin Association of Patriotic Women Comrades. The Tianjin Alliance, inaugurated on June 14, 1919, embraced a large number of educators, businessmen, students, journalists, religious leaders, and other civic notables. The chairman was Bian Yueting, who was president of the Tianjin Chamber of Commerce, and the two vice chairmen were Ma Qianli, a Protestant representative and one of Zhou Enlai's former teachers at Nankai Middle School, and Liu Junqing, a Catholic representative and general manager of the newspaper *Yishibao*. The council of the Tianjin Alliance included Shi Zizhou, a Moslem representative and another of Zhou Enlai's former teachers at Nankai, Chen Zhidu, chairman of the Tianjin Student Union, and Liu Qingyang, chairman of the Tianjin Association of Patriotic Women Comrades. This association had 600 members, the youngest only thirteen years old, and it published a weekly journal, *Xingshi Zhougan* (Awakening World Weekly). Later, Liu joined Zhou Enlai in organizing the Awakening Society (*Juewushe*) in 1919, and the Chinese communist cell in Paris in 1921.

In cooperation with the Tianjin Alliance and the Tianjin Association of Patriotic Women Comrades, the Tianjin Student Union held mass rallies, led general strikes, sponsored street speeches, and organized a campaign to boycott Japanese goods. It spearheaded drives to burn Japanese products, to harass Japanese shops and offices, and to attack Chinese merchants who collaborated with Japan. Chen, the chairman of the Union, was a veteran student leader even before the May Fourth Movement. In 1918 he was active in cooperating with the Chinese students who returned from Japan after the May demonstrations in Tokyo. He joined Zhang Guotao, Xu Deheng, Zeng Qi, and other student leaders in editing a magazine, *Guomin* (Nation), in the spring of 1919. Distinctive because of his unusually long beard, Ma was a widely recognized student leader not only in Tianjin but also in Beijing and Shanghai; he was a brilliant orator and tireless agitator. When the Tianjin Student Union decided to publish a daily newspaper, *Tianjin xuesheng lianhehuibao* (Tianjin Student Union *Bulletin*), toward the end of June 1919, Ma turned to his old friend Zhou Enlai as an ideal person to be in charge of its editorial work. This was precisely the sort of task that Zhou Enlai felt most comfortable with. It was an effective way for him to use his journalistic abilities and draw upon his rich experience, and it was a way in which he could become a real part of the student movement without assuming a position of frontline leadership.

In an article that appeared in the *Nankai Daily* on July 12, 1919, Zhou Enlai stated that the *Bulletin* was being published in response to the current student movement in China; he compared the movement with the rice riots in Japan and the independence movement in Korea, which represented new worldwide ideological trends as well as a growing popular awareness in East Asia.[16] He went on to list twenty specific principles of the new publication. The most important were: to advance the spirit of reform and renewal (*gexin*), to emphasize the spirit of democracy (*minzhu zhuyi*), to criticize government policies, to make recommendations to the Tianjin Student Union, to present scientific analysis and fair criticism on social life and academic issues, to introduce the most recent thoughts (*zuixin sichao*), to exchange news with other newspapers, and to represent the public opinion (*yulun*) of all students in Tianjin.

The first issue of the *Bulletin* was dated July 21, 1919; it had an English title, "The Tientsin Student," and the top of the front page proclaimed, "DEMOCRACY: A GOVERNMENT FOH [*sic*] THE PEOPLE BY THE PEOPLE AND OF THE PEOPLE—OUR MOTTO." This was indicative of Zhou's continuous adherence to Abraham Lincoln's democratic ideals. Although he emphasized reform (*gexin*) as a leading principle, he was not yet ready to advocate socialism or revolution openly in this newspaper.

Zhou Enlai, as editor, insisted on using the vernacular Chinese language style (*baihua*) so that the contents of the *Bulletin* would be easily accessible to students and other less well-educated ordinary readers. He himself contributed a variety of pieces to the *Bulletin* under the pen names Feifei and Xiangyu. His friends who collaborated with him on the *Bulletin* testify that just as at Nankai Middle School, Zhou Enlai was totally devoted to his editorial responsibilities; according to Pan Shilun, one of the *Bulletin*'s staff members, Zhou Enlai came to the editorial office early in the morning and worked until midnight.[17] He was extremely meticulous about small details and worked with the utmost seriousness every day. Since the staff was limited, he also spent much of his time in the printing house, encouraging the typesetters and facilitating printing and distribution procedures, and he was active in generating publication funds by means of advertisements and dramatic performances. He refused to accept any advertisements for Japanese products, but he offered a 50 percent discount to advertisers of Chinese goods. At the outset, the paper printed about 4,000 copies a day, but it was so immediately popular that the run was soon increased to around 20,000. It was not simply a local paper. Student leaders in urban areas all over China read it. It was favorably reviewed by the Beijing *Chenbao* (Morning Daily) and by a Nanjing magazine, *Shaonian Shijie* (Youthful World). A Shanghai magazine, *Xinren* (New Person), praised the *Bulletin*'s editorial and commentary sections and called it the best student newspaper in the nation.[18] The *Bulletin* published about 100 issues until early 1920, but only a few issues are still extant.

In the pages of the *Bulletin* Zhou Enlai closely followed the student movements and government policy in Beijing as well as Shandong province, whose status was the initial focus of the May Fourth Movement. In early August when Ma Liang, the martial law commander of Shandong province and a protégé of Duan Qirui, who led the powerful Anfu clique, brutally suppressed the anti-Japanese demonstrations in Shandong and summarily executed a Moslem doctor, Ma Yunting, and two other Moslems, Zhou Enlai denounced the incident in a moving article entitled "The Forces of Darkness" (August 6, 1919):

> Fellow citizens! The forces of darkness are sweeping toward us like a tidal wave. Following the Shandong students' demonstration, over three hundred of them have been locked up in the First Normal School by the police. We hear that some are to be shot. Students of Beijing University have been arrested. Now the police have issued a notice that even arrests may not

be announced in the press. The Japanese attitude toward the Nine Resolutions on Shandong (see yesterday's paper) shows that Japan does not regard China as an independent country. Citizens! The dark forces are gathering their strength. How are we to resist them? We must be prepared, we must devise practical means, and we must be ready to sacrifice ourselves. Down with the Anfu clique! Down with the bosses who back the Anfu clique! Down with the warlords on whom the Anfu clique depends! Down with the foreign forces that the Anfu clique has invited in! Citizens, awake! Now is the hour![19]

Zhou joined his friend Pan Shilun in writing another commentary, "A Criticism of Ma Liang," that appeared in the *Bulletin* on August 7. That issue was printed in blue ink in memory of the patriotic Moslems who were killed in Shandong and it was filled with news of Ma Liang's repressive measures. The August 9 issue contained another commentary by Zhou, "A denunciation of the Anfu clique's methods," in which he pointed out the strength of the mass movements organized by students, workers, and other citizens. He declared that China required a "fundamental reform" to get rid of the Anfu clique's oppressive rule.

Toward the end of August, the Tianjin Student Union sent a delegation to Beijing to join other student demonstrators in protesting Ma Liang's brutality. Zhou, for the first time that we know of, was actively involved, to the extent of joining the several hundred students from Tianjin who went to Beijing to demonstrate in front of the Presidential Office. Zhang Boling, Sun Ziwen, president of the Zhili Fishery School, and other Tianjin educational leaders also went to Beijing to support the protest movement, and several thousand people held overnight sit-in demonstrations at Xinhuamen (New China Gate), where the Presidential Office was located. In Beijing, Ma Jun, Liu Qingyang, Guo Longzhen, and Guan Xibin were the most outspoken student representatives from Tianjin.[20] Ma Jun delivered major speeches at the Xinhuamen rallies, and he was among those who were arrested by the police. Zhou Enlai printed a special issue of the *Bulletin* to publicize the government's action.

Ma Jun and other arrested student leaders were released on August 30, and on September 2 Zhou Enlai returned to Tianjin along with several other student leaders, including Guo Longzhen, Zhang Ruoming, Guan Xibin, and Chen Xiaochen. In the course of the four-hour train journey, they agreed to organize a new core organization of top leaders from the Tianjin Student Union and the Tianjin Association of Patriotic Women Comrades. They would publish a journal and lead a movement for cultural reform. As a result, on September 16, twenty persons gathered at the office of the Tianjin Student Union and launched the Awakening Society (*Juewushe*).[21]

The increasing popularity and influence of the *Bulletin* had made it subject to police surveillance and harassment. The Tianjin police confiscated one issue on August 3, 1919. In an attempt to form a united front against increasing police suppression, Zhou Enlai was instrumental in organizing the Tianjin Union of Student Publications on August 9; the union included *Nankai Rigan* (Nankai Daily), *Beiyang Rigan* (Beiyang School Daily), *Xingshi Zhougan* (Awakening World Weekly), and *Shifan Rigan* (Normal School Daily).[22] He agreed to coordinate activities, which would include guest speakers and in general promote the exchange of "new knowledge."

A secret document submitted to the Ministry of Home Affairs at Beijing in mid-September by Zhili Provincial Governor Cao Rui reported that the *Bulletin* carried extensive reports on mass rallies, protests in Beijing, strikes, and the campaigns against taxation and conscription. Cao concluded that the publication was harmful to public safety and social order.[23] Less than ten days after this report, Police Commissioner Yang Yide forced the Xiecheng Publishing House to stop printing the *Bulletin*. On September 22 Zhou Enlai announced in *Yishibao* that Yang Yide's interference had caused the suspension of the *Bulletin*, which had published 62 issues.[24] But Yang Yide had not revoked permission for publishing the *Bulletin* altogether, and on October 7, 1919, after *Yishibao* agreed to do the printing, Zhou Enlai was able to resume publication. Liu Junqing, *Yishibao*'s general manager and vice chairman of the Tianjin Alliance of All Circles for National Salvation, was an enthusiastic supporter of the Tianjin Student Union, and he apparently had enough prestige to withstand Yang Yide's pressure.

In the first issue of the revived *Bulletin* Zhou Enlai promised to wage a determined struggle in accordance with "conscience" and "justice" and not to retreat at all, in spite of the repressive measures taken by Yang Yide, who considered the *Bulletin* a "mote in one's eye."[25] He reiterated his editorial policy and declared his intention to continue to discuss new trends in international affairs, to transcend narrow parochial views, and to seek a "liberated China." Henceforth, however, the *Bulletin* would appear twice a week rather than daily, probably because of practical printing and financing problems and also because schools had just reopened for the fall semester.

Throughout this period, despite his increasing political activism and public struggle against the Tianjin authorities, Zhou Enlai was still on cordial personal terms with Yan Xiu and his friends, who epitomized the rich and powerful elite groups in Tianjin. Yan Xiu's diary of September 21, 1919, notes that Zhou Enlai enjoyed a sumptuous and leisurely dinner with Yan Xiu, Zhang Boling, Fan Jingsheng (former minister of education), Wang Zhanggu (education commissioner), and other Tianjin notables.[26] Zhou was apparently the only young person present. A few months earlier, Zhou Enlai had characterized President Zhang as undemocratic and arbitrary, and student activists such as Ma Jun and Chen Zhidu regarded Commissioner Wang as a villain.[27] Under pressure from the Xu Shichang government and Governor Cao Rui, Commissioner Wang constantly instructed Tianjin's educational administrators to control student demonstrations and strikes, and he repeatedly scolded student leaders.

That very day, September 21, Zhou Enlai had written the depressing announcement about the *Bulletin*'s suspension to appear in the next day's issue of *Yishibao*. That morning, at the Wesley Methodist Church, in the French concession, he had heard a passionate talk by Beijing University Professor Li Dazhao about the Bolshevik revolution and had then invited Li to a group discussion at the Awakening Society that afternoon.[28] Afterward, he saw Li off at the railway station and then went to the Yan Xiu residence. In the *Bulletin* published two days earlier (September 19, 1919), Zhou had severely criticized the Ministry of Education as an agent of the "forces of darkness" and as a means of sustaining an old-fashioned and moribund educational policy. One can interpret this episode as another striking example of Zhou Enlai's flexibility, pragmatism, and dualism. It may have been that he saw no serious contradiction between his activist political stand and his personal and social association with the local oligarchs. On the other hand, Yan Xiu may have been deeply concerned about the fact that his friends—Xu Shichang, Cao Rulin, Zhang Zongxiang, Yang Yide, and Wang

Zhanggu—were targets of student attacks and for that reason purposely invited his favored student leader, whom he still considered a possible husband for his youngest daughter (Yan Zhian), in an effort to ease the situation. It is conceivable, too, that Zhou Enlai took advantage of the opportunity to articulate his political views and to urge Wang Zhanggu to understand the patriotic aspirations of student activists. As we shall see later, Zhou's relationship with the Yan Xiu family was to be further solidified, despite his increasing political activism and ideological radicalization.

A few days after this dinner, Zhou Enlai attended an elaborate inaugural ceremony for the new Nankai University.[29] He had given up his earlier intention to enter either Qinghua or Beijing university, probably for academic as well as financial reasons; because he was a graduate of Nankai Middle School, he was admitted to the newly opened Nankai University without having to take entrance examinations. Following their visit to the United States in 1918, Yan Xiu and Zhang Boling had succeeded in generating sufficient funds to open a new university on the grounds of the Nankai Middle School. (Zhou had, of course, severely criticized the fund-raising, especially the substantial gift from Cao Rulin.) There were many notables at the convocation: Yan Xiu, Wang Zhanggu, Li Yuanhong (former President of the Republic), Fan Jingsheng, Sun Ziwen (president of the Zhili Fishery School), Lu Muzhai (former Zhili education commissioner), and a representative of Governor Cao Rui.[30]

Zhou Enlai was one of 96 freshmen who took part in the inauguration of Nankai University. His classmates included Ma Jun and Pan Shilun. Zhou Enlai had finally achieved his goal of entering college. Yet his Nankai University transcript shows no grades at all. School started, but he was too busy with political activities to attend classes regularly. Students were required to enroll in twenty hours of classes, and they were supposed to complete about two hours of outside study for each hour of class. Pan Shilun frankly admitted later that he and Zhou Enlai rarely went to classes at Nankai University and had only nominal affiliations with it.[31] Furthermore, Nankai University was affected by a series of student strikes, demonstrations, and campaigns. Only 21 out of the 96 members of that first class were able to graduate four years later. Zhou was still very loyal to the Nankai educational community, however. He set up a Nankai alumni liaison office on campus, drafted its charter, and directed its initial operations. In a letter to Nankai graduates at home and abroad that December, he urged them to forward news, letters, inquiries, and suggestions to the liaison office.[32]

On October 1, 1919, Zhou Enlai joined other delegates from Tianjin on a trip to Beijing for a mass demonstration on the Shandong question. The delegates from Tianjin included other members of the Awakening Society—Guo Longzhen, Chen Xiaochen, Guan Xibin, Zhao Guangchen, and Huang Zhengpin: Zhou's former Nankai Middle School teachers Ma Qianli and Shi Zizhou were also there. The huge gathering, sponsored by the All-China Student Union, had delegations from all the major cities—Shanghai, Nanjing, Wuhan, and Shandong, Hunan, and Henan provinces, as well as Tianjin and Beijing. As before, the demonstration was staged in front of the Xinhuamen Gate and demanded a meeting with President Xu Shichang. According to his fellow participants, Zhou Enlai was mainly responsible for managing propaganda and communications with student representatives of other areas and organizing supplies for the Tianjin delegation.[33] Again, he was not an active agitator but rather concentrated on strategy and logistics, and also gathered information for a full report that was to appear in the first edition of the resumed *Bulletin* on October 7. Zhou himself explained that another reporter (Zhao Guangchen) wrote the eyewitness account of what took place at Xinhuamen Gate, and Zhou edited it at his hotel. The police arrested 32 students at the gate; among them were Guo Longzhen, Zhao Guangchen, Guan Xibin, Huang Zhengpin, and Feng Fuguan, whom Zhou had traveled with to Beijing. They were detained for 40 days, until November 7.[34] Zhou, meanwhile, was free to return to Tianjin and publicize the events. Here again Zhou seemed to be acting from a strong survival instinct, born of his childhood experiences, and a characteristic caution that kept him from plunging into situations rashly before weighing various courses of action. His interest lay in the broader problem, and he could maintain a degree of journalistic objectivity and detachment in the face of highly emotional and violent events.

Zhou returned to Tianjin on October 4. On October 7, along with Ma Qianli and Chen Zhidu, he attended a meeting of the Tianjin Alliance council in the French concession. After listening to Zhou's firsthand report, the council decided to collect and send clothes and other necessary items to the Tianjin students who were detained in Beijing and to hold a protest demonstration on the National Holiday, October 10.[35] That same day Zhou spoke to the Tianjin Union of Student Publications; he was elected one of the four persons in charge of the Press office, which was entrusted with the task of publishing articles both in Chinese and in English for foreign organizations. The union decided to attach a high priority in their publications to world affairs, academic research, economic problems, and social issues. The increasing importance of diplomacy and popular movements was especially noted.

The demonstrations on October 10 turned out to be massive and bloody, and for Zhou they were decisive in that they prompted his ascendancy in the student movement and ignited his angry protest against the Tianjin government authorities. Because several of the leaders were still being held in Beijing, and others (Ma Jun and Liu Qingyang) were away in Shanghai, Zhou Enlai for the first time assumed a central role in the demonstration. About 40,000 people from fourteen schools and various civic and religious organizations showed up in the Nankai Middle School stadium for the rally on October 10. The police were there also, some 100 of them, to surround the stadium in hopes of keeping the demonstrators inside. Ma Qianli was the chairman, but the students took charge. Shouting, "Long live the Republic of China!" they followed the student marching band, playing the national anthem, and forced their way through the police into the streets and began handing out patriotic leaflets to onlookers. The police responded, and in the ensuing clashes several students were seriously injured. Two of the girls in the Awakening Society, Deng Yingchao and Li Xijin, had to be hospitalized. After things died down, Zhou Enlai, who had avoided attack by the police, went with three other student representatives to the police station to lodge a protest against police brutality and to request that students be allowed to have peaceful street demonstrations.[36] They did not see the commissioner, Yang Yide, but they did see Yang's deputy, who answered their protests by saying, "Why don't you pursue your complaints in the court?" A group of ten other leaders, among them Ma Qianli, Shi Zizhou, and Chen Zhidu, tried unsuccessfully to see Governor Cao, but they met with his deputy and Education Commissioner Wang Zhanggu and demanded that Governor Cao dismiss Yang Yide. It is important to note that even during this time of bloody confusion and extreme anger, Zhou was willing to assume responsibility for negotiating and reasoning with the hostile authorities. He felt confident of his ability to serve as an effective delegate for others, to articulate his views, and to persuade his adversaries in understanding, if not accommodating, these views. His negotiating tactics were to be repeated in January 1920, and they came to constitute a distinct hallmark of his future political and diplomatic career.

In the absence of any positive response from Governor Cao and Police Chief Yang, several thousand students scattered across Tianjin to denounce Yang's excessive use of force. On behalf of the Tianjin Student Union and the Tianjin Alliance of All Circles for National Salvation, Zhou Enlai drafted an eloquent declaration for the student strikes that were planned for October 13. The declaration stated that students had conducted a well-disciplined and orderly demonstration but that police had blocked the demonstration and had attacked students with bayonets and rifle butts.[37] It denounced Yang Yide as the "chief villain" of police brutality. The short-term student strike was being organized, the declaration said, to protest Yang's crimes and to stimulate an "awakening" in society. Zhou also put out a special issue of the *Bulletin* on October 12 that was devoted to the October 10 incident. It was full of such phrases as "Tianjin in deep water and burning fire," "the dark Double-Ten Day with no sun," "the unprecedented calamity," "the heroic cries of female students," "the public outrage by all citizens," "venomous beating by police," and "Yang Yide's sabotage of the National Holiday."

The anti-Yang campaign escalated throughout the winter. He was vilified as a second Ma Liang. Students gave street-corner speeches and handed out leaflets, and there was propaganda in the newspapers. A number of civic and religious organizations in Tianjin adopted anti-Yang resolutions, and a meeting of all presidents and principals of Tianjin schools asked Governor Cao to dismiss Yang. On October 20 about 10,000 students and citizens held an anti-Yang rally at the YMCA auditorium and marched to the Zhili Provincial Office. A group of eleven representatives, including Ma Qianli, Shi Zizhou, Liu Junqing, Chen Zhidu, Zhang Ruoming, and Li Yitao, and three reporters of the *Bulletin* arranged a meeting with Governor Cao and Education Commissioner Wang, at which nothing was resolved.[38] The All-China Student Union and several provincial student organizations also called for the removal of Yang Yide. A number of influential legislators in Beijing joined the anti-Yang bandwagon. But Yang, solidly supported by the powerful Anfu clique led by Duan Qirui, did not lose his job. On the contrary, his political fortunes soared in subsequent years; he was appointed Zhili provincial governor as well as Zhili provincial commissioner of police in 1924.[39]

Organizational Leadership

The Awakening Society, which Zhou and others had initiated on the way back from Beijing at the beginning of September 1919, was becoming important as a vehicle of student activism—a nucleus for discussing strategies and tactics, stimulating intellectual discourse on political and social issues, and in general inculcating a sense of belonging to a common cause. The founding organization had twenty members, ten men and ten women. Six more persons were accepted somewhat later (some as "friends"), after a unanimous vote by all members. The roster of the society embraced all the top-level leaders of the Tianjin Student Union (Chen Zhidu, Ma Jun) and the Tianjin Association of Patriotic Women Comrades (Liu Qingyang, Li Yitao, Guo Longzhen, Deng Yingchao). Most of them were in their early twenties (the youngest was Deng Yingchao, who was sixteen) and were connected with Nankai University (or Nankai Middle School) or with the First Zhili Women's Normal School (see Table 6).[40] Instead of going by their real names, each member was known by a number (between one and 50) to assure secrecy and confidentiality. Zhou Enlai was "wuhao" (number five); he signed some of his future writings and correspondence with this code name (*yinming*).

According to Chen Zhidu's recollections, at the inaugural meeting on September 16, Zhou Enlai, who was instrumental in initiating and organizing the Awakening Society, was nominated as chairman but declined the position "out of modesty," and so a collective administration was entrusted to the Organization Committee.[41] At this first meeting, the society chose as its guidelines for action, the spirit of "reform," "self-awakening," and "self-determination." It vowed to emphasize "sacrifice," "mutual help," and "struggle," and to conduct joint research on "family reform," "collective living,"

TABLE 6
Original Members of the Awakening Society, 1919

Name	Sex	Status	CCP/YSL[a]
Deng Yingchao [Deng Wenshu]	F	First Zhili Women's Normal School student	yes
Zhou Zilian	F	First Zhili Women's Normal School student	—
Zhou Enlai	M	Nankai University student	yes
Zhao Guangchen	M	Nankai Middle School student	yes
Xue Hanyue	M	Nankai University student	—
Guo Longzhen	F	First Zhili Women's Normal School student	yes
Guan Xibin [Guan Yiwen]	M	First Normal School student	yes
Pan Shilun	M	Nankai University student	—
Hu Weixian	M	Nankai University student	yes
Wu Ruiyan	F	First Zhili Women's Normal School graduate	yes
Liu Qingyang	F	First Zhili Women's Normal School graduate	yes
Li Baosen	M	Nankai University student	yes
Ma Jun	M	Nankai University student	yes
Li Xijin	F	not known	—
Zheng Jiqing	F	First Zhili Women's Normal School student	—
Zhang Ruoming	F	First Zhili Women's Normal School student	yes
Zhang Siqing	F	First Zhili Women's Normal School student	—
Chen Xiaochen	M	Beiyang School of Law and Politics student	yes
Li Yitao	F	Primary School teacher	yes
Chen Zhidu	M	Hebei Higher Technical School student	yes

NOTE: Another member, Zhang Shuwen, female, joined the Awakening Society at a later date. Five "friends" of the society were also voted in: Tao Shangzhao, Huang Zhengpin (Huang Ai), Yang Naixian, Han Xunhua, and Wang Zuowu.
[a]Participation in the Chinese Communist Party or the Socialist Youth League.

and "work-study." They agreed to use *baihua* exclusively in their publications and communications; it was an important part of the New Culture Movement.

The first issue of *Juewu* (Awakening), which appeared in January 1920, contained the society's "declaration" written by Zhou Enlai and adopted in December 1919.[42] It stated:

The voices and waves of "awakening" [*juewu*] are surging high in the new tide of the 20th century. Because the Peace Treaty in Europe last year had such an effect on us, the Chinese, even those who have little common sense, have acquired a profound degree of awakening. All the evils that do not belong in an advanced society—such as militarism, capitalists, party cliques, bureaucrats, sexual inequality, outmoded ideas, old morals, and old ethics—must be abolished or reformed. Once we have an awakening, which gave birth to our nationwide student movement, it will affect students all over China. Everyone wants to follow the direction of awakening. Under these circumstances, we, students in Tianjin, decided to join together in an impassioned publication, a small pamphlet called "Awakening." Hence our newly organized association is also called the "Awakening Society."

The pamphlet went on to point out the weaknesses of Chinese students: they were often pessimistic, arrogant, lazy, superstitious, jealous, selfish, and extravagant. To rectify those weaknesses, reminiscent of Zhang Boling's characterization, the society urged Chinese students to awaken themselves, reform their attitudes, and follow the spirit of "equality," "mutual help," and "universal love" —concepts associated with socialism and anarchism but also, in "universal love" (*boai*), Buddhism. From the outset, the Awakening Society invited distinguished scholars to speak. These were mostly from Beijing University, which under President Cai Yuanpei had established itself as the outstanding center of progressive thinking in China during the May Fourth era.[43]

The first and most important guest speaker was Li Dazhao, who held a seminar on September 21, 1919. He applauded the concept of equality between male and female Awakening Society members and the socially conscious direction of its activities. He also presented his views on Marxism and the Bolshevik revolution. Li, the director of the Beijing University Library, where Mao Zedong worked, was a well-known advocate of Marxism as an ideological solution to China's problems. In his essay "The Victory of the Common People," which appeared in *Xinqingnian* in January 1919, he argued that the outcome of the First World War signaled the failure of all "big isms," including capitalism, and the victory of democracy and workers. In another essay, "The Victory of Bolshevism," in the same issue of *Xinqingnian*, he saluted Lenin as the great leader of the proletarian revolution. He articulated his new beliefs in "My Views on Marxism," published in two consecutive issues of *Xinqingnian* (September and November 1919). His "views" were based on almost exact translations of Kawakami Hajime's articles.[44] (Zhou Enlai presumably read the original articles in *Research in Social Problems* before he left Japan). Li's highly publicized conversion to Marxism was enormously influential on Chinese youth, who were seeking a prominent intellectual leader who could offer a relatively simple but coherent program of action to cure China's internal ills and external weaknesses. Li paid keen attention to the student movements in Tianjin, where he had attended the Beiyang School of Law and Politics from 1907 to 1913.

One of Zhou Enlai's friends, Chen Xiaochen, remembers that as a result of Li Dazhao's visit and influence, quite a few members of the Awakening Society cemented important relations with Li and received his guidance in regard to Marxism.[45] Another member of the Awakening Society, Liu Qingyang, admits that Li Dazhao's views on Marxism exerted a great influence over her revolutionary awakening.[46] This was the time when China's early Marxist converts learned from each other and reinforced their newly found belief system through mutual support. To Zhou Enlai, who had already learned something about Kawakami Hajime's Confucianist as well as Marxist writings in Japan, Li's arguments were both familiar and, one can infer, attractive, for this direct association with Li Dazhao in Tianjin was the beginning of a close political cooperation between the two men that was to last until Li's execution in 1927.

The Awakening Society was not the purposeful prototype of a Marxist study association, similar to Li Dazhao's Marxist study group at Beijing University, because its members espoused a diverse array of political orientations and ideological dispositions, including anarchism, which was fairly popular in China during the May Fourth Movement. And yet the Awakening Society tended to promote progressive thinking among its members. It is also conceivable that some members were in contact with Sergei A. Polevoy, a professor of Russian literature at Beijing University who visited Tianjin in 1919. Polevoy, a graduate of the Far Eastern University at Vladivostok, was not a communist himself but he was known to be sympathetic with the Bolshevik revolution. According to a Soviet source, Zhou Enlai took a few friends to Beijing University to have a discussion with Polevoy.[47]

In the next few years, about three-fourths of the Awakening Society's members joined the Chinese Communist Party or the Socialist Youth League in China or Europe. An important personal as well as political by-product of Zhou Enlai's involvement in the Awakening Society was his relationship with his future wife, Deng Yingchao, who had already distinguished herself as a courageous female leader in Tianjin. Zhou Enlai and six other members of the

Awakening Society went to Europe; Zhou Enlai joined Liu Qingyang and Zhao Guangchen in constituting an initial core group of the Chinese Communist Party in Europe. In 1946, Zhou Enlai told Henry Lieberman that during the May Fourth Movement "my thought was already inclined to agree with revolution and socialism. However, owing to my feudalistic family background, my initial socialist thought was rather utopian. Once I myself suffered from agony and understood the difficulties of life, I became a Marxist materialist in a short span of time."[48]

Manifesting the spirit of equality and cooperation between men and women displayed in the Awakening Society's organizational framework, Zhou Enlai advocated a merger between the male-dominated Tianjin Student Union and the Tianjin Association of Patriotic Women Comrades. Extending his admiration for his adoptive mother to women in general, he continued to express high esteem and respect for women. In early December he participated in a series of meetings of representatives from Tianjin schools, and an agreement on the merger was finally reached. On December 10, about 500 student representatives met at the Chamber of Commerce and started a new Tianjin Student Union. Zhang Ruoming, chairman of the Student Council at the First Zhili Women's Normal School and a member of the Awakening Society, presided over the event. Several speakers—Ma Qianli, Ma Jun, Zhang Ruoming, Bian Yueting—emphasized the recurring themes of the May Fourth Movement, that is, national salvation by students, the boycott of Japanese goods, the condemnation of Chinese collaborators with Japan, and the liberation of women. The Governing Council elected Zhang Ruoming as one of two co-chairmen.[49] The most important ten-member Committee on General Affairs included four members of the Awakening Society—Ma Jun, Chen Zhidu, Liu Qingyang, and Li Yitao. Deng Yingchao was elected as member of the Committee on Education and of the Committee on Speeches; she was soon elected chairman of the Committee on Speeches. The new Tianjin Student Union also had committees on publications, investigations, and economic affairs. Zhou Enlai was not a member of the Governing Council or of any decision-making committees, but he was made director of the Executive Bureau, which was equivalent to a secretariat responsible for the union's day-to-day operations. Once again, he did not seek a prominent top position in the new organization that he helped restructure but preferred instead to carry out its actual administrative and organizational work behind the scenes. The Committee on Publications also chose him as director of the Weekly Publications Division.

Zhou Enlai's two-year experience in Japan became a major asset for his political activism. In his *Bulletin* articles, he referred confidently to Japanese events such as the rice riots and the newspaper strikes, and he cited reports and articles that appeared in Japanese newspapers, in particular, *Osaka Asahi Shimbun*, which was critical of the Terauchi loans to Duan Qirui.[50] He also translated and published Japanese articles in the *Bulletin*; he particularly liked an essay by Miyazaki Ryūnosuke that accused Japanese capitalists of invading China and obstructing peace in Asia. As the son of Miyazaki Tōten (an influential Japanese friend of Sun Yat-sen and Huang Xing) and a disciple of Yoshino Sakuzō (pro-China professor at Tokyo Imperial University), Miyazaki Ryūnosuke was sympathetic with the May Fourth Movement in China and espoused a progressive ideology.[51] Like Yoshino Sakuzō and Miyazaki Ryūnosuke, Zhou Enlai believed that it was not the Japanese people but the Japanese militarists and capitalists who were hostile to China's national interests, and that Japan needed radical internal reforms to change its anti-China policy.

In a brief commentary entitled "Respectful Advice to the Japanese Students in China" that he wrote in August 1919, Zhou Enlai welcomed a group of Japanese students who visited China in early August after they had issued an open letter at Tokyo on July 30, 1919.[52] In this letter they said, "Only our young generation has enough absolute sincerity to save our nations, and to thoroughly understand the general trends of the world. Goodwill between China and Japan can only be realized by our generation." In response, Zhou Enlai observed: "You are speaking frankly to our Chinese students, and your words have never before been said by the Japanese who came to China. You really make us see some measure of hope for goodwill between the peoples of the two East Asian nations in the future." Yet he gave them pointed advice:

"Combining knowledge with practice" [*zhixing heyi*] is the teaching of Wang Yangming, and the Japanese worship this approach the most. Now that you realize that warlords are evil, that invasion is wrong, that society needs reform, that the force of the common people should be strengthened, and that all human beings should be equal, you should make a real effort to promote the egalitarian movement, to overthrow your warlords, and to break the Japanese national ambition of foreign invasion. Only by so doing can the social movements in the two nations join together. . . . In short, the real goodwill between the peoples in the two nations can never be expressed by talking and writing. Of the utmost importance is the actualization of fundamental social reform by the peoples on both sides.

This advice is reminiscent of the poem Zhou wrote in Kyoto in April 1919 in which he criticized warlords and capitalists. Quite correctly, he recognized the domestic sources of Japan's aggressive policy toward China. In order to achieve domestic reforms in Japan, he called for cooperation between the "intellectual class" and "working classes." This was his first explicit published statement in support of social reforms pursued jointly by intellectuals and workers. Although he did not in this instance specifically mention a need for cooperation between intellectuals and workers in China, it is not difficult to infer that he recognized such a requirement for social reforms in China as well.

Zhou's quotation from the Ming dynasty philosopher Wang Yangming (1472–1529) indicates his enduring adherence to the Chinese traditional philosophies—Confucian or Neo-Confucian—despite his support of the New Culture Movement, which ran counter to the central contents of the Confucian social order. Jon L. Saari points out that Neo-Confucian thought had a wide-ranging impact on educated young men like Zhou Enlai who grew up in the period 1890–1920.[53] Zhou Enlai's article also suggests that his participation in the anti-Japanese boycott was directed as much against the Anfu clique as against Japan per se. In this context Yang Yide was viewed as a concrete incarnation of the Anfu power in Tianjin. Zhou's usage of such terms as "reform" (*gaizao*), "equality" (*pingdeng*), "common people" (*pingmin*), and "working class" (*laodong jieji*) clearly suggests his advocacy of progressive ideas as early as August 1919. It is important to note that the Chinese phrase "common people" (*pingmin*) also meant the "proletariat" as used in Marx's *Communist Manifesto*.

Prison Experience

The nationwide boycott of Japanese goods reached an emotional climax in November 1919 when Japanese Consulate guards and Japanese residents in Fuzhou killed and wounded a number of Chinese students involved in boycott activities. Students and citizens in Tianjin responded to the Fuzhou incident with angry meetings, protest messages, and an accelerated boycott movement. They demanded that the Chinese government protect its own citizens against Japanese atrocities. In the *Bulletin* Zhou Enlai set forth the details and implications of the Fuzhou incident and urged his fellow students to take active parts in the anti-Japanese operations. Students distributed 50,000 leaflets a day, printed by *Yishibao*, concerning the Fuzhou incident.[54] The Tianjin Student Union chose Zhou Enlai as a member of a five-person delegation to visit with Governor Cao and Education Commissioner Wang in late November, but, for unknown reasons, he did not join this delegation.[55] He may have been too busy putting out the *Bulletin*; possibly, also, he did not want to confront Commissioner Wang, whom Yan Xiu had introduced him to two months before. In his capacity as director of the Tianjin Student Union's executive bureau, Zhou did visit with Bian Yueting (president of the Chamber of Commerce) and other local business leaders to discuss student boycott issues.[56] Some Chinese merchants opposed the boycott because it undermined their business interests and they therefore collaborated with the Japanese Consulate General and the Japanese Chamber of Commerce and Industry in Tianjin. As Table 7 shows, the boycott already adversely affected Japanese commerce in China: there was a significant drop in the quantities of Japanese consumer goods imported via Shanghai.[57] Japanese authorities set up a special low-interest bank loan program to help Japanese companies that went bankrupt in China, and it exerted a great deal of diplomatic pressure upon the Chinese government to stop the boycott and to honor the Sino-Japanese Commercial Treaty.[58]

On December 20 about 30,000 students and citizens in Tianjin met at Nankai University to protest the Fuzhou tragedy. As usual, Ma Qianli, Shi Zizhou, Guo Longzhen, and Li Yitao played prominent roles in the rally: press reports did not mention Zhou Enlai as one of some 30 leaders.[59] Demonstrators heard passionate patri-

TABLE 7

Effects of Anti-Japanese Boycott in China: Decline in Imports from Japan, 1918–1919

Commodity	Unit[a]	July 1918 (first 10 days)	July 1919 (first 10 days)
Cement	dan	4,000	0
Clothing	da	42,150	15,417
Cotton yarn	dan	4,042	737
Cotton	dan	5,112	0
Coarse cloth	pi	241,550	27,000
Utensil	da	51,173	233
Match	luo	107,900	15,900
Mirror	da	2,634	0
Brass	dan	3,511	119
Copper	dan	283	572
Iron	dan	2,162	24
Paper	dan	3,936	607
Cloth	pi	104,299	77,604
Sugar	dan	22,828	7,093
Umbrella	ba	78,403	0

SOURCE: *Yishibao*, Aug. 12, 1919. The imports from Japan were those listed by the Shanghai customs office.

[a]dan = 100 kilograms; da = dozen; luo = basket (50–100 kilograms); pi = roll (33.1 meters); ba = piece.

otic speeches, adopted an anti-Japanese resolution, burned a huge pile of confiscated Japanese goods, and marched in the streets. The Tianjin Student Union and the Tianjin Alliance of All Circles for National Salvation jointly devised an elaborate scheme to investigate and expose Chinese merchants who imported Japanese goods and to confiscate and burn those items (towels, parasols, pencils, hats, clothes, toys, wallets, shoes). Shortly thereafter, in response to rising popular sentiment and Japanese pressure, Governor Cao issued an order banning all boycott activities, and he cracked down on the Tianjin Student Union and the Tianjin Alliance. These actions only served to spur anti-Japanese activities in Tianjin. Finally they reached a crisis in the Kuifacheng incident.

On January 23, 1920, investigative members of the Tianjin Student Union discovered seventeen baskets of Japanese lamp shades at the Kuifacheng Foreign Goods Store in Tianjin. When they began confiscating them in accordance with their boycott, the Chinese store owners called in a number of Japanese *ronin* (masterless samurai), who attacked the students and then escaped into the Japanese concession.[60] This incident was immediately followed by a series of protest demonstrations, and a number of Tianjin leaders, including Ma Qianli, Shi Zizhou, and Ma Jun, rushed to the Governor's Office. In the ensuing confrontation with demonstrators and petitioners, Police Commissioner Yang Yide arrested some twenty civic and student leaders, including Ma Qianli, Shi Zizhou, and Ma Jun. Yang also closed the offices of the Tianjin Student Union and the Tianjin Alliance of All Circles for National Salvation.

Zhou Enlai, though not in the forefront of the demonstrations and petition drives, joined other members of the Awakening Society in holding overnight strategy meetings in the basement of the Wesley Methodist Church.[61] They decided to seek the release of the arrested leaders and to urge the government to find and punish the Japanese *ronin* and Chinese collaborators.

On January 29, several thousand students gathered before the YMCA building and marched toward the Governor's Office. According to an extensive account reported in *Yishibao*, Zhou Enlai was identified as the "general commander" of this student march.[62] Only when his friends and teachers fell victims to police repression and became incapacitated did he step forward to assume frontline leadership. He had a particularly strong sense of loyalty and solidarity toward Ma Qianli and Ma Jun. Even at this critical juncture, however, he sought to negotiate and reason with the government authorities rather than seek violent confrontation. Local newspapers vividly described his preeminent leadership role and quoted a segment of the speech he delivered at the rally: "This petition is of the utmost importance. I hope that those directing the activity of each school will maintain discipline, avoid unnecessary disturbance, be fully prepared spiritually, and pay close attention to the activities of the police."[63]

Zhou Enlai was one of the four student representatives designated to present the patriotic petition to the Governor; the others were Guo Longzhen and Zhang Ruoming (of the Awakening Society) and Yu Fangzhou, a student leader at the Public Middle School. As soon as the four entered the gate of the provincial government office, the police and security force, on the alert, arrested them and used fire hoses, clubs, and bayonets to disperse the student demonstrators. As they were being carried off by the police,

Zhou Enlai and three other student representatives shouted, "Long live the Republic of China," "Long live the people," and "Long live students."[64] This incident was described as an "unprecedentedly bloody tragedy." About 60 students were severely wounded and 800 others received varying degrees of minor injuries.[65] The injury list compiled by local newspapers included several members of the Awakening Society and Zhang Xilu, Zhang Boling's eldest son, who was a student at Qinghua School and had returned to Tianjin during the winter vacation.[66]

During six months of imprisonment, Zhou made detailed notes of the whole experience. His two accounts, "The Record of Detention in the Police Station" (*Jingting juliuji*) and "The Diary in the Public Prosecution Prison" (*Jianting rilu*), are our main source of information on the episode. Zhou started compiling "The Record" in May and completed it on June 5, 1920.[67] As a companion account to "The Record," he completed "The Diary" on November 24, 1920, while he was aboard ship on his way to Europe.[68] Both accounts are meticulously organized and very informative, and devoid of bitterness and emotionalism.

For the first week following the arrest, Zhou Enlai and the three other student representatives were detained in the garrison barracks—the two young men in one room and the two young women in another. As soon as they entered the barracks, they all signed a statement addressed to the barracks commander in which they claimed full responsibility for all actions taken by student demonstrators. An uncle of Zhou's former Nankai classmate Li Fujing worked in the barracks and came to visit with Zhou Enlai.

On February 6 all four students were transferred to the police station. They joined Ma Qianli, Ma Jun, Shi Zizhou, and other inmates who were already detained there. Thus there were at that time a total of 26 detainees in the police station, separated in several rooms. The only place where direct communications could take place among them was in the common restroom. In the police station Zhou Enlai encountered Police Commissioner (and Martial Law Commander) Yang Yide, probably for the first time. When Zhou asked why he was arrested, Yang told him that the students were expressing their patriotism in the wrong way and were being used by politicians. He added that he had no personal animosity against the students and that he was only following the central government's instructions.

Zhou explained that the students' actions were noble and that they only wanted to present a petition to the Governor. Thereafter Yang and Zhou continued to have contacts and discussions.

The detainees in the police station included several respected civic leaders—Ma Qianli (director of business affairs at Nankai University), Shi Zhizhou (teacher at Nankai Middle School), Meng Zhenhou (manager of a local Chinese newspaper, *Taiwushibao*), and Yang Mingseng (manager of an insurance company)—who were well connected with the Tianjin establishment. Yang Yide was careful not to offend them personally. He was apologetic toward Ma Qianli, a brother-in-law of Zhang Boling, whom Yang had regarded as a friend for more than twenty years; Yang also had made a substantial financial contribution to Nankai. Yang allowed the inmates to correspond with their relatives, to receive visitors, and to read *Xinqingnian*, *Xinchao*, and other liberal magazines. No newspapers were available, however. On the eve of the Lunar New Year, Yang gave a dinner for all the detainees and arranged their gathering on New Year's Day. This was the first opportunity for them to be together after a month of separation; Zhou Enlai described the event as "very joyful." Yang assembled them on a few other occasions also and held long and intense discussions with them. He released several who were unwell, including Ling Zhong, a younger brother of Ling Bing (dean of academic affairs at Nankai University) and one of Zhou Enlai's classmates at Nankai Middle School and Nankai University.[69] Yang did not release others, however, on the grounds that he had no authority to do so, or to hand them over to the office of a local public prosecutor.

On April 2 the detainees staged a hunger strike to demand an immediate release or prompt trial. A number of Christian, Islamic, business, media, and other leaders in Tianjin expressed their support and encouragement for the detainees. There is no evidence that any immediate member of the Zhang Boling and Yan Xiu families, except for Ma Qianli's wife, came to the police station. In a discussion session Yang referred to Zhou Enlai's uncles as government officials in Heilongjiang province, but neither Zhou's father nor his uncles came to see him.

On April 5, in a remarkable demonstration of solidarity, 24 representatives of the Tianjin Student Union went to the police station and requested that they be permitted to replace all the detainees

TABLE 8
List of Prison Inmates, Tianjin, 1920

Name	Age	Occupation	Sentence (July 1920)
Ma Qianli	37	Nankai University staff	2 mos.[a]
Ma Jun	26	Nankai University student	2 mos.
Meng Zhenhou	35	Newspaper manager	2 mos.
Yang Mingseng	51	Manager, insurance company	2 mos.
Xia Qingxi	30	Leader, Chamber of Commerce	2 mos.
Shi Zizhou	42	Nankai Middle School teacher	2 mos.
Yu Junwang	18	Commerce School student	2 mos.
Guo Xurong	21	Commerce School student	2 mos.
Chen Baocong	23	Dehua Middle School graduate	2 mos.
Shi Jingrang	20	Nankai Middle School student	NG[b]
Li Sanren	25	Businessman	NG
Sha Zhupei	20	Chengmei School student	NG
Li Yanhao	23	Beiyang School of Law and Politics student	NG
Li Peiliang	18	Commerce School student	NG
Qi Shiliang	19	Nankai Middle School student	NG
Shang Moqing	20	Businessman	10 days
Zhou Enlai	23	Nankai University student	2 mos.
Yu Fangzhou	21	Public Middle School student	2 mos.
Zhang Ruoming	20	Women's Normal School student	Fine
Guo Longzhen	25	Women's Normal School graduate	Fine

SOURCE: ZZ, pp. 383–85.
NOTE: Other inmates released earlier included Ling Zhong and Tao Shangzhao.
[a]Sentenced to two-month imprisonment.
[b]NG = not guilty.

currently in custody. The group included Zhou Enlai's close associates and members of the Awakening Society—Deng Yingchao, Chen Zhidu, and Zhao Guangchen. Yang Yide refused the request, but permitted them to meet the detainees. In "The Record" Zhou Enlai wrote of his "happy" reunion with his student associates. A few days after that, Yang Yide moved all the detainees to the office of a Hebei provincial public prosecutor, where they were then transferred to the prison of the Public Prosecutor. The trial was still three months off, and the new prison gave them greater privileges. All the male detainees were housed in five rooms, but were allowed to have a partial communal life. The two female inmates, Guo Longzhen and Zhang Ruoming, were confined in a separate room with limited communication with the male group.

There was great diversity among the inmates in terms of age, occupation, educational level, religious affiliation, and ideological orientation (see Table 8). A majority of them were high school or college students in their late teens and early twenties. The youngest one (Tao Shangzhao) was fifteen years old, but he was soon released, presumably because of his age. A few adults were in their thirties and forties and the oldest was 51 years old. There were at least three Moslems—Shi Zizhou, Ma Jun, and Guo Longzhen. In spite of this diversity, they were able to sustain a mutually supportive and cooperative pattern of living and struggling together. Their camaraderie transcended the old-fashioned social boundaries in prison.

Zhou Enlai noted with pleasure the new freedom to read newspapers. For the first time in what he called "75 days of darkness," he was allowed to read *Yishibao* and other local newspapers. He now had a deeper understanding of the development of China's domestic and foreign affairs. Deng Yingchao, Chen Zhidu, and other student leaders and members of the Awakening Society came regularly to visit, bringing encouragement and outside news, and students from Beijing came to show their support. Other people in Tianjin donated money, flowering plants, fans, beverages (including Shaoxing wine), herbal medicines, and other items for the inmates. The inmates were never subjected to physical torture or cruel treatment, and they were permitted to hold group discussions and to organize collective activities. They had regular exercises, held birthday parties, and enjoyed recreational activities together. In their dramatic presentations they asked Zhou Enlai to reenact the famous play performed at Nankai, *One Dollar*, in which he had played the role of the heroine.

Every evening at eight o'clock the inmates held a general meeting, and they worked out a well-structured daily schedule, reminiscent of the highly regimented program at Nankai Middle School: 8:00 A.M., rising time; 8:30, calisthenics; remainder of the morning, working on preparations for investigations and their trial; 2:00–5:00 P.M., reading and discussion; 7:00–9:00 P.M., group study of social problems; 9:00–11:00 P.M., recreation; 12:00 midnight, retire. Zhou Enlai joined Ma Qianli and Yu Fangzhou in developing a program for the study of social problems and a schedule for readings, which were divided into four categories—English and Chinese literature, history, and mathematics. Zhou Enlai himself, who was considered something of an expert, delivered a series of lectures on Marxism in which he talked about historical materialism, the history of class struggle, the theory of the surplus value of labor, and *Das Kapital*. It may well be that during his prison experience he came close to espousing Marxism as his own political belief. On May 1 he joined other inmates in celebrating International Labor Day, and they all agreed that after they were released they would work for the interests of the "common people" (*pingmin*). Zhou Enlai also gave talks on other political and historical topics such as the history of Japanese control over Qingdao, the Shandong question, and the May Fourth Movement. On May 4 he presided over an elaborate program to celebrate the first anniversary of the movement. He also taught the Japanese language to his prison comrades. Ma Jun talked about anarchism, and Ma Qianli discussed Christianity and held prayer meetings.

During all this time, the Public Prosecutor continued to investigate the inmates' "crimes" and to question them about their political activities, especially the anti-Japanese boycott, the Kuifacheng incident, and demonstrations. The Tianjin Student Union, the *Bulletin*, and the Tianjin Alliance of All Circles for National Salvation were the focus of intense investigations and inquiries. On June 30, four days after the trial date was announced, the detainees were notified of the formal charges against them. Zhou Enlai was charged with the crime of "social disturbance" according to Article 164 of the Criminal Law; specifically, he was accused of having violently threatened the government authorities and of having refused to disperse the student demonstrators on January 29. For their defense, he and his fellow inmates chose a team of eminent lawyers headed by Liu Chongyou, who had gained a national reputation by defending the leaders of the May Fourth Movement in Beijing. Representatives of the Tianjin Student Union and the Tianjin Alliance went to Beijing to request Liu's legal assistance.[70] In a letter that he wrote to Liu on July 1, 1920, Zhou Enlai, along with other student representatives, argued that the Public Prosecutor's charge was groundless because on January 29 they only wanted to see the Governor and present their patriotic petition to him, and that once they were arrested inside the Governor's Office, they had no way to influence the demonstrators outside.[71]

The trial began July 6. The courtroom was crowded and several hundred people who were unable to enter waited outside. For the next ten days or so, while the trial was under way, Tianjin was engulfed in armed clashes between the Zhili clique, led by Wu Peifu (and Zhang Zuolin and Cao Kun), and the Anfu clique, headed by Duan Qirui. Many citizens sought refuge in the foreign concessions. There was some concern about the safety of the inmates during the political and military commotion, but there was no way for them to be moved to a secure place. Wu Peifu conducted a brief but successful military campaign, and the Anfu clique's long-standing control over Tianjin was weakened. Afterward, the Public Prosecutor was abruptly replaced. The Tianjin Student Union planned to hold massive demonstrations if the inmates were given severe punishment. On July 17 the judge handed down his relatively lenient decisions: Zhou Enlai, Ma Qianli, Ma Jun, Shi Zizhou, Yu Fangzhou, and six others were sentenced to two months in prison. The two women, Guo Longzhen and Zhang Ruoming, received a fine of 60 yuan each, and another person was sentenced to ten days in prison. The rest were found not guilty.[72] Since they had already remained in detention longer than the judge's sentences required, all the inmates were immediately released.

A large crowd of Tianjin citizens—students, religious leaders, legislators, politicians, and businessmen—turned out to welcome their release as "heroes." The liberated inmates were driven through the downtown area in a caravan of nine cars with white flags fluttering; they were followed by several hundred admirers on foot. Each was presented with a mirror and a bouquet of flowers. The Congregational Church gave each of them a medallion with the inscription, "A Sacrifice for the Nation."[73] At the welcoming ceremony Ma Qianli and Shi Zizhou spoke, and Zhou Enlai and Zhang Ruoming reported on the conditions of life in prison. They gathered for a commemorative group photograph. In the evening, Bian Yueting, president of the Tianjin Chamber of Commerce, and Sun Ziwen, president of the Zhili Fishery School, were the official hosts at a dinner meeting held in honor of the "heroes."

Communism in Europe

The six months in prison did not dampen Zhou Enlai's political and organizational activities in Tianjin; on the contrary, as he later made clear, his budding revolutionary consciousness was decisively aroused by his prison experience.[74] After he was released, he resumed his part in the Awakening Society, which was now dedicated to the formation of a nationwide coalition of reformist organizations in China.

As the first step toward this goal, Zhou Enlai and ten other members of the Awakening Society went to Beijing in August for a meeting at Taoranting Park with representatives of four progressive Beijing organizations.[75] At this meeting, chaired by Liu Qingyang, Deng Yingchao described the achievements of the Awakening Society, and Zhou Enlai outlined the goal of coordination among progressive organizations in Beijing and Tianjin. Li Dazhao and Zhang Shenfu (a Beijing University lecturer) applauded Zhou Enlai's goal, and the participants then agreed to found a Reform Federation (*gaizao lianhe*). On August 18 about twenty representatives, headed by Li Dazhao, met at the Beijing University library and adopted the Reform Federation's Declaration and Charter, which had been drafted by Zhang Shenfu.[76] The declaration proclaimed that under the "red flag" of reform the federation was committed to promoting "liberty" and "equality" and to the task of "going to the people" (*dao minjian qu*), after the pattern of the Narodnik movement in Russia in the 1870's. Li Dazhao spearheaded that campaign and exerted a great impact upon Chinese youth in the early 1920's.[77] This populist movement, with its romantic attitude toward rural life, was committed to nationalist and progressive ideals. The federation adopted a program of investigating social conditions, organizing peasants and workers, spreading education for the "common people," and advancing "women's independence" (*funü duli*). In this federation, Zhou Enlai had the opportunity to strengthen his association with Li Dazhao and to become acquainted with Zhang Shenfu, who was Liu Qingyang's boyfriend. There is no indication that Zhou Enlai had any contact with the Comintern agent Gregori Voitinsky, who met with Li Dazhao at Beijing and Chen Duxiu at Shanghai in 1920.

Meanwhile, Zhou Enlai assisted his Nankai teachers and former prison comrades Ma Qianli and Shi Zizhou in starting a new newspaper, *Xinminyibao* (New Popular Voice), in Tianjin. Both Ma and Shi had resigned from their positions at Nankai after their release from prison. Zhou Enlai's journalistic experience made him an important part of the staff not only for practical reasons but also for matters of editorial policy.[78] At the same time he was preparing for his departure to Europe. It is clear that he had already decided to

In Tokyo, circa 1918, Zhou Enlai with his old friends from Nankai Middle School (from left, standing): Wu Hantao, Wang Pushan, Zhou Enlai, and Zhang Ruifeng. The person seated is not identified. (Zhou Enlai Memorial Museum)

Zhou Enlai (far right) with his friends in Tokyo, circa 1918; he is the only person without a school hat because he was not enrolled in a college or a higher school. (Zhou Enlai Memorial Museum)

Members of the Nankai Alumni Association in Japan, together with other students from Tianjin, gathered to welcome Zhang Boling and Yan Xiu to Tokyo in December 1918: Zhou Enlai (seated third from left in the front row), Zhang Boling (behind Zhou Enlai, with mustache), Yan Xiu (on Zhang Boling's left, with glasses), Fan Jingsheng (left of Yan Xiu), and Zhang Pengchun (behind Yan Xiu). Other participants included Zhang Zongxiang, Chinese Minister to Japan. (Zhou Enlai Memorial Museum)

Kawakami Hajime, a leading Japanese Marxist and professor at Kyoto Imperial University who introduced Marxism to Zhou Enlai in Japan. (Nishikawa Tsutomu, *Arubamu hyōden—Kawakami Hajime*, Tokyo: Shinhyōron, 1980.)

Zhou Enlai (right) with Pan Shilun in Tianjin in 1919. They were members of the Awakening Society, editors of the Tianjin Student Union *Bulletin*, and classmates at Nankai University. (Zhou Enlai Memorial Museum)

Members of the Awakening Society in 1920. From left in the back row: Chen Xiaochen, Pan Shilun, Ma Jun, Li Yitao, Guo Longzhen, Hu Weixian, and Zhou Enlai. From left in the front row: Chen Zhidu, Xue Hanyue, Zheng Jiqing, Zhou Zilian, Deng Yingchao (Zhou Enlai's future wife), Liu Qingyang, and Li Baosen. (Not pictured: Zhao Guangchen, Guan Xibin, Wu Ruiyan, Li Xijin, Zhang Ruoming, Zhang Siqing.) (Zhou Enlai Memorial Museum)

Prison inmates in Tianjin, 1920. From left in the front row: Zhang Ruoming and Guo Longzhen. From left in the second row: Li Peiliang (first), Ma Jun (second), and Tao Shangzhao (third). From right in the third row: Ma Qianli (first). From right in the fourth row: Yu Fangzhou (first) and Zhou Enlai (second). From right in the back row: Shi Zizhou (third). (Zhou Enlai Memorial Museum)

Zhou Enlai with his old friends from Nankai Middle School—Li Fujing (middle) and Chang Ceou (right)—in London, 1921. (Zhou Enlai Memorial Museum)

Zhou Enlai and his friends in Paris, 1921. From left in the back row: Zhang Shenfu (first), Tao Shangzhao (second), Zhou Enlai (third), and Zhao Guangchen (fifth). From left in the front row: Liu Qingyang and Li Yuru. (Zhou Enlai Memorial Museum)

From left: Zhang Shenfu, Liu Qingyang, Zhou Enlai, and Zhao Guangchen at Lake Wannsee in Berlin, 1922. Leaders of the Chinese Communist Movement in Europe, they had known each other since the May Fourth Movement in China. (Zhou Enlai Memorial Museum)

Zhou Enlai in front of the Godefroy Hotel in Paris, 1923, where he had an office as general secretary of the Chinese Communist Youth League in Europe. (Zhou Enlai Memorial Museum)

In July 1924, the Chinese Communist Youth League in Europe held a meeting in Paris before Zhou Enlai's return to China. From left in the front row: Nie Rongzhen (first), Zhou Enlai (fourth), Li Fuchun (sixth). From left in the second row: Lin Wei (second). From left in the back row: Mu Qing (first) and Deng Xiaoping (seventh). (Zhou Enlai Memorial Museum)

Leaders of the Guomindang's European Branch met in Paris to bid farewell to Zhou Enlai in July 1924. From left in the front row: Wang Jingqi (first), Zhou Enlai (second), and Zhao Dong (third). From right in the back row: Li Fuchun (first) and Lin Wei (second). (Zhou Enlai Memorial Museum)

In November 1924, Zhou Enlai, shown here in a Guomindang military uniform, was appointed director of the Political Department at Whampoa Military Academy in Canton. (Zhou Enlai Memorial Museum)

In 1917, before his departure for Japan, Zhou Enlai gave this memento in his calligraphy to his friend Guo Shiling. It says: "I hope that China will fly aloft all over the world when I see you again." (*Zhou Enlai shoujixuan*, Beijing: Wenwu chubanshe, 1988)

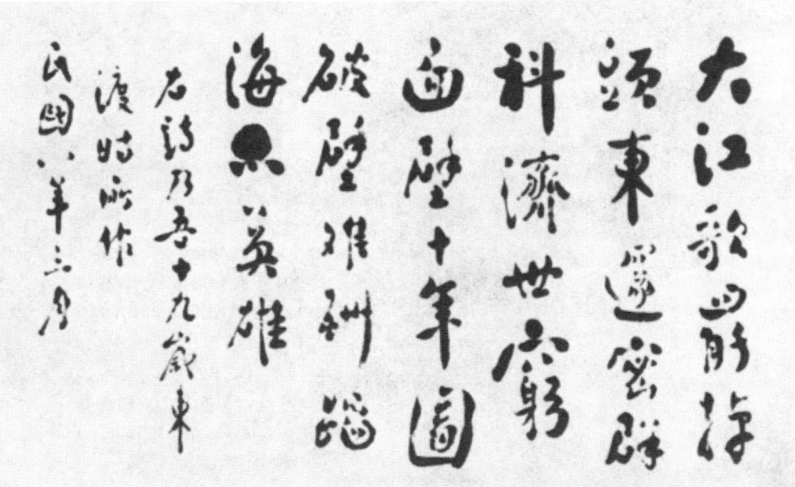

At a farewell party given by Zhang Honggao in Tokyo in March 1919, Zhou Enlai wrote this poem, which he had composed two years earlier in China before departing for Japan. (*Zhou Enlai shoujixuan*, Beijing: Wenwu chubanshe, 1988)

go to Europe while in prison, in part because he, Ma Jun, and other Nankai detainees in the police station had been expelled by Nankai University. While in prison, Zhou composed a long poem for Li Yuru, who was a student at the First Zhili Women's Normal School and the fiancée of Pan Shilun, as she was about to leave for France. One part read:

> Coming back some day,
> You'll unfurl the standard of freedom,
> Strike up the song of independence.
> You'll fight for women's rights,
> Seek equality,
> Plunge yourself into action.
> You'll overthrow the outdated ethics,
> All by dint of a thought in your mind!
> Three months from now,
> On the wharf of Marseilles,
> In the suburbs of Paris,
> Maybe you and I shall meet.[79]

He referred to France as a "home of liberty" (*ziyou guxiang*), suggesting that he held a favorable view of France. Zhou had studied the democratic principles of Rousseau and Montesquieu at Nankai and had learned from Chen Duxiu and other Chinese intellectuals during the May Fourth Movement that the French were the creators of modern Western civilization.[80] When one of his friends expressed anxiety about going to Europe, Zhou Enlai said: "Didn't you read *Xiyouji* [*The Journey to the West*]? Going to France requires the same spirit that the Tang dynasty monk [in *Xiyouji*] showed in going to India in search of the Buddhist scriptures. Don't worry! We have many [Nankai] schoolmates there and they will help us."[81]

Zhou's plans were arranged smoothly and quickly. Finances were of course a great problem, but early in the fall he was selected as one of the first two recipients of the Yan Xiu Scholarship for study abroad; the other recipient was one of Zhou's closest Nankai friends, Li Fujing. On October 4 Zhou and Li met with Yan Xiu to discuss their European plans, and a few days later, with a letter of introduction from Yan Xiu, the two went to Beijing and easily obtained the certificate to travel to France from the Chinese-French Educational Commission, which was directed by one of Yan Xiu's friends, Cai Yuanpei, the president of Beijing University.

This certificate identified Zhou and Li as students (*jianxue*) rather than work-study students (*qingong jianxue*) and authorized them to carry "gold bars" for educational expenses in Europe.[82]

In 1912 Cai Yuanpei, who was at that time Minister of Education, had joined his associates in organizing the Society for Frugal Study in France, in an attempt to encourage young Chinese to go to France. A few years thereafter, Cai, a dedicated Francophile, and his Chinese and French friends established the Chinese-French Educational Commission, with offices in both Paris and Beijing. After the war ended, the program became very popular: the number of Chinese students who went to France under the Commission-sponsored work-study program increased from 400 in 1919 to 1,200 in 1920. Cai's plan was based on the assumption that Chinese students could get work in France to earn the money to pay for their college tuition, learn from the advanced aspects of Western civilization, and then return and lead China's modernization efforts.[83] During the war, there had been approximately 200,000 Chinese contract workers in France and other European countries, and after the war ended, it became the fashion for ambitious young Chinese to flock to France and other European countries.

Besides his scholarship, Zhou Enlai was also promised financial support by Yan Xiu and Liu Chongyou, who as a defense lawyer was much impressed by Zhou Enlai's intellectual ability and personal charm;[84] and *Yishibao*—perhaps at his request—made him a special correspondent in Europe. Once again Zhou Enlai capitalized on his reputation and connections and demonstrated his resourcefulness in generating multiple sources for his financial support in Europe. His departure was to be from Shanghai; on his way, he visited his uncle Zhou Tiaozhi and also a cousin, Chen Shizhou (a nephew of his adoptive mother), in Nanjing; both of them may have given him money also. On November 7, 1920, Zhou Enlai left Shanghai on the French postal ship *Porthos*. He was one of 197 persons who constituted the fifteenth work-study group traveling to Europe. Li Shizeng was the trip supervisor. Among the others from Tianjin were several of Zhou's friends, including Li Fujing, Zhang Ruoming, and Tao Shangzhao.[85]

The voyage was five weeks long, and there were numerous ports of call. Zhou Enlai spent one night in Hong Kong and three days in Saigon, from where he sent a postcard to his youngest brother, Zhou

Enshou, listing his itinerary.[86] He saw Singapore and Colombo, crossed the Indian Ocean, and sailed through the Suez Canal and the Mediterranean Sea. Xie Shuying, who became acquainted with Zhou Enlai and Li Fujing on board ship, remembers that they all often talked about China's weakening international status.[87] He also recalls that at times the voyage was rough, and that many passengers became ill because of the violent waves in the Indian Ocean. On the ship Zhou Enlai, showing self-discipline and, apparently, a strong constitution, was able to complete "The Diary in the Public Prosecution Prison."

The *Porthos* docked at Marseilles on December 13. There was no time to sightsee in this first European city Zhou had ever been in; he took an overnight train to Paris as arranged by a representative of the Chinese-French Educational Commission. In Paris, he was met by a welcoming group of friends from Nankai and Tianjin, including Li Yuru, Yan Zhikai (Yan Xiu's youngest son), Zhao Guangchen, and Guo Longzhen.[88] Altogether, there were about twenty Nankai alumni scattered throughout France. Both Zhou and Li Fujing were bound for England, Zhou, ultimately, for Scotland where he meant to attend the University of Edinburgh.

Li Fujing left Paris at once, but Zhou Enlai was stranded in France for three weeks because of a minor illness. In the first week of 1921, he was finally able to continue his journey.[89] In London, he stayed with his old Nankai friend Chang Ceou, who was studying economics at the University of London, and met with Li Fujing, who planned to study civil engineering at the University of Manchester. With a letter of introduction from Yan Xiu, Zhou Enlai went to the Chinese Legation in London to see Minister Gu Shaochuan in the hope that he would help him with his educational and financial plans in the United Kingdom, but Minister Gu was away in Geneva at a League of Nations meeting.

Zhou Enlai reported to Yan Xiu that he was admitted to the University of Edinburgh and that he would not be required to take the entrance examinations except for one test in English.[90] He may have chosen the University of Edinburgh because Zhang Shizhao, an outstanding publicist and a frequent speaker at Nankai Middle School, had graduated from that school. Zhou Enlai also informed Yan Xiu that he had submitted an application for a government scholarship to the supervisor of Chinese Students in Europe and to the education commissioner of Zhejiang province (his ancestral province), and he asked Yan Xiu to communicate with Education Minister Fan Jingsheng so that Fan could speak to the Zhejiang education commissioner on his behalf. Zhou Enlai had seen Fan Jingsheng in China and Japan on several occasions, notably in April and December 1918, when Yan Xiu and Fan visited Tokyo, and in September 1919, when Yan Xiu gave a dinner for Fan, Zhou, and other guests. In spite of his explicit espousal of Marxism by this time, Zhou Enlai evidently had no scruples about seeking favors from the Chinese establishment if that could help solve his educational and financial problems. Zhou Enlai asked for financial support from his wealthy uncle Zhou Tiaozhi, but unfortunately for Zhou Enlai, his uncle died in the fall of 1921.

In letters written to relatives and friends, Zhou Enlai expressed enthusiasm for London as the "world's largest city" and mentioned that, even without attending lectures, he could obtain material for study from London's "several hundred phenomena."[91] From London, he dispatched his first report to *Yishibao*, with the title, "The Crisis in Europe After the European War."[92] He was very critical of the work-study program in France. He told Yan Xiu that Chinese students in France were physically weak, ill-prepared in French, unable to find suitable jobs, and too exhausted from manual labor to concentrate on their studies. He observed that whereas Chinese students in the United States worked only part time to supplement their tuition and living expenses, Chinese students in France became full-time workers.

Zhou Enlai stayed in England only a few weeks before returning to Paris in February 1921. He had found that enrolling in the University of Edinburgh was not going to be as easy as he had hoped. In the first place, the new academic year would not begin until October, and the university required competence in another European language besides English for graduation. Living in Paris would cost only half as much as it would in London or Edinburgh, and in France he could learn the French language so that he could fulfill the language requirement at Edinburgh. An additional reason for returning to Paris may have been that he regarded continental Europe as a better base than England for his reports to *Yishibao*. His long-range plans still included the University of Edinburgh: he told his cousin Chen Shizhou that he intended to study there for three or four years under a Chinese government scholarship and then study for one year in the United States.[93]

After leaving London, Zhou Enlai apparently studied French in Paris for a while and worked briefly in a Renault automobile plant, probably with Li Lisan, although the amount of work he actually did seems to have been negligible. Sometime during the winter or early spring of 1921 he and four friends from Tianjin moved to Blois, about 100 miles south of Paris, for further study.[94] As had been the case in Japan, he did not enter any college, or meet his original academic goal, mainly because he was unable to obtain a Chinese government stipend, even with Yan Xiu's and Fan Jingsheng's assistance. Yet Yan Xiu continued to send Zhou Enlai (and Li Fujing) money, even after Zhou's radical activities in Europe were well known in Tianjin. Criticized for his financial support of Zhou Enlai, Yan Xiu justified his assistance by quoting a Chinese proverb, "Every intelligent man has his own purposes!"[95] Yan Xiu also met with Zhou Enlai's father in February 1922; they may have discussed either the problem of financial support for Zhou Enlai or the possibility of marriage between Zhou Enlai and Yan Xiu's youngest daughter, Yan Zhian.[96]

Nonetheless, although Zhou Enlai's deficiencies in foreign languages were still a distinct handicap to his academic pursuits, he had the advantage over many Chinese students in Europe because he had undergone extensive training in English at Nankai Middle School. For his *Yishibao* reports, for instance, he relied heavily on *The Times* (London) and other English-language publications in Europe. His friend Chang Ceou often mailed *The Times* to Zhou Enlai in France and Germany.[97] From March 22, 1921, to May 1, 1922, *Yishibao* printed quite a number of detailed investigative reports and critical commentaries by Zhou Enlai, covering a wide range of contemporary political and economic concerns relating to Europe and China. These show a sympathetic attitude toward the Soviet Union, particularly Lenin's New Economic Policy. Among other issues, Zhou paid special attention to the complicated and turbulent dynamics of the Chinese student movements in Europe. Nearly 1,700 Chinese students were in France in 1921 (see Table 9), many from the populous hinterland (Sichuan, Hunan), the southern coastal region (Guangdong, Fujian), and the eastern coastal region (Zhili, Zhejiang, Jiangsu). As Zhou Enlai reported in *Yishibao*

TABLE 9
Chinese Students in France: Provincial Origins, January 1921

Province	Number	Province	Number
Sichuan	378	Shanxi	28
Hunan	346	Henan	20
Guangdong	251	Shandong	15
Zhili	147	Guizhou	9
Fujian	89	Shaanxi	9
Zhejiang	85	Guangxi	7
Jiangsu	69	Yunnan	6
Anhui	40	Fengtian	5
Hubei	40	Others	100
Jiangxi	28	TOTAL	1,672

SOURCE: Lin Zexun, *Zhongguo liuxue jiaoyushi*, p. 365.

(December 20, 1921), an overwhelming majority of Chinese students from Sichuan, Hunan, Zhili, Zhejiang, and Jiangsu provinces joined the work-study program in France, but only a small portion of the Chinese students from Guangdong and Fujian provinces participated in the program because, being adequately subsidized by their rich provincial governments, they had no need to do so.

As a correspondent for *Yishibao*, Zhou Enlai made it his responsibility to observe and analyze all major Chinese student activities and problems in France. As their counterparts had done in Japan, the discontented Chinese students frequently demonstrated in front of the Chinese Legation in Paris to denounce a variety of China's domestic and foreign policy decisions. In the summer and fall of 1921 Zhou Enlai was directly involved in a number of these demonstrations and meetings, and for the first time he had the opportunity to collaborate with radical Chinese students from other parts of China—Cai Hesen, Zhao Shiyan, Li Lisan, Chen Yi, Li Weihan, Li Fuchun, Wang Ruofei, Xiang Jingyu, Cai Chang, and others. Cai Hesen (1895–1930) had been a close classmate of Mao Zedong at the First Normal School in Changsha, Hunan province, and together they had organized the New People's Study Society (*Xinmin xuehui*) at Changsha in April 1918. This group was largely responsible for recruiting the huge number of Hunan students to the work-study program in France.[98] While he was in France, Cai gave Mao specific recommendations for organizing the Chinese

Communist Party, and Cai's letters and articles were published in *Xinqingnian*.[99]

During the course of 1921, the Chinese government became increasingly unhappy with the radicalization of work-study students in France and finally suspended its financial support and set up a new Sino-French University at Lyons. This university, headed by Wu Zhihui, one of Cai Yuanpei's colleagues, would not give priority to the work-study students who were already in Europe but would instead invite new students directly from China. In September 1921, about 120 work-study Chinese students convened in Lyons from various parts of France and after holding protest rallies forcibly occupied the Sino-French University. When the news of this reached Paris, Zhou Enlai, Nie Rongzhen, Wang Ruofei, and Xu Teli hurried to Lyons to give their support to the demonstrators.[100] There is no evidence to indicate that Zhou Enlai participated actively in the occupation of the university, but he did send *Yishibao* several long and vivid reports on what he titled "The Last Destiny of the Work-Study Students in France."[101] In October the French government deported 104 Chinese demonstrators; they included Cai Hesen, Li Lisan, Chen Yi, and Wang Jingqi.[102]

More important than Zhou Enlai's journalistic and political activities in France was the beginning of his formal association with the communist movement in China. In the spring of 1921 Zhou Enlai joined a small Chinese communist cell in Paris, upon the recommendation of Zhang Shenfu and Liu Qingyang (a member of the Awakening Society).[103] This was a few months before the Chinese Communist Party was formally launched in Shanghai. Zhang Shenfu, whom Zhou Enlai had met at the Taoranting Park meeting in August 1920, had come to France with Liu Qingyang to assume a teaching position at the Sino-French University in Lyons. He had been a lecturer in philosophy and logic at Beijing University and a contributor to *Xinqingnian* and *Meizhou Pinglun*, and he was a recognized intellectual leader of the May Fourth Movement in China. He also had a clear mandate from Chen Duxiu to organize communist activities in Europe.[104] Regarding Zhang's prominence in France, Vera Schwarcz writes: "When he arrived in Paris on New Year's Day 1921, Zhang Shenfu considered himself the most senior Chinese Bolshevik in Europe. He was a trusted intimate of Chen Duxiu and Li Dazhao and had been included in party founding discussions since the summer of 1920. On the basis of these credentials, he proceeded to become the self-styled mentor of younger intellectuals who became communists in Europe."[105] Zhou Enlai later acknowledged that Zhang Shenfu and Liu Qingyang had introduced him to the Chinese Communist Party. He said: "Zhang Shenfu's thought was very complicated. He studied [Bertrand] Russell most intensely. His aim was to integrate the ideas of Confucius, Russell, Marx, Freud, and Einstein."[106] Zhou Enlai seems to have accepted Zhang Shenfu, a strong-willed and domineering person, as his mentor in Europe, and to have listened to Zhang's lectures on philosophical issues and Marxist theory.

In addition to Zhang Shenfu, Zhou Enlai, and Liu Qingyang, the Paris cell included Zhao Shiyan and Chen Gongpei (a former student at Beijing University). According to Vera Schwarcz, "The coming together of these five young people was directed more by circumstance than by ideology. Love affairs, school friendship, and physical proximity played a role in their associations, even greater, perhaps, than the ideas that they held in common." The Paris cell led by Zhang Shenfu did not get along well with a group of Hunanese radicals in Montargis, who were led by Cai Hesen. The Montargis group included Li Weihan, Li Fuchun, Cai Chang, Li Lisan, Chen Yi, Xiang Jingyu, Nie Rongzhen, Su Shan, and Deng Xiaoping; Guo Longzhen, a member of the Awakening Society, participated in this group. The initial Paris-Montargis tension was probably caused by Zhang Shenfu's arrogant, eccentric, and mercurial personality. As a result of mediation by Zhao Shiyan and Zhou Enlai, however, the two groups agreed to form a new united organization for communist activities in Europe.[107]

Because of his deep involvement in political and ideological developments in France, Zhou Enlai did not take the English test at the University of Edinburgh in September 1921 as originally planned. At this point, he put aside academic goals and turned to writing reports and commentaries and to promoting communism in Europe. He also had quite a few friends in France who could help him financially and politically, and he apparently had no close friend at Edinburgh. As in Japan, he was active in the Nankai Alumni Association in Europe (he was elected one of its directors in 1922), and he continued to send letters and postcards to his Nankai friends in China, Japan, and the United States.[108] In January 1922 Zhou

Enlai visited London again, and in March he went to Berlin with Zhang Shenfu and Liu Qingyang, who were then married. This was a practical move—the cost of living in Berlin was one-third what it was in Paris—but also a political one. The Social Democratic government in Germany was relatively lenient toward radical activities by foreign residents, and the three hoped they could coordinate the growing Chinese communist movement in Europe as a whole. Zhou Enlai set about reorganizing the Berlin communist cell and held weekly discussion sessions at Zhang Shenfu's apartment; they recruited several new members, among them Zhu De, the former warlord and opium addict, Sun Bingwen, who had been a student at Beijing University, and Zhao Guangchen, a member of the Awakening Society. Zhou Enlai and Zhao Guangchen had collaborated in editorial and political work in Tianjin and in petition campaigns in Beijing in 1919. When Zhu De encountered Zhou Enlai in Berlin in 1922, he found him "serious," "intelligent," "quiet," "thoughtful," and "even a little shy."[109]

The Awakening Society served Zhou Enlai well as an enduring personal and political network in Europe; four of his fellow members—Liu Qingyang, Guo Longzhen, Zhao Guangchen, and Zhang Ruoming—extended their May Fourth Movement activities to Europe and supported the Chinese Communist Party. Attracted by Zhang Ruoming's beauty and intelligence, Zhou Enlai evidently fell in love with her, but their relationship did not last long in France; Zhang eventually left the communist movement and concentrated on her doctoral work on André Gide at the University of Lyons.[110] Zhou Enlai showed some interest in Li Fujing's sister, Li Fumin, by sending her a postcard (with a painting *Girls with Cherries*, by John Russell) from Paris, but he maintained frequent correspondence with Deng Yingchao throughout his European stay. Another member of the Awakening Society, Guan Xibin, was also in France from 1919 to 1921 as a participant in the work-study program, but he did not join the Chinese Communist Party at that time.[111] Another associate was Tao Shangzhao, a "friend" of the Awakening Society, who was Zhou Enlai's youngest fellow inmate in Tianjin. Tao was accidentally burned to death during a picnic in Lyons in 1922; Zhou Enlai arranged for the funeral and mailed Tao's belongings to his family in China.[112] Zhou Enlai continued to contribute articles, letters, and poems to *Jueyou* [Awakening Letters], a successor to *Juewu*, which Ma Qianli agreed to publish as a supplement to *Xinminyibao* during 1923 and 1924.

One poignant poem Zhou Enlai composed in Germany for *Jueyou* was inspired by the news that Huang Zhengpin (Huang Ai), a "friend" of the Awakening Society, had been arrested and executed by a warlord during the cotton mill workers' strike at Changsha in January 1922. Huang had collaborated with Zhou Enlai during the May Fourth Movement in Tianjin. In memory of his martyred friend, Zhou Enlai wrote:

A heroic death.
A wretched life.
Clinging fondly to life in dread of death—
Is it not better to die a weighty death
That makes light of life!

Parted in life or separated by death—
The worst that could happen to me.
Parted—in sorrow, in anguish,
Dead—for naught that counts—
Is it not better to bid a farewell that inspires!

No sowing done,
No reaping possible.
Hankering for the blooms of communism
But not sowing the seed of revolution,
Dreaming of Red Flags flying triumphant
Without consecrating them with blood:
Such a cheap gain—could there ever be?

Sit and talk—
Better rise and act!
They that cling to life
Will wail over partings,
Will let life or death lead them by the nose.

They will never understand
A farewell that inspires,
A soul-stirring farewell.
Hope resides in yourself and no one else.
The way of life or death lies open to all.
Fly towards light—
All's up to you!
So take up your hoes,
Open up the untilled land,

Seeds strewn among men,
Blood watering the earth.

Partings have always been.
More farewells are yet to come.
See life and death steadily,
And see both through:
Strive and make the best of your life,
Strive and make the best of your death.
What of it if it comes to bidding farewell?[113]

A note by Zhou at the end of the poem says: "The news of his death has thoroughly strengthened my commitment to communism. I believe I shall prove worthy of my dead friend." He also promised his Awakening Society friends, "I will never change my ideology, and I will continue resolutely to work for it and propagate it."[114] Needless to say, Zhou Enlai never deviated from this heartfelt pledge for the rest of his life.

As a specific proof of his promise, Zhou Enlai met with 22 other Chinese communists in Paris in June 1922; they agreed to set up the Chinese Youth Communist Party in Europe (CYCPE) as an overseas branch of the Chinese Communist Party, established a year earlier. This meeting in Paris adopted the party's new charter drafted by Zhou Enlai. The party's three-member executive committee consisted of Zhao Shiyan (general secretary), Zhou Enlai (director of propaganda), and Li Weihan (director of organization). This troika leadership structure could be viewed as symbolizing a coalition of the three May Fourth organizations in China—the China Youth Association (led by Li Dazhao) in Beijing, the New People's Study Society (led by Cai Hesen and Mao Zedong) in Changsha, and the Awakening Society in Tianjin. Li Weihan, who had graduated from the First Normal School in Changsha (Mao's alma mater) in 1917 and had taken part in the inauguration of the New People's Study Society in 1918, inherited the leadership of the progressive Montargis group after Cai Hesen was deported in October 1921.[115] It was most appropriate for Zhou Enlai to be responsible for the party's propaganda because he excelled in journalistic work and public debates. When the party decided to publish a magazine, *Shaonian* (The Youth), it was Zhou Enlai who received a 1,000-franc contribution from Zhang Shizhao, who was visiting Europe at that time.[116] Beginning with its first issue, published in August 1922, *Shaonian* carried a number of articles and reports written by Zhou Enlai and Zhang Shenfu. The French title of this journal, "La Jeunesse," was exactly the same as that of Chen Duxiu's *Xinqingnian*. Chen's two sons—Chen Yannian (b. 1898) and Chen Qiaonian (b. 1902), who had earlier advocated anarchism—participated in the publication of *Shaonian*.

After Li Weihan's departure for China, the CYCPE elected five members of its executive committee in October 1922—Zhao Shiyan, Zhou Enlai, Chen Yannian, Wang Ruofei, and Yin Kuan. Wang and Yin were Li Weihan's friends from Montargis. Upon Chen Duxiu's instruction, 42 representatives of the CYCPE met at Billancourt in February 1923 and adopted a new name for their organization—the Chinese Communist Youth League in Europe (CCYLE). This organization functioned as a European branch of the Chinese Socialist Youth League, which had been established in May 1922. They passed another charter drafted by Zhou Enlai, elected a five-member executive committee, and chose Zhou Enlai as its general secretary. Other members of the executive committee were Yin Kuan, Wang Zejie, Ren Zhuoxuan, and Xiao Pusheng.[117] In spite of Zhou Enlai's objections, at this meeting it was decided to expel Zhang Shenfu from the CCYLE, but the decision was overturned by the Chinese Communist Party.[118] At the age of 25 Zhou Enlai reached the highest leadership position in the League, which had a total of 72 members—58 in France, eight in Germany, and six in Belgium. When the Chinese Communist Party instructed twelve members of its European Branch to go to the University of the Toilers of the East in Moscow, Zhou Enlai in Berlin arranged their visas and other necessary documents in cooperation with the Comintern agents. The departing comrades included Zhao Shiyan, Wang Ruofei, Chen Yannian, Chen Qiaonian, and Xiong Xiong. (Later they were followed by Zhu De, Sun Bingwen, Nie Rongzhen, Li Fuchun, Deng Xiaoping, Guo Longzhen, Cai Chang, and other Chinese communists in Europe.)[119] The Comintern agents may have provided funds for Zhou Enlai's operations. A few Chinese students (Chen Yannian and Su Shan) joined the French Communist Party, but Zhou Enlai apparently did not do so.

In the summer of 1923 Zhou Enlai returned to Paris to oversee the League's day-to-day affairs. His office was set up in a small room in the Godefroy Hotel at 17 rue Godefroy near the Place d'Italie.[120] As an articulate and sophisticated intellectual, he was very effective in projecting the Chinese Communist Party's revolutionary messages among Chinese students and workers in Europe. He was also entangled in heated ideological debates and political contests with several competing forces in France, particularly statists (*guojia zhuyi*) and anarchists. He encountered the most ferocious challenge from the China Youth Party, which Zeng Qi and Li Huang organized in 1923. Although they were members of the Li Dazhao-led China Youth Association, they criticized the Chinese Communist Party for its subservience to the Soviet Union and the Guomindang for its loss of revolutionary spirit.[121] Yet Li Huang respected his rival, Zhou Enlai, as a capable political leader.

When the Third National Congress of the Chinese Communist Party in June 1923 accepted the Comintern's instructions to form a united front with the Guomindang led by Sun Yat-sen and to let its individual members join the Guomindang, Zhou Enlai negotiated with Wang Jingqi for the purpose of uniting Communist and Nationalist forces in Europe. Wang Jingqi had been deported to China in October 1921 after the Lyons incident, but Sun Yat-sen sent him back to France to organize the Guomindang group. Just as the Chinese Communist Party and the Guomindang did in China, Zhou Enlai and Wang Jingqi agreed to allow all members of the CCYLE to join the Guomindang as individual members. Approximately 80 CCYLE members became affiliated with the Guomindang at that time. As a new member of the Guomindang, Zhou Enlai spoke at the inaugural meeting of the Guomindang's European Branch held in Lyons in November 1923. At this meeting Wang Jingqi was elected as chairman of the executive committee, Zhou Enlai as director of general affairs, and Li Fuchun as director of propaganda. Nie Rongzhen was made director of the Paris liaison office of the Guomindang. While working as a prominent leader of the Guomindang's European branch, however, Zhou Enlai still directed the CCYLE's active operations. When the CCYLE decided to replace *Shaonian* with a new semimonthly journal, *Chiguang* (Red Light), Zhou Enlai asked Deng Xiaoping, a nineteen-year-old work-study student from Sichuan province, to manage its printing. (His associates jokingly gave him the title, "Ph.D. in mimeographing.")[122] Hence the Zhou Enlai–Deng Xiaoping connection was firmly cemented in Paris. Upon Zhou Enlai's suggestion, Deng Xiaoping opened and managed a successful bean-curd shop in Paris.[123]

In terms of both experience and temperament, Zhou Enlai was an ideal person to carry out the dual political responsibilities for the Guomindang and the CCP simultaneously and to implement the concept of a united front in Europe. He was able to promote the tactics of "democratic revolution" without compromising the ultimate goal of "socialist revolution." He was quick to gain confidence and trust from the Guomindang leadership so that he served as acting chairman of the Guomindang's European branch in the absence of Wang Jingqi. In a letter written to his father, Wang Jingqi lavishly praised Zhou Enlai's "intelligence" and "attractiveness."[124] Indeed, Zhou Enlai demonstrated his pragmatic flexibility and the extraordinary ability to iron out policy differences and personality conflicts in the united front and to strike a compromise among diverse ideological tendencies and rival factions. This experience in Europe proved very useful to Zhou Enlai's subsequent political career in China.

Zhou Enlai's ability, experience, and achievements were widely known, and the Chinese Communist Party asked him to return to China because it needed an increasing number of competent and committed young cadres. It is also claimed that Zhang Shenfu, who had returned to China with Liu Qingyang in 1924 and had become deputy director of the Political Department at the newly established Whampoa (Huangpu) Military Academy at Canton, recommended Zhou Enlai and Zhou Fohai (a founding member of the Chinese Communist Party) to Liao Zhongkai (1876–1925), a Guomindang representative at Whampoa, and that Zhang Shenfu asked Zhou Enlai to come to the Whampoa Military Academy.[125] In any event, at the meeting of the CCYLE on July 13–15, 1924, Zhou Enlai handed over his leadership position to Lin Wei. Other persons present at the meeting included Deng Xiaoping, Li Fuchun, Nie Rongzhen, and Mu Qing. The League's new executive committee adopted a very favorable report on Zhou Enlai's personality and ability. It said:

> He [Zhou Enlai] is a man of honesty and fairness who operates actively and energetically. His speech is persuasive and his essays are written with ease. Since he has conducted profound studies on "ism," he is completely

proletarianized. He speaks English relatively well, and he can also read newspapers and books in French and German. In addition, he is one of the founders of the League. As a member of its Executive Committee, he worked enthusiastically and patiently and established a record of outstanding achievements.[126]

Zhou Enlai also took part in the Second Congress of the Guomindang's European branch on July 20, 1924; Wang Jingqi and other leaders of the European branch assembled to bid him farewell. Shortly thereafter, Zhou Enlai left France with a few work-study students and Chinese workers who were returning to China; he did not have to pay for his passage. It is incorrect to suggest that he returned to China via Moscow. As an admirer of the Bolshevik revolution, he was probably tempted to visit the Soviet Union and to see his comrades at the University of the Toilers of the East, but he headed directly to China via ship, heeding the Chinese Communist Party's urgent recall. He reached Hong Kong in late August and immediately met with Tan Pingshan, a top leader of the Chinese Communist Party and the Guomindang. On September 1 he sent a brief report to the Central Executive Committee of the Chinese Socialist Youth League in which he said that he would proceed to Canton; he ended his report with "a salute to communism."[127]

Zhou Enlai was soon appointed chairman of the reconstituted Guangdong District Committee of the Chinese Communist Party as well as its director of propaganda. He worked under the central leadership of Li Dazhao and Chen Duxiu, whose two sons, Chen Yannian and Chen Qiaonian, had cooperated with Zhou Enlai in France. Thanks to Zhang Shenfu's assistance, Zhou started teaching political economy at the Whampoa Military Academy, first as deputy director of the Political Department under Director Dai Jitao and then, in November 1924, as director of the Political Department. In his new position Zhou Enlai was intimately associated with Chiang Kai-shek, commandant of the Academy. From the beginning, this relationship was very complicated, at once both cooperative and adversarial. Around the same time Zhou Enlai also met Mao Zedong, who worked at the Peasant Education Institute in Canton. The Zhou-Mao relationship, too, was very complex. Even though Zhou enjoyed a highly visible and influential status in the Chinese Communist Party during the late 1920's, he would eventually assume a secondary role in their essentially symbiotic linkage that would last until their deaths in 1976. And in August 1925 Zhou Enlai married Deng Yingchao, who had moved from Tianjin to Canton as Director of Women's Affairs at the Chinese Communist Party's Guangdong District Committee. Hence Zhou Enlai embarked on a new phase of his political career and personal life in China.

During the five-year period 1919–24, Zhou Enlai confronted a variety of critical challenges and opportunities, first in Tianjin, then in Paris and Berlin, and as he became more intellectually and politically mature he moved from the careful but alert background position that he maintained in Tianjin during May and June 1919 to the powerful vortex of China's historic movement. In Tianjin, drawing on his growing literary and journalistic expertise and his old Nankai ties, he was a capable editor of the Tianjin Student Union *Bulletin*, which articulated his views on China's domestic and foreign affairs and provided a unified direction for the students in Tianjin. He criticized political repression, social injustice, and foreign intrusion, and upheld the principles of reform, equality, and nationalism. His earlier exposure to the Bolshevik revolution and Kawakami Hajime's progressive writings was nurtured and reinforced by Li Dazhao's influential propagation of Marxist doctrines in China. Maurice Meisner suggests that Li Dazhao was not only a teacher, an intellectual guide, and a "political oracle" for his students and followers, but also a "fatherly adviser" on their personal and financial matters.[128]

While neglecting his academic pursuits as a freshman at Nankai University, Zhou Enlai was preoccupied with a variety of political activities—assisting the Tianjin Student Union, organizing the Awakening Society, writing political commentaries, and attending protest campaigns in Tianjin and Beijing. It was only after his teachers and friends were arrested that he came forward to assume a direct and prominent role in the May Fourth Movement. His six-month imprisonment for these actions was decisive in his subsequent commitment to the communist cause.

In Europe, Zhou Enlai again forsook an academic life, first for political journalism, then for the active life of politics leading to revolution. His responsibilities as a special European correspondent for *Yishibao* compelled him to understand and analyze the postwar developments in Europe as well as the dynamics of the increasingly radical activities of the Chinese work-study students in France. Though not a regular work-study student himself, Zhou Enlai shared their ideology and belief in political activism. His rise in the first Chinese communist cell in Paris led to organization of the Chinese Communist Youth Party in Europe (and of the Chinese Communist Youth League in Europe). From there, as the League's general secretary, the next step was the Chinese Communist Party.

Conclusion

Neither truculent nor jovial; faultlessly urbane. And as reticent as a cat. . . . He [Zhou Enlai] is the perfect embodiment of the Confucian sage.
—André Malraux, *Anti-Memoirs*

An astute and sympathetic observer of China's contemporary political turmoil, André Malraux, who visited China as the French Minister of Culture on the eve of the devastating Cultural Revolution in 1965, described Premier Zhou Enlai as having the "bizarre attentiveness" of a studious cat. After four decades of communist struggle Zhou Enlai still seemed the perfect embodiment of the Confucian sage: a virtuous, rational, and cultivated man with extraordinary self-control. Malraux's description, however, might have applied equally to the young Zhou Enlai when he returned from France to China 40 years earlier. At that time China was in the throes of great revolutionary upheavals and the young Zhou Enlai took over the leadership of the Guangdong District Committee of the Chinese Communist Party as well as the Political Department of Whampoa Military Academy. A photograph taken at that time shows him wearing a neatly tailored Guomindang military uniform, sitting in a calm, attentive, and alert posture. In the relatively short span of 26 years Zhou Enlai had indeed traversed a long and tortuous road leading to his ardent Marxist experiment in Canton: emerging from a protected Confucian environment in Shanyang (Huaian) and eventually traveling to Tokyo, Paris, London, and Berlin. His formative years culminated in the making of an earnest and enthusiastic revolutionary leader.

As suggested in Chapter 1, Zhou Enlai presumably inherited

dual and potentially contradictory personality traits from his biological parents—sociability, cheerfulness, and optimism from his mother, and shyness, gentleness, and intelligence from his father. It is certainly plausible that his unassertive father's weakness as an authority figure led Zhou Enlai to seek a surrogate father figure and made it easier for him to work effectively with strong and dominant male personalities such as Zhang Boling. Zhou Enlai's introverted tendencies were reinforced by his reclusive adoptive mother, who exerted a profound influence over his life and education during his infancy and boyhood. This duality was further compounded by his early experiences in contrasting geographical regions—the mild and cultured Jiangsu province and the rugged Manchurian frontier—and by his exposure to divergent philosophical systems, Confucianism and Marxism.

As the firstborn son reared in an established gentry family, Zhou Enlai learned and practiced the Confucian teachings. In particular, during his childhood he recognized the importance of social order, moral rectitude, self-cultivation, and proper etiquette. He was immensely proud of his ancestors' illustrious grandeur recorded in Shaoxing, Zhejiang province, and of his close family ties. In times of crisis and adversity, he fell back on his extended family as a source of comfort and inner fortitude. Even after he espoused Marxism, his essentially "correct" Confucian code, with emphasis on moderation, virtue, grace, and self-discipline, enabled him to function effectively in the tradition-bound social milieu of China. This was a distinctive advantage that not many of his revolutionary colleagues possessed. It was therefore not surprising that Yan Xiu, an eminent Confucian scholar-official, wished to accept Zhou Enlai as his son-in-law or that, just as had André Malraux, Wu Guozhen, one of Zhou Enlai's Nankai friends, appreciated his lifelong Confucianist orientations.[1] Moreover, his upper-class family background, coupled with Zhang Boling's exhortations on *gong* (public-spiritedness) and *neng* (ability), instilled in the young Zhou Enlai a strong sense of obligation to his country and a conviction that he was competent to rescue China from its national calamities and restore its proper international respectability. Growing up and maturing in a volatile period of political decay and social disorder, Zhou Enlai faced the challenge of being alert, sensitive, and quickly adaptable to the dynamics of China's shifting environment, which had encompassed the fall of the Qing dynasty, the Republican revolution, and the warlord conflicts.

Zhou Enlai was by nature careful, prudent, meticulous, and versatile. He consciously attempted to practice what he wrote in his Nankai essay, "Sincerity Moves Things." He was antithetical to displays of arrogance, flamboyance, dogmatism, and extremism. As a child, he developed the ability to deal with the tense and complicated emotional interplay among his three mothers (natural mother, adoptive mother, and wet nurse) and with the declining fortunes of his family. All these conflicting conditions compelled him to seek compromises, to adjust himself to turbulent circumstances. In situations of conflict, he learned how to identify the causes of tension. He was able to understand how underlying contradictions contribute to disorder, to grasp quickly the aspirations and agonies of other people, and to accommodate the interests of all parties involved in tense and threatening circumstances. He was intensely loyal to his friends and very generous in giving them recognition and credit while maintaining his own self-effacing manner. Henry Lieberman observes that Zhou Enlai had "the fantastic talent of making other people feel important."[2] In addition, he was excessively diligent and a perfectionist, though he in turn expected his friends and co-workers to be equally loyal, dedicated, and meticulous. He was a demanding, albeit understanding, leader to his followers. Above all, Zhou Enlai learned how to transform adversity into positive opportunity. He was willing and able to admit his limits, mistakes, and failures. As demonstrated in the situations involving his family tragedies, academic failures, imprisonment, and financial difficulties, Zhou Enlai did not despair, but instead utilized his extraordinary patience, personal connections, and creative resourcefulness to find alternative ways to achieve his goals. At times, it must be said, he appeared to be so flexible and ambiguous that his critics characterized him as elusive, enigmatic, or even opportunistic.

In his formative years, Zhou Enlai manifested a high degree of intellectual curiosity and social consciousness. Even though he was not destined to become a brilliant scholar, as evidenced in his abortive attempts to enter the Qinghua School, the Tokyo Higher Normal School, and the First Higher School in Japan, he was a good listener with varied interests and a quick learner, able to absorb a broad range of knowledge about political and social problems. In addition to being instructed at an early age by his adoptive mother, Zhou Enlai eagerly learned from his farsighted relatives (such as Gong Yinsun and Chen Shizhou) and his schoolteachers (such as Gao Gewu and Zhao Xiwen). Among all his teachers, Zhang Boling exercised the most significant and lasting impact upon Zhou Enlai's mode of behavior, and he introduced Zhou to the basic principles underlying modern enlightenment and nationalist consciousness that Zhou enthusiastically embraced. Yet Zhou Enlai was cautious and eclectic in accommodating new ideas and fashionable trends and in avoiding the pitfalls of premature judgment or facile solutions; at Nankai he advocated a discriminating approach—*qushe quliu* (lit. "to accept some and reject some").

Zhou Enlai readily attributed his literary advancement to his adoptive mother's devoted teaching and tender care. Firmly grounded in the Confucian classics and other traditional Chinese literature, he felt at ease composing essays and poems during his childhood and adolescence. After he won a prize for an essay at the Dongguan Model School in Fengtian (Shenyang), he gained self-confidence in his creative abilities, and though he was never a first-rate poet by any means, he had the training, and the desire, to express his feelings and views in poetic form. He continued to assert his literary prowess at Nankai Middle School, during the May Fourth era, and in Europe.

He was a superbly skillful journalist. This talent, too, appeared early and gave him confidence and then experience. After his editorial work on the *Jingye Review* and *Xiaofeng* at Nankai established his reputation as a good writer, he was an obvious person to edit the Tianjin Student Union *Bulletin* and then to be a leading contributor to *Juewu* (Awakening) during the May Fourth Movement. His journalistic work in Europe was an integral part of his life there and a direct connection to his subsequent dedication to communist revolutionary activity. His rich, diverse journalistic experiences in China and Europe sharpened his analytic ability to understand and synthesize important events as they were occurring, and they also taught him how to report on complex issues in a succinct and comprehensible fashion and to articulate his views and commentaries in a persuasive way. Even though he was neither an original thinker nor a creative author, he was a good analyst and an effective publicist. These abilities were enormously useful assets in Zhou Enlai's political activities and interpersonal relations.

Another means that Zhou Enlai acquired at Nankai to express himself was through oratorical and dramatic performances, and this performing experience helped him in overcoming his natural shyness. In spite of his shrill voice, he became adept at public speaking, using animated gestures to enhance the utmost seriousness of his manner. He was, in a sense, a born actor: he liked to entertain, and he enjoyed his dramatic experiences at Nankai and in prison and liked the spectators' applause. At Nankai Zhang Boling urged his students to broaden their horizons and to play important roles on the world stage. In this regard, Zhou Enlai did not disappoint his mentor. Henry Lieberman remembers: "I always thought that Zhou Enlai, in addition to all his other talents, was one of the world's greatest actors. He had a great sense of the dramatic and used a lot of actor tricks."[3]

Beyond that, however, Zhou Enlai faithfully followed his mentor's constant admonition that the Chinese needed to understand the concept of group (*tuanti*) and to organize and unite themselves. From the early days of the Jingye Society at Nankai, which Zhou conceived and led, Zhou took tremendous satisfaction from his participation in structured group activities, which gave him an avenue for stable and close associations. He always preferred to be part of a team rather than working in isolation. Zhou Enlai was involved in organizations wherever he went—in Japan, in the Nankai Alumni Association and the New China Study Society; during the May Fourth Movement, in the Awakening Society, the Tianjin Union of Student Publications, and the Reform Federation under Li Dazhao's leadership. He was instrumental in reorganizing the Tianjin Student Union along the principle of gender equality. And he assumed a position of leadership in organizing the Chinese Communist Youth Party and the Chinese Communist Youth League in Europe, and the Guomindang's European branch. He excelled in drafting charters, manifestos, and reports and in managing executive and administrative affairs. In his ensuing career, he became widely recognized as a capable and dependable leader who would fulfill his responsibilities gracefully and competently.

In general, Zhou Enlai performed best in dyadic situations and in small groups of intimate friends and associates with whom he could develop direct rapport and mutual respect. His combination of modesty, sophistication, and personal charm rendered him readily acceptable to many different sorts of people—different ages, different provincial origins, and even different ideological orientations. Perhaps because he was a Confucian, he remained loyal and helpful to his friends and was tolerant of his adversaries. He was particularly courteous and respectful toward his teachers and senior colleagues. As far as possible, he wanted to avoid direct personal confrontations and to reason with his adversaries, searching for understanding and compromises. Though critics may argue that he was too deferential or submissive to his chosen authority figures, such as Zhang Boling, even his rivals and enemies found it difficult to hate or criticize Zhou Enlai as a person.[4]

In view of his introverted tendencies, childhood experiences, and conscientious style, Zhou Enlai was reluctant to seek self-serving publicity or to assume the supreme position in an organization. He preferred to work diligently behind the scenes and to exert influence through his outgoing friends, such as Zhang Ruifeng at Nankai, Gong Debai in Tokyo, Ma Jun in Tianjin, Cai Hesen in Lyons, and Zhao Shiyan in Paris. He was temperamentally hesitant to plunge into any situation without an adequate analysis or without examining the many options available. Before committing himself formally to the communist cause, Zhou Enlai, characteristically, had to be satisfied about the merits of this new political development. In Japan, China, and finally in Europe, he studied, analyzed, discussed. The Bolshevik revolution aroused his curiosity about Marxism, and he then studied Marxist theory in such writings as Kawakami Hajime's *Research in Social Problems*. He subsequently became favorably impressed by Li Dazhao, who confessed his conversion to Marxism in *Xinqingnian* during the May Fourth period. Zhou Enlai discussed this important ideological issue with other members of the Awakening Society and in meetings and discussions with Li Dazhao in Tianjin and Beijing. Toward the end of 1919, Zhou Enlai, like many other politically inspired Chinese young people at that time, came to agree with Li's ideological manifestation. This agreement was solidified during Zhou Enlai's political activities and imprisonment. A further opportunity to discuss Marxism with Zhang Shenfu and Liu Qingyang occurred in France. In the spring of 1921 Zhou Enlai took the crucial step of joining the communist cell in Paris on Zhang's and Liu's recommendation. Nothing in his personality, family background, and Confucian education predisposed Zhou Enlai toward rebellious acts, and he probably would have preferred reform (*gaige*) to revolution (*geming*); but once he had made his revolutionary commitment, he pursued his professed objective with obvious determination and complete devotion.

It now seems clear that Zhou Enlai espoused Marxism not simply because he was influenced by Kawakami Hajime, Li Dazhao, and Zhang Shenfu, but because he found Marxism compatible with his nationalistic, humanistic, and idealistic orientations. The concept of dialectical materialism was the least important factor in his ideological transformation. At this time in his political career, Zhou Enlai was not particularly interested in such ideas as class struggle and proletarian dictatorship. What he did believe was that Marxism presented both an analytic tool and a program of action to help China to achieve national salvation, to bring about justice for the common people [*pingmin*], and to establish an ideal society for humanity. From the beginning, he had no illusions that Marxism was a panacea for all of China's chronic internal and external problems, but he did believe that Marxism was an appropriate and convenient means of achieving China's long-term national interests.

At the initial stage of his communist activities, Zhou Enlai developed a mutually reinforcing personal network of support and cooperation with his old acquaintances from the May Fourth era (Li Dazhao, Zhang Shenfu, Ma Jun, Guo Longzhen, Deng Yingchao, Liu Qingyang, Zhao Guangchen, Yu Fangzhou, and Zhang Guotao) and with his new colleagues from Europe (Cai Hesen, Zhao Shiyan, Zhu De, Deng Xiaoping, Li Fuchun, Li Weihan, Li Lisan, Nie Rongzhen, Wang Ruofei, Chen Yi, Xu Teli, and Cai Chang). The Chinese returnees from Europe continued to constitute a powerful group in the Chinese Communist Party (and later on in the People's Republic of China).[5] Yet it is very important to point out that Zhou Enlai did not follow a considerable number of early Chinese communists, including his associates from Europe—Zhang Shenfu, Liu Qingyang, Zhao Guangchen, Ren Zhuoxuan, Zhang Ruoming, and Yin Kuan—who eventually left the Chinese Communist Party.[6] One reason for this difference was that Zhou Enlai, unlike many Chinese communists, had the rare opportunity to study and understand Marxism before it became a fashionable doctrine in China. His communist commitment was therefore not a sudden, emotional, or precipitous act, but was rather a consequence of intellectual discourse and deliberate preparation. Moreover, as graphically expressed in his poem about Huang Zhengpin's death, Zhou Enlai had an uncompromising sense of loyalty and solidarity toward his friends and colleagues who became revolutionary martyrs during the 1920's. He was especially saddened over the deaths of his close friends and comrades—Li Dazhao, Ma Jun, Guo Longzhen, Yu Fangzhou, Sun Bingwen, Zhao Shiyan, Cai Hesen, Chen Yannian, Chen Qiaonian, Xiong Xiong, Xiang Jingyu, and Mu Qing.[7] The idea of betraying these fallen comrades was completely alien to Zhou Enlai's character. Most importantly, he felt that his abilities and credentials would enable him to make a significant contribution toward the Chinese Communist Party's ultimate victory and that his associates and followers respected and appreciated his ascending leadership.

As a young adult (age 26), Zhou Enlai was well equipped with a unique set of attractive personal attributes, journalistic and organizational experiences, wide-ranging political activities, and supportive human connections. As a person who spent five and a half years of his formative period in Japan and Europe (mostly Paris and Berlin), he had a cosmopolitan outlook and sophisticated demeanor. Toward the end of 1924 not many young Chinese communists were in a position to match Zhou Enlai's achievements and promise. Hence he was destined to assume an increasing number of important positions in the Chinese Communist Party in the years ahead.[8] In the process of fulfilling his growing political responsibilities, Zhou Enlai was bound to adjust, refine, and modify the overall framework of his Confucian behavioral code, Marxist ideological commitments, organizational and communication skills, and cosmopolitan sophistication that he had already acquired during his first 26 years.

REFERENCE MATTER

Notes

Abbreviations used in the Notes can be found in the References Cited, p. 213.

Introduction

1. Snow, *Red Star Over China* (1961), pp. 50–51.
2. White, *In Search of History*, pp. 117–26.
3. Kissinger, *White House Years*, pp. 743–45.
4. Nixon, *Leaders*, pp. 218–19.
5. The most comprehensive and authoritative biography written in China on Zhou Enlai's pre-1949 period is Jin Chongji, ed., *Zhou Enlai zhuan 1898–1949*.
6. For example, see Li Tien-Min, *Chou En-lai*.
7. See Hsu, *Chou En-lai: China's Gray Eminence*, and Wilson, *Zhou Enlai: A Biography*.

Chapter One

1. The year 1899 is cited by Snow, *Red Star Over China* (1978), p. 46; Li Tien-Min, *Chou En-lai*, p. 14; Yan Jingwen, *Zhou Enlai pingzhuan*, p. 12; and *Who's Who in Communist China*, p. 137. The year 1896 is cited by Nakano Akira, *Ajia no kaiki—Chūkyō*, p. 77; Matsuno Tanio, *Chūgoku no shidōsha*, p. 20; *Gendai Chūgoku jinmei jiten*, p. 234; and Nashimoto Yūhei, *Shū Onrai*, p. 14. For his birthplace, Shaoxing is given by Nashimoto, p. 14, and by Hsu, "Chou En-lai," p. 519. Huaiyin is cited by Archer, *Chou En-lai*, p. 3; Hunan is cited by Hatano Kanichi, *Chūgoku kyōsantōshi*, 1: 34.
2. For example, in 1918 Zhou wrote February 13, 1898, as his birth date in his application form for Kyoto Imperial University in Japan.
3. When Zhou died in January 1976, the Revolutionary Committees

of Zhejiang and Jiangsu provinces sent special delegations to the funeral at Beijing in recognition of his connections with both provinces. In 1986, on the tenth anniversary of his death, his ancestral home in Shaoxing was opened with Chen Yun's inscription, "The Home of Zhou Enlai's Ancestors." See *Renmin Ribao*, Jan. 9, 1986. On what would have been his 90th birthday, the Zhou Enlai Memorial Museum was inaugurated in Huaian with Deng Xiaoping's inscription; the Zhou statue was also unveiled there. See ibid., Mar. 7, 1988.

4. For Zhou's family background, see Chen Duo, "Zhou Enlai shaoxing jiashi," pp. 58–62.

5. Quotation from Giles, *History of Chinese Literature*, p. 219. Another prominent ancestor was Zhou Mao, who served as a deputy prime minister under the Yuan dynasty.

6. Cole, *Shaohsing*, pp. 98–105.

7. A recent study shows that Zhou Panlong bought a title to the position of *zhixian* but did not serve in that capacity because of his sudden death. See Sun Zhiyao, "Zhou Enlai jiashi tongnian," pp. 1–8.

8. This is the contention of Wilson, *Zhou Enlai: A Biography*, p. 21.

9. Several studies have mistakenly identified Zhou Enlai's father as Zhou Panlong's seventh and youngest son: see Hsu, *Chou En-lai*, pp. 3–4, Roots, *Chou: An Informal Biography*, and Weidenbaum, "Chou En-lai: Creative Revolutionary."

10. Upon Cai Yuanpei's introduction, Wang Shiyu (1874–1944) joined Sun Yat-sen's Revolutionary Alliance and had a very close association with a famous female revolutionary martyr, Qiu Jin (1875–1907). When Zhou Enlai visited Shaoxing in 1939, he composed a poem in memory of Qiu Jin and gave it to his cousin Wang Qubing. He also met with Wang Shiyu and they had their picture taken together. For this information, see Ogawa Heishirō, "Shūkin joshi to Shū Onrai."

11. Hsu, *Chou En-lai*, pp. 5–6.

12. Interview, October 1988.

13. See Wilson, *Zhou Enlai*, p. 20.

14. Lieberman, a special correspondent of the *New York Times*, conducted a series of interviews with Zhou Enlai at Nanjing in August and September 1946. See the Chinese-language text in "Zhou Enlai tong Li Boman tan geren jingli," pp. 26–29. The *New York Times* failed to print Lieberman's detailed report on Zhou Enlai and his own notes were lost (Lieberman's letter to the author dated Oct. 31, 1985). Zhang Wenjin, who in the mid-1980's served as China's ambassador to the United States, was an interpreter (interview with Zhang Wenjin, Beijing, October 1988).

15. "Zhou Enlai tong Li Boman."

16. Hsu, *Chou En-lai*, p. 5.

17. Ogawa Heishirō, *Chūgoku saihō*. The book reproduces the photographs of Zhou Enlai's parents.

18. See Wang Jingru, *Zhou Enlai qingshaonian shidai*, pp. 17–18.

19. "Zhou Enlai tong Li Boman."

20. For this information, see *Zhou zongli yu guxiang*, pp. 2–3.

21. Wilson, *Zhou Enlai*, pp. 20–21.

22. All major Western biographers of Zhou Enlai repeat this speculation; see Hsu, Wilson, and Weidenbaum, for example.

23. See Ma Shunyi, *Taochura chisede jiating*. This is a bitter denunciation of the Zhou Enlai family and the Chinese Communist Party, which she blames for her father's death in China. Evidently both Kai-yu Hsu and Li Tien-Min interviewed her extensively in Taipei.

24. Zhou Enzhu, "Wode tangxiong—Zhou Enlai."

25. For example, see Zhou Enlai's letter to Zhou Tiaozhi from London in *Zhou Enlai nianpu*, p. 45. Zhou Enlai also sent Zhou Enzhu postcards and gifts from Europe. (Interview with Zhou Enzhu's relative, Beijing, October 1988).

26. Snow, *Red Star Over China* (1978), p. 46.

27. As quoted in Jin Chongji, ed., *Zhou Enlai zhuan*, p. 3.

28. See Wang Jingru, *Zhou Enlai tongzhi*, p. 18, and *Zhou zongli yu guxiang*, p. 6.

29. See ZZ, p. 7.

30. See "Zhou Enlai tong Li Boman," and *Zhou zongli yu guxiang*, p. 13.

31. *Zhou zongli yu guxiang*, pp. 9–10.

32. Zhou Enpu died when he was still young. Zhou Enshou graduated from the Whampoa Military Academy but left the military service in the late 1920's. After the establishment of the People's Republic of China, he held a relatively minor position in the Ministry of Metallurgical Industry. He was imprisoned during the Cultural Revolution. Afterward he retired from government service because of ill health. As Premier, Zhou Enlai did not show any favoritism toward his youngest brother and his family. (Interview with his relative, Beijing, October 1988).

33. Saari, *Legacies of Childhood*, p. 79. For the concepts of "ego strength" and "personal trustworthiness" as a foundation of strong leadership, see Erikson, *Young Man Luther* and *Childhood and Society*.

34. Lieberman's letters to the author dated Oct. 31 and Dec. 8, 1985.

35. *Zhou zongli yu guxiang*, pp. 15–16.

36. See *Zhou Enlai nianpu*, p. 7. Kai-yu Hsu is in error when he says that Wan Donger died when Zhou Enlai was four years old (*Chou En-lai*, p. 5). Ma Shunyi (*Taochura chisede jiating*, p. 7) is also in error: she says that Zhou Enlai's natural mother died when he was one year old.

37. In 1920, before leaving for Europe, Zhou Enlai visited with Chen Shizhou at Nanjing (Su Shuyang, *Dadide erzi*, pp. 10 and 61), and he also corresponded with Chen during 1921. His long letters to Chen from London and Paris discussed a wide range of issues—his political ideas, his academic plans, his brothers, British conservatism, Soviet reforms, and the Chinese family system. See *SX*, pp. 23–27.

38. *Zhou Enlai nianpu*, p. 8.

39. Ibid., p. 24.

40. For Zhou Enlai's 1952 meeting with Gong Zhiru, who had become a kindergarten teacher and a devout Christian, see *Zhou zongli yu guxiang*, pp. 68–76.

41. Hu Hua, *Early Life of Zhou Enlai*, pp. 3–4.

42. It is also suggested that Zhou Enlai retained his Baoying accent because he was reared by his adoptive mother, a Baoying native in Jiangsu province. (Interview with his relative, Beijing, October 1988.)

43. *Zhou zongli yu guxiang*, pp. 104–6.

44. Ibid., pp. 112–13.

45. Wilson, *Zhou Enlai*, p. 22.

46. Hsu, *Chou En-lai*, pp. 5–6.

47. Weidenbaum, "Chou En-lai," pp. 12–33.

48. See Pye, *Mao Tse-tung*. For Mao's characterization of his father as a "hot-tempered man" and a "severe taskmaster," see Snow, *Red Star Over China* (1978), pp. 121–34.

49. Saari, *Legacies of Childhood*, pp. 104–5.

50. See Erikson, *Gandhi's Truth*.

51. "Zhou Enlai tong Li Boman." Lieberman, however, says that he does not remember anything about any references by Zhou Enlai to his father. Lieberman's letter to the author.

52. Discussion with Professor Yamaguchi Kazuko of Soka University (Japan), Tianjin, October 1988. Professor Yamaguchi was born and raised in Tieling.

53. For example, Zhou Enlai met with his father in Shanghai in 1927. See Zhou Enzhu, "Wode tangxiong," p. 2.

54. See *Zhou Enlai nianpu*, pp. 535–37. Both Mao Zedong and Chiang Kai-shek conveyed messages of condolences to Zhou Enlai. After the establishment of the People's Republic of China, the Chongqing Municipal Committee of the Chinese Communist Party moved Zhou Yineng's wooden coffin to the public cemetery for revolutionary martyrs. When Zhou Enlai heard of this, he instructed the Chongqing Committee to remove the coffin from the cemetery. In 1964, the Chongqing Committee having not acted, he sent a staff member of the State Council to Chongqing to transfer the

coffin to a remote grave with no tablet. See *Zhou zongli yu guxiang*, pp. 87–88.

55. For his speech at Wannan in March 1939, see *Zhou Enlai xuanji*, 1: 101–9.

56. In 1906 the Yingang Academy established a primary school with five classes. For the history of the Yingang Academy, see *Renmin Ribao*, Mar. 7, 1987, and Wang Jingru, *Zhou Enlai tongzhi*, p. 32.

57. Zhou Yigeng's résumé was discovered in the archives of the Heilongjiang Provincial Government; it was written in 1921 when he received a special meritorious award from the Heilongjiang Government. The author obtained a copy of the résumé from the Zhou Enlai Memorial Museum in Tianjin. See Chen Zilai, "Zhou Yigeng de liangfen ziliao," pp. 32–33.

58. See his meeting with Han Nianlong (Vice Minister of Foreign Affairs) and other government officials on Aug. 16, 1970, in Wang Jingru, *Zhou Enlai tongzhi*, p. 44.

59. Christie, *Thirty Years in Moukden*, p. 251.

60. Ibid., p. 1.

61. "Zhou Enlai tong Li Boman."

62. As quoted in Hammond, *Coming of Grace*, p. 6, and Wang Yongxiang and Liu Pinqing, *Weile Zhonghua zhi jueqi*, p. 18.

63. See Wang Jingru, *Zhou Enlai tongzhi*, p. 45.

64. For Zhou Enlai's discussions of his teachers (Gao and Mao), see "Zhou Enlai tong Li Boman," and Wang Jingru, *Zhou Enlai tongzhi*, pp. 36–38.

65. *Zhou Enlai tongyi zhanxian wenxuan*, pp. 211–12. For details on Zhang Binglin, see Furth, "The Sage as Rebel." In the People's Republic of China Zhang is considered a "democratic revolutionary"; his memorial hall was established at Hangzhou in 1988. See *Renmin Ribao*, Jan. 13, 1988.

66. For Zou Rong (1885–1905) and the text of *Revolutionary Army*, see Schiff, "Life and Writings of Tsou Jung."

67. For Chen Tianhua (1875–1905), see Young, "Problems of a Late Ch'ing Revolutionary."

68. Dai Jitao (1891–1949) studied law at Nihon University. He was a member of Sun's Revolutionary Alliance and one of Sun's assistants. He started *Minquanbao* in Shanghai toward the end of 1911. In 1912 he became Sun's personal secretary and the following year he fled to Japan. Zhou Enlai after returning from Europe in 1924 served briefly under Dai as deputy director of the Political Department at Whampoa Military Academy in Canton. Subsequently, Dai served as president of the Examination Yuan under Chiang Kai-shek.

69. "Zhou Enlai tong Li Boman."

70. Fairbank, Reischauer, and Craig, *East Asia*, p. 633.

71. See Zhang Jingxuan's recollection in *Zhou Enlai zongli*, pp. 147–48.

72. Wang Jingru, *Zhou Enlai tongzhi*, pp. 38–41.

73. The original texts of the two poems are exhibited in the Zhou Enlai Memorial Museum in Tianjin.

74. Christie, *Thirty Years in Moukden*, pp. 194–95.

75. Jin Chongji, ed., *Zhou Enlai zhuan*, p. 7.

76. Zhang Zuolin was a good friend of Zhang Boling and made substantial financial contributions to Nankai Middle School. In December 1936 Zhou Enlai went from Yanan to Xian at the invitation of Zhang Zuolin's son, Zhang Xueliang, and negotiated the release of Chiang Kai-shek from Zhang Xueliang's arrest.

77. For the text of this early essay, see ZZ, pp. 3–5.

78. Fairbank, Reischauer, and Craig, *East Asia*, p. 662.

79. For various comments, see ZZ, p. 3.

80. See the Zhou Yigeng résumé.

81. This memento was given to Guo Chengzhen. See Wang Jingru, *Zhou Enlai tongzhi*, p. 58.

82. See the recollection by Wei Yuanjin, one of Zhou Enlai's classmates, "Youguan daze buxi xuexiao de yiduan huiyi."

83. For the Qinghua School, see *Xuefu jiwen—Guoli Qinghua daxue*, and Lin Zexun, *Zhongguo liuxue jiaoyushi*, pp. 252–78.

84. For the employment of American-educated Chinese intellectuals in 1925, for example, see Y. C. Wang, *Chinese Intellectuals*, p. 516.

85. Hsu, *Chou En-lai*, p. 10.

86. Personal communication (dated Mar. 14, 1983) from one of Zhou Enlai's schoolmates, Meng Chih, who took the Nankai Middle School examination in 1912.

Chapter Two

1. The biographical information about Zhang Boling is derived from the work by his son Zhang Xizuo, "Zhang Boling xiansheng zhuanlüe," and from Wang Wentian, *Zhang Boling yu Nankai*.

2. For more on Yan Fu, see Schwartz, *In Search of Wealth and Power*.

3. See Zhang Boling's statement in Wang Wenjun, ed., *Zhang Boling jiaoyu yanlun xuanji*, pp. 143–45.

4. This is my revision of Hu Shih's original translation; see Hu Shih, "Chang Poling: Educator," in *There Is Another China*, pp. 4–14. This book was published in celebration of the granting of the honorary degree of Doctor of Letters to Zhang Boling by Columbia University in June 1946.

5. Meng, *Chinese-American Understanding*, p. 56.

6. Stuart, "Introduction," in *There Is Another China*, pp. 1–3.

7. See Boorman, ed., *Biographical Dictionary of Republican China*, 1: 100–105.

8. Hersey, "A Reporter at Large: China—Part II," p. 52.

9. See Zheng Zhiguang, ed., *Zhang Boling zhuan*, pp. 16–19.

10. As quoted in *Xuefu jiwen—Guoli Nankai daxue*, p. 3.

11. Hu Shih, "Chang Poling," p. 7.

12. For Yan Xiu's biographical information, see Yan Renzeng, ed., *Yan Fansun xiansheng nianpu*, and the excerpts of Yan Xiu's diary in *QS* 4 (1983): 34–35. I am greatly indebted to Yan Renzeng (Louis Yen) for his cooperation in July 1984. Yan Renzeng is the son of a nephew of Yan Xiu who died in 1913; after his father's death, Yan Renzeng was raised at the Yan Xiu household. He studied chemistry at Hillsdale College in Michigan and at Cornell University. Also see Qi Zhilu, "Tianjin jindai zhuming jiaoyujia Yan Xiu."

13. Yan Xiu also opposed the practice of foot binding for Chinese girls. His poem "Music for Foot Liberation" (*fangzuge*) deplored the suffering of girls caused by their distorted bones. For the text, see *TJ* 25 (1983): 52.

14. Schwartz, *In Search of Wealth and Power*, p. 83.

15. See Garrett, *Social Reformers in Urban China*, p. 201. At least four of Yan Xiu's sons studied in Japan: Zhichong, Zhiyi (Tokyo Higher Engineering School), Zhizhong (Tokyo Imperial University, where he studied medicine), and Zhikai (Tokyo School of Fine Arts, where he studied Western painting).

16. Other high positions that Yan Xiu rejected included speaker of the House of Councillors (1917) and president of Beijing University (1925).

17. For example, see Huang Yusheng, "Zaoqide nankai zhongxue," p. 131. Huang went on to study at the University of Chicago and later was a professor of education and psychology at Nankai University.

18. *Xiaofeng*, Apr. 17, 1916.

19. Meng, *Chinese-American Understanding*, p. 57.

20. *Xiaofeng*, Mar. 27, 1916.

21. The auditorium (*Weitingtang*) was named after Yuan Shikai's courtesy name (Weiting) in appreciation of his large financial contribution to Nankai. After Yuan declared himself Emperor in 1916, the name was removed from the Nankai auditorium because of student pressure. See Huang Yusheng, p. 132.

22. Interview with Wu Guozhen (K. C. Wu) in Savannah, Georgia, Apr. 1, 1984.

23. See the recollection by Wang Zuxiang in *Zhang Boling xiansheng bainian danchen jiniance*, pp. 15–17.

24. In addition to the above-mentioned memorial volume, see another memorial collection of reminiscences and essays, Guo Rongsheng and Zhang Yuan, eds., *Zhang Boling xiansheng jinianji.*

25. The school charged 36 yuan for tuition and 24 yuan for a dormitory room for a year. Students could choose either a low-cost meal plan (three yuan and four jiao per month) or a more expensive one (four yuan and nine jiao); this difference determined the variety of food students were allowed to choose. See *Xiaofeng*, June 12, 1916.

26. As quoted in Jin Chongji, ed., *Zhou Enlai zhuan*, p. 12.

27. Zhang Honggao, "Huiyi xuesheng shidaide Zhou Enlai tongzhi."

28. Hsu, *Chou En-lai*, p. 267. Li Fujing is also identified as one of Zhou Enlai's roommates in Zhang Xilu, "Zhou Enlai—Nankai zuihaode xuesheng."

29. This information is based on Meng Chih's letter dated Mar. 14, 1983, and on an interview with Wu Guozhen on Apr. 1, 1984.

30. See Chen Zilai, "Zhou Yigeng de liangfen ziliao."

31. Zhang Honggao, "Huiyi xuesheng shidaide Zhou Enlai tongzhi," p. 396.

32. This information comes from Chang Ceou's children, Chang Zuochao and Chang Jingchao, "Zhou Enlai yu Chang Ceou de youyi."

33. Detailed comments on Zhou Enlai, as on other graduates, were included in *Dishice biye tongxuelu* (The Tenth Graduation Book), as reprinted in *Zhou Enlai qingnian shidai.*

34. Zhang Xilu, "Zhou Enlai—Nankai zuihaode xuesheng," p. 4. After Nankai, Zhang Xilu studied at Qinghua School and the University of Chicago. Later he taught mathematics at Nankai, Xiamen, Zhongfa, and Beijing universities and at the Beijing Aeronautical Engineering Institute.

35. Duan Molan entered Nankai Middle School in 1913 with Zhou Enlai; Zheng Daoru entered a year later. Duan received a Ph.D. from Columbia University and became Chiang Kai-shek's ambassador to France. Zheng Daoru was a minister in Chiang's cabinet.

36. For a detailed daily program, see Huang Yusheng, "Zaoqide nankai zhongxue," pp. 144–46.

37. Zhang Xilu, "Zhou Enlai," p. 3.

38. See the recollection by Shi Kuiling, who worked with Zhou Enlai in school publications and drama programs, in Guo Rongsheng and Zhang Yuan, eds., *Zhang Boling*, pp. 13–14.

39. Interview with Wu Guozhen.

40. Meng Chih's letter dated Mar. 14, 1983.

41. Hu Shih, "Chang Poling," p. 8.

42. *Xiaofeng*, May 1, 1916.

43. Meng, *Chinese-American Understanding*, p. 58.

44. See Garrett, *Social Reformers*, pp. 93–103.

45. Feifei (one of Zhou Enlai's pen names), "Wo zhi rengeguan" (My Views on Human Dignity), in *Jingye Review* 5 (Oct. 1916), as reprinted in ZZ, pp. 95–99.

46. Meng, *Chinese-American Understanding*, pp. 59–61.

47. Interview with Wu Guozhen.

48. In his summit meeting with President Nixon in 1972, Zhou Enlai observed approvingly that Lincoln had waged the Civil War to free the slaves and had won the war because the people supported him. See Nixon, *Leaders*, p. 222. For Zhou Enlai's other comments on Lincoln, see *Quotations from Premier Chou En-lai*, p. 93.

49. See Huang Yusheng, "Zaoqide nankai zhongxue," pp. 135–38, and Wang Yongxiang and Liu Pinqing, *Weile zhonghua zhi jueqi*, p. 20.

50. "Zhou Enlai tong Li Boman."

51. See Zhou's praise of Mei Yilin's valedictory speech delivered in English at the ninth graduation ceremony (December 1916) in *Xiaofeng*, special edition, Jan. 15, 1917. Mei Yilin studied at Qinghua School and earned an M.D. degree at Rush Medical College in Chicago. His older brother, Mei Yiqi, who studied at Nankai, Qinghua, and Worcester Polytechnic Institute, served as Qinghua University's president and as Minister of Education in Taipei in the 1960's. Mei Yilin's younger brother, Mei Yibao, who also studied at Nankai and Qinghua and received a Ph.D. from the University of Chicago, served as acting president of Yanjing University during the Pacific War. Later he retired from the University of Iowa.

52. The Tenth Graduation Book.

53. See Zhou's report on this contest as well as the text of his essay in *Xiaofeng*, May 15, 1916. The text is reprinted in ZZ, pp. 54–57. The list of the top 40 contestants included two of his roommates, Zhang Honggao and Chang Ceou, Zhang Boling's eldest son, Zhang Xilu, and Zhang's two other student assistants, Duan Molan and Zheng Daoru.

54. For the teachers' comments, see ZZ, p. 54.

55. See *Xiaofeng*, Mar. 20, 1916; ZZ, pp. 40–43.

56. Yan Renzeng, "Zhou zongli yu Yan Fanlao," and interview with Yan Renzeng in Tianjin, July 17, 1984. Yan Xiu's diary entry of Sept. 29, 1915, notes that Zhou Enlai came to the Yan residence and asked Yan Xiu to write the title page of the *Jingye Review*, of which Zhou Enlai was editor.

57. This information is based on a letter from Julia Yen, Yan Xiu's granddaughter, to the author dated Mar. 31, 1983. The text of Yan Xiu's letter concerning his daughter's possible marriage to Zhou Enlai is exhibited in the Zhou Enlai Memorial Museum, Tianjin.

58. See Zhang Honggao, "Huiyi Zhou Enlai zai Nankai xuexiao he liuri shiqide xuexi yu shenghuo." Yan Zhian graduated from the famous Keen's School in Tianjin and then from Yanjing University in 1924 with a B.S. degree in mathematics. She first taught at Keen's School and then at Yanjing University as a part-time lecturer. Her teaching position is listed in *Yenching University Student Directory* (Oct. 1938). I wish to thank Dr. Philip West for sharing this directory with me. Yan Zhian died in January 1949, ten months before Zhou Enlai became the first premier of the People's Republic of China.

59. Yan Renzeng, "Zhou zongli yu Yan Fanlao," p. 4. Zhou Enlai urged Yan Renzeng to compile a comprehensive biographical record on Yan Xiu so that the Chinese people could learn from his integrity and accomplishments.

60. Meng, *Chinese-American Understanding*, p. 58.

61. *Xiaofeng*, Nov. 8, 1916, as reprinted in ZZ, pp. 102–7. Other top award-winners were Zheng Daoru (first), Ma Jun (second), and Duan Molan (third). *Xiaofeng*, Oct. 9, 1916.

62. Interview with Wu Guozhen.

63. See Zhou Enlai's report on Ma Jun's speech in *Xiaofeng*, Oct. 25, 1916.

64. *Xiaofeng*, Apr. 17, 1916.

65. See Wang Jingru, *Zhou Enlai tongzhi*, pp. 67–70, and Hu Hua, *Early Life of Zhou Enlai*, pp. 11–12.

66. As recorded in *Zhou Enlai nianpu*, p. 12.

67. See Zhou Enlai's two-part report on Liang's speech at Nankai, in *Xiaofeng*, Feb. 27 and Mar. 7, 1917. Yan Renzeng remembers that because of Liang's heavy Guangdong accent, his speech was not easily understood by Nankai students.

68. See Zhou Enlai's discussion of Huxley in *Xiaofeng*, Mar. 20, 1916.

69. Schwartz, *In Search of Wealth and Power*, p. 99.

70. After his prison experience, Shi left Nankai School and joined Ma Qianli in publishing the newspaper *Xinminyibao*. In the late 1920's he managed a bookstore in Beijing and served as a secretary-general to the Education Department of Hebei province under Governor Yan Zhiyi. He joined the Guomindang and served on its Central Committee; later, in Taiwan, he was active in the Islamic temple and translated the Koran into Chinese. See Shi Zizhou, "Huinian Boling xiansheng."

71. For Ma's brief biography written by his son, see Ma Cuiguan, "Xianfu Ma Qianli xiansheng shilüe." For his daughter's reminiscences on Zhang Boling and Ma Qianli, see Ma Zhuguan, "Wo de wujiufu." Ma's association with Zhou Enlai during the May Fourth Movement is discussed

in Chapter 4. During the 1920's, as co-publisher of *Xinminyibao*, he wrote an article on Lenin. He joined the Guomindang in 1927 and became a member of the Tianjin City Council. He died in February 1930. His diary for twenty years (in 23 volumes) is in the Tianjin Historical Museum.

72. Interview with Kang Nairu's son, Kang Tiejuan, in Tianjin, July 18, 1984. Kang Nairu died in 1948 at Tianjin. Kang Tiejuan, a graduate of Nankai University and a professor of chemical engineering there, was also, in 1984, a vice chairman of the Chinese People's Political Consultative Conference in Tianjin.

73. For Zhou Enlai's appreciation of his teachers' editorial help, see *Xiaofeng*, May 2, 9, 16, and 23, and June 6 and 15, 1917. He regretfully mentions Zhang Shiling's death and Zhang Gaoru's departure from Nankai.

74. See the texts of Zhou's and Zhang's poems in ZZ, pp. 100–101. For the English translation, see N. Lin, *In Quest*, p. 7.

75. Reprinted in ZZ, pp. 12–13, and translated in N. Lin, p. 1.

76. This appeared in the fourth issue of *Jingye Review* (Apr. 1916); reprinted in ZZ, pp. 45–47 and translated in N. Lin, pp. 3–4. In his speech at Shanghai in 1984, President Ronald Reagan quoted this poem; see *Renmin Ribao*, May 1, 1984, and *Current Policy* 575 (1984).

77. N. Lin, p. 5.

78. Hu Hua, *Early Life of Zhou Enlai*, p. 15.

79. Feifei and Guzhu yaren, "Benhui chengli xiaoshi."

80. This personal network was to be extended to Japan in 1917 when Zhou Enlai had a close association with Zhang Ruifeng, Zhang Honggao, and Wu Hantao, and to England in early 1921 when Zhou relied upon Chang's assistance.

81. See Wang Jingru, *Zhou Enlai tongzhi*, p. 73, and Huai En, *Zhou zongli qingshaoniandai*, p. 39.

82. See the charter in ZZ, pp. 38–39.

83. See *Jingye Review* 4 (Apr. 1916).

84. Interview with Wu Guozhen.

85. Wu Guozhen's letter to the author dated Apr. 20, 1984.

86. After graduating from Nankai, Wu studied at the Qinghua School and Grinnell College in Iowa; he received a Ph.D. in politics from Princeton University and returned to China to join Chiang Kai-shek's government. In this capacity he had many dealings with Zhou Enlai during the late 1930's and the 1940's. Wu held a number of important positions during that period: mayor of Hankou in the late 1930's, mayor of Chongqing in the early 1940's, vice minister (and acting minister) of foreign affairs at Nanjing in the mid-1940's, and mayor of Shanghai in the late 1940's. Wu

recalls that in October 1938 when the Japanese forces threatened Hankou, he and Zhou went to the airport to see Chiang Kai-shek off. Afterward, Zhou came to Wu's house with a bottle of wine to celebrate the latter's birthday. In Chongqing they met frequently to argue their political differences. And in the process of postwar CCP-Guomindang negotiations they sat on opposite sides of the table. Wu says, "If Zhou had been captured by Chiang Kai-shek's forces, I would have saved his life." "If I had been captured by Mao Zedong's forces," he states confidently, "Zhou would have done the same for me." Such a test of their Jingye Society friendship did not occur, however. Wu later served as governor of Taiwan province and cabinet minister (1949–53), but went to the United States in 1953 after a dispute with Chiang Kai-shek. When he died in June 1984 in Savannah, Georgia, Wu's wife received a telegram of condolence from Zhou Enlai's widow, Deng Yingchao. See Deng Yingchao's telegram in *Renmin Ribao*, June 12, 1984. For Wu's biographical data, see Boorman, ed., *Biographical Dictionary of Republican China*, 3: 438–40.

87. Wang Yongxiang and Liu Pinqing, *Weile Zhonghua zhi jueqi*, p. 35.

88. Zhou gave many items, including copies of *Dongfang Zazhi* (Eastern Miscellany), *Datongbao* (a newspaper), *The Foundations of National Reconstruction*, *Model for a Soldier*, *Model for Self-Government*, *Problems of the Life and Death of the Republic*, *History of the American War of Independence*, and *Qingnianbao* (Youth Newspaper). See the lists of contributions in *Jingye Review* 1 (Oct. 1914) and 2 (Apr. 1915).

89. As reported in *Xiaofeng*, May 29, 1916.

90. Ibid., May 30, 1917. Cai became president of the Academy of Science at Nanjing in 1928. Li Shizeng studied chemistry in France, edited an anarchist journal (*Xinshiji*) in Paris in 1907, wrote several books advocating anarchism, and ran a tofu plant in France to support students. He rose to a high position in the Guomindang and served as adviser to Chiang Kai-shek in 1948. Wu Yuzhang joined Cai Yuanpei in organizing the work-study program for Chinese students in France in 1916 and set up a preparatory school for France-bound Chinese students in Beijing. In 1920 Zhou Enlai used this program to go to Europe. Wu was elected to the Central Committee of the Chinese Communist Party in 1938 and 1956 and to the First National People's Congress in 1954. He was appointed president of Yanan University in 1941, Huabei University in 1948, and the Chinese People's University in 1949. He was also made a member of the Central People's Government in 1949, together with Zhou Enlai, and he was a member of the Political and Legal Commission in the State Council headed by Zhou Enlai. For Wu's biographical data, see *Renmin Ribao*, Jan. 14, 1984.

91. As cited in *Zhou Enlai nianpu*, p. 22.

92. For the origin of this pen name, Huai En refers to a poem by Cao

Zhi, which uses the term "feifei" to describe a flying yellow bird. See Huai En, *Zhou zonglide qingshaoniandai*, p. 40. The "fly" is also related to Zhou's other name, Xiangyu, because he sometimes split one Chinese character "xiang" into two different Chinese characters—"yang" (lit. "sheep") and "yu" (lit. "plumage").

93. For Zhou Enlai's relationship with *Xiaofeng*, see Liao Yongwu, "Zhou Enlai tongzhi yu Nankai xiaofeng."

94. *Xiaofeng*, May 2, 9, 16, and 23 and June 6 and 15, 1917, as reprinted in *ZZ*, pp. 118–33.

95. The Tokyo group, the Spring Willow Company (*Chunliushe*), produced a new drama called *A Girl of Tea Leaves* (*Chahuanü*). See Wang Yongxiang and Liu Pinqing, *Weile Zhonghua zhi jueqi*, p. 50.

96. As recorded in *Zhou Enlai tongzhi qingnianshiqi*.

97. For his set-designing and directing roles, see Zhou's report on a play in *Jingye Review* 5 (Oct. 1916). It is interesting to note that Deng Yingchao, Zhou's future wife, acted a male role in her school drama. See Cao Yu, "Huiyi zai Tianjin kaishede xijushenghuo."

98. The text of *One Dollar* is included in Xia Jianshan, ed., *Nankai huoju yundong shiliao*, pp. 185–239.

99. This information is based on Meng Chih's letter dated Mar. 14, 1983.

100. *Jingye Review* 4 (Apr. 1916).

101. Wang Yongxiang and Liu Pinqing, *Weile Zhonghua zhi jueqi*, p. 58. For the meeting between Zhou Enlai and Mei Lanfang in June 1949 when they reminisced about Zhou's student performance, see Wang Jingru, *Zhou Enlai tongzhi*, pp. 81–82. Mei was president of the Peking Opera Academy in the People's Republic of China as well as president of the Chinese Theater Research Center and a member of the National Committee of the Chinese People's Political Consultative Conference.

102. See the recollection by Zhang Lunyuan (who attended Nankai from 1914 to 1918), "Huiyi Zhou zongli zai Nankai."

103. Mei Yibao's letter written to the author dated Apr. 13, 1984.

104. See Zhou's assistance to Zhang Pengchun in the drama program in *Jingye Review* 5 (Oct. 1916). For Zhang's drama program at Nankai, see Ma Ming, "Zhang Pengchun yu Zhongguo xiandaihuaju." Zhang Pengchun joined China's diplomatic service during the Sino-Japanese War. He served as minister in Turkey and as ambassador at the United Nations until 1952. Interview with Dr. Y. F. Chang (Zhang Yuanfeng), one of Zhang Pengchun's sons, in Claremont, California, July 10, 1990.

105. See Zhou Enlai's article, "Woxiao xinjuguan."

106. Hu Shih's comment appeared in *Xinqingnian*, Mar. 15, 1919. Hu Shih and Zhang Pengchun entered the Qinghua program at the same time

and sailed to the United States on the same ship. They often met each other and attended plays together in the United States. Interview with Y. F. Chang.

107. See Zhou Enlai's "Woxiao xinjuguan."

108. See *TJ* 15 (1981): 13–17.

109. See *Jingye Review* 1 (Oct. 1914).

110. Meng Chih's letter dated Mar. 14, 1983.

111. For a summary of Zhou Enlai's speech, see *Nankai xingqibao* (Nankai Weekly) 49 (June 14, 1915). For Zhang Boling's statement, see ibid., 46 (May 24, 1915).

112. As reported in *TJ* 15 (1981): 9.

113. *Xiaofeng*, June 12, 1916.

114. Meng, *Chinese-American Understanding*, p. 58.

115. Usui Chūsan, *Tenshin kyoryū mindan sanjū shūnen kinenshi*, p. 486. For a critical assessment of Japan's activities in Tianjin, see Sun Limin and Xin Gongxian, "Tianjin rizujie gaikuang."

116. As discussed in *TJ* 15 (1981): 11–12.

117. See *Xiaofeng*, Nov. 8, 1916, as reprinted in *ZZ*, pp. 102–7.

118. For Zhou Enlai's summary of Xiong's speech made at the ninth graduation ceremony of Nankai Middle School in December 1916, see *Xiaofeng*, special edition, Jan. 15, 1917. Xiong had studied in Japan after graduating from the Hanlin Academy. He was appointed minister of finance in 1911 and was prime minister during 1913–14 under Yuan Shikai. Cai Yuanpei, also a graduate of the Hanlin Academy, studied in Germany; he was minister of education and then (1916) president of Beijing University. Fan Jingsheng (1876–1927) studied at the Tokyo Higher Normal School. He was a high official in the ministry of education of the Qing government and minister of education in the early 1920's; in 1921 Zhou Enlai asked for his assistance in obtaining a Chinese government scholarship to study in the United Kingdom. Lu Muzhai (1856–1947), who published Yan Fu's books in Tianjin, was education commissioner of Zheli and Fengtian provinces under the Qing government and was a trustee of Nankai Middle School.

119. *Xiaofeng*, Nov. 29, 1916.

120. *Jingye Review* 5 (Oct. 1916), as reprinted in *ZZ*, pp. 95–99.

121. *Xiaofeng*, Nov. 29, 1916, as reprinted in *ZZ*, pp. 108–12.

122. As quoted in *Zhou Enlai nianpu*, p. 21.

123. It is interesting to note that Zhou Enlai attempted to follow in the educational footsteps of Chen Duxiu (1879–1942) and Zhang Shizhao (1881–1973), but failed in his efforts to enter the Tokyo Higher Normal School in 1918 and the University of Edinburgh in 1921. After the CCP's victory in China, Zhang Shizhao was a member of the National Committee of the Chinese People's Political Consultative Conference and a member of the Political and Legal Commission in the State Council headed by Zhou

Enlai. He also served as president of the Central Historical Museum in Beijing.

124. *Xiaofeng*, Sept. 6, 1917.

125. See Chang Zuochao and Chang Jingchao, "Zhou Enlai yu Chang Ceou de youyi."

Chapter Three

1. See Jansen, *Japan and China*, pp. 149–50, Ayers, *Chang Chih-tung and Educational Reform*, p. 136, and Bays, *China Enters the Twentieth Century*, pp. 132–62.

2. See Liang Qichao's essay in Itō Teruo, *Chūgokujin no Nihonjinkan hyakunenshi*, pp. 66–67.

3. The most frequently used figure (4,000) in 1916 is quoted from Sanetō Keishū, *Chūgokujin Nihon ryūgaku shi*, p. 544. Chinese government data indicate 2,326 students; see Lin Zexun, *Zhongguo liuxue jiaoyushi*, pp. 399–400. For the first decade of Chinese students' study in Japan, see Harrell, *Sowing the Seeds of Change*.

4. One of these was Zhang Ruifeng. Zhou Enlai reproduced his correspondence with Zhang, who went to study in Tokyo in early 1916, in *Jingye Review* 4 (Apr. 1916).

5. See Zhou Enzhu, "Wode tangxiong—Zhou Enlai," pp. 1–3.

6. His friend, Guo Shiling, preserved Zhou Enlai's calligraphy for 40 years and gave it to the Central Archive. See Wang Jingru, *Zhou Enlai tongzhi qingshaonian shidai*, pp. 59–60, and *Guangming Ribao*, Jan. 12, 1978.

7. Exhibited in the Chinese Museum of Revolutionary History, Beijing.

8. Translated and annotated by N. Lin in *In Quest: Poems of Chou Enlai*, p. 9. The poem was composed in 1917 but was rewritten for Zhou's Nankai classmate Zhang Honggao in March 1919. Zhang gave the original poem to the Chinese Museum of Revolutionary History in 1976 after Zhou Enlai's death.

9. Guo Moruo, *Shaonian shidai*, p. 392.

10. Hu Hua, *Early Life of Zhou Enlai*, p. 18.

11. The Donghua School was opened on April 1, 1918, and several members of its teaching staff were graduates of Nankai Middle School. See Ye Zufu, "Zhou Enlai tongzhi yu haerbinshi Donghua Xuexiao," pp. 199–201. Another of Zhou's Nankai classmates, Zhang Honggao, also remembered Zhou's Harbin visit in 1917.

12. See Chen Zilai, "Zhou Yigeng de liangfen ziliao."

13. For Zhou Enlai's travel through Korea in September 1917, see Huai En, *Zhou zonglide qingshaoniandai*, p. 61.

14. This group of teachers meticulously recorded the exact time of the

train schedules from Tianjin to every major stop (Fengtian, Andong, Seoul, Pusan). See Cao Hongnian's document, published by Zhili shuju in 1918, in the Sanetō Keishū Collection at Tokyo Metropolitan Library.

15. See Wang Gongbi's poem in Sanetō Keishū, *Nitchū hiyūkō no rekishi*, p. 271.

16. See Roy, *Kuo Mo-jo*, pp. 54–55 and 75.

17. In his letter written to Feng Liuqi (Feng Wenqian, 1896–1963) on Nov. 26, 1917, Xue Zhuodong said that he and Zhou Enlai lived together at Tamatsukan. Interview with Feng Liuqi's son, Feng Chengbai, a Nankai University lecturer, at Tianjin in July 1984. See also *TJ* 15 (1981): 19.

18. The full text of Zhou's letter dated Dec. 22, 1917, to Chen Songyan (1900–1978) is in *ZZ*, pp. 137–39; a partial text of his letter dated Dec. 19, 1917, to Feng Liuqi is in *Nankai Daxue Xuebao* (Nankai University Review), 1 (1979): 12–13.

19. For Zhou's references to Buddhism, Madame Chen, celibacy, love, and marriage, see *Zhou Enlai nianpu*, pp. 22–24.

20. Okamoto Ryūzo, "Shū Onrai shushō," pp. 178–96.

21. Sanetō Keishū, *Chūgokujin Nihon ryūgaku shi*, pp. 217–18.

22. Ibid., pp. 119–20.

23. See Zhou's letter to Feng Liuqi.

24. See Zhou's letter to Chen Songyan.

25. As reported in *Xiaofeng* 83 (Dec. 17, 1917).

26. See *TJ* 15 (1981): 20.

27. As reported in *Xiaofeng* 92 (Mar. 1918).

28. As reported in ibid., 95 (Apr. 1918). See also Yan Renzeng, ed., *Yan Fansun xiansheng nianpu*, and the excerpts of Yan Fansun's diary in *QS* 4 (1983): 34–35. Wu Hantao, a Jilin native, studied at the First Higher School in Tokyo and then the Third Higher School in Kyoto and graduated from Tokyo Imperial University. He received a Ph.D. degree from the University of Illinois in 1930 and then taught at Dongbei and Beijing universities. He was a Chinese staff member for the Lytton Commission of the League of Nations. Chiang Kai-shek appointed him governor of Hejiang province in 1945 and made him a key leader in the fight against the Chinese Communist Party in Manchuria. In 1960 Wu was appointed a Special Councillor for Chiang in Taipei. For his background, see *Dongbei wenxian* (Northeastern Journal) (Aug. 1973), pp. 43–46. Later in the 1940's, Tong Qiyan served as chairman of the Legislative Yuan under Chiang Kai-shek.

29. As quoted in Liao Yongwu and Jiang Hai, "Zhou Enlai tongzhi zaoqi geming sixiang fazhanchutan." For an extensive reference to and quotations from Zhou Enlai's Japan diary, see Liu Jianqing, "Zhou Enlai liurishiqide sixiang bianhua," and *Zhou Enlai nianpu*.

30. One of Zhou's Nankai classmates, Shen Tianmin, who was a stu-

dent at the Qinghua School in Beijing, recalls that Zhou sent him an English-language book called *The Japanese Spirit*. See Shen Tianmin, "Huiyi yu Zhou Enlai tongban tushude shiqi."

31. See *TJ* 15 (1981): 23. For Zhou's participation in the New China Study Society, see Yang Fuqing, "Xinzhongxuehui jiyao."

32. See the report of an oral history project with Chen Gang (Chen Tieqing), one of Zhou Enlai's Nankai friends in Japan, in *QS* 3 (1982): 37.

33. "Zhou Enlai tong Li Boman."

34. They were Yan Zhikai, a son of Yan Xiu and a student at the Tokyo School of Fine Arts, Zhang Ruifeng, Cai Shijie, an aspirant for the Military Academy, and two other friends, probably Wu Hantao and Wang Pushan; see Hsu, *Chou En-lai*, pp. 16–17 and 236, and Zhang Honggao, "Huiyi xuesheng shidaide Zhou Enlai tongzhi." Zhou Enlai's friend called "Mr. Han" in Kai-yu Hsu's book is identified by Yan Jingwen as Han Dage, but I believe that he was Wu Hantao. See Yan Jingwen, *Zhou Enlai pingzhuan*, p. 24.

35. As quoted in Jin Chongji, ed., *Zhou Enlai zhuan*, p. 24.

36. See Shinobu Seisaburō, *Taishō seijishi*, p. 541.

37. For the detailed police reports, I examined the archival records in the Diplomatic Archives of the Japanese Ministry of Foreign Affairs (*Nihon gaimushō gaikō shiryōkan*) in Tokyo.

38. For the text of this letter dated Apr. 3, 1918, see *Nankai Daxue Xuebao* 1 (1979): 13. It was common among Chinese youth in the 1910's to eat lightly, for both health and economic reasons. Half a century later, Zhou Enlai told Japanese trade delegates that while in Japan, he had cooked Japanese food with bean curd and observed that bean curd with its protein was good for health. See Maiya Kenichirō, ed., *Shū Onrai Nihon o kataru*, pp. 68–69.

39. Zhou's Tokyo addresses have been identified as follows: c/o Mr. Takemura, 3 Omodesarugakuchō, Kandaku; c/o Mr. Naitō, 30 Koishikawa, Sasugayachō; a three-tatami room on the second floor of a Kanashima furniture store in Yamafukuchō, Ushigomeku; a rented room at 112 Tsurumakichō, Ushigomeku; a rented room in Jimbochō, Kandaku; a room shared with Xu Yiqiao in Sekiguchichō near Waseda University; and a room shared with Xu Kuijiu on the second floor of a wooden house rented by Wang Pushan and his wife in Mizakichō of Kandaku.

40. Both Kai-yu Hsu and Wilson suggest the Kyoto residence during 1918; see Hsu, *Chou En-lai*, p. 18, and Wilson, *Zhou Enlai*, pp. 39–40.

41. See Okamoto Ryūzo, "Shū Onrai shushō," p. 174, *Asahi Shimbun*, Jan. 23, 1969, and *Renmin Ribao*, Apr. 15, 1979.

42. See Zhou's letter of Apr. 3, 1918, to Feng Liuqi.

43. Other preparatory schools for Chinese students in Japan included

Kōbun Gakuin (established in 1902), *Seijō Gakkō* (originally set up in 1898 as a military preparatory school), *Nikka Gakudō* (1898), *Kōtō Daidō Gakkō* (opened by Liang Qichao in 1899), *Tōkyō Dōbun Shoin* (1902), and *Tōa Shōgyō Gakkō* (1901).

44. For Matsumoto's background and career, see Sanetō Keishū, *Chūgoku ryūgakusei shidan*, pp. 340–66, and Hirano Hideo, *Matsumoto Kamejirōden*. For his relationship with Zhou Enlai, see *Renmin Ribao*, Apr. 3, 1985.

45. As quoted in Sanetō Keishū, *Chūgoku ryūgakusei shidan*, pp. 351–52.

46. See Zhang Honggao, "Huiyi xuesheng shidaide Zhou Enlai," p. 396, and Okamoto Ryūzo, "Shū Onrai shushō," p. 175.

47. Zhang Honggao, "Huiyi Zhou Enlai zai nankai xuexiao."

48. For the agreement, see Huang Fuqing, *Qingmo liuri xuesheng*, pp. 94–105; Shu Xincheng, *Jindai zhongguo liuxueshi*, pp. 65–69; and Futami Tsuyoshi, "Senzen Nihon ni okeru Chūgokujin."

49. For a detailed two-part report prepared by the Nankai Alumni Association in Japan in regard to the examinations for the First Higher School and the Tokyo Higher Normal School, see *Xiaofeng* 56 (Feb. 28, 1917) and 57 (Mar. 7, 1917).

50. Xu Kuijiu, "Huiyi zairiben yu Zhou Enlai tongzhi xiangchude rizi."

51. See Zhou Fohai, *Wangyiji*, pp. 20–23. Zhou Fohai went on to study economics under Kawakami Hajime at Kyoto Imperial University. He was a founding member of the Chinese Communist Party, but later betrayed its cause. For his complicated political career, see Marsh, "Chou Fo-hai: The Making of a Collaborator," and H. Lin, "Chou Fo-hai: The Diplomacy of Survival."

52. See *Zhou Enlai nianpu*, p. 27, and Zhang Honggao, "Huiyi xuesheng shidaide Zhou Enlai."

53. See Roy, *Kuo Mo-jo*, p. 54. Guo Moruo studied the Japanese language for several years in China before going to Japan. When he passed the entrance examination for the First Higher School in June 1914 after six months of study in Japan, he said that no other Chinese student had ever passed the examination so quickly.

54. A few years later in England, Zhou acknowledged that he was not a genius in foreign languages. See the letter he wrote to Chen Shizhou on Feb. 23, 1921, from London in *SX*, pp. 30–33.

55. As quoted in Maiya Kenichirō, ed., *Shū Onrai Nihon o kataru*, p. 129.

56. See Lin Zexun, *Zhongguo liuxue jiaoyushi*, pp. 401–2.

57. This is suggested by Hsu, *Chou En-lai*, p. 20.

58. The papers were discovered in 1944 by Ota Teijiro, a farmer in a

suburb of Kyoto who grew rice and vegetables and distributed them to his relatives and friends in Kyoto who were suffering from the wartime food shortage. To return the favor, one of his relatives gave him a bundle of wastepaper (paper was also in short supply), within which Ota found two papers with handsome calligraphy in black ink. He decided to preserve them, though he knew nothing about their author. When his son returned from China after the war and talked about Zhou Enlai, Ota took out the two papers bearing Zhou Enlai's name and framed them. In April 1979 during a visit to Japan, Deng Yingchao, Zhou Enlai's widow, confirmed the authenticity of Zhou's calligraphy. Later, the Ota family sent the two original documents to Deng Yingchao. See Nishikawa Tsutomu, *Arubamu hyōden—Kawakami Hajime*, p. 40.

59. For the exchange of letters between Pan Shien and Zhou in early 1918, see *TJ* 15 (1981): 20. In his letter dated Dec. 19, 1917, to Feng Liuqi, Zhou Enlai was critical of Jinling University's church connections. Interview with Feng Chengbai in July 1984.

60. See *Zhou Enlai nianpu*, p. 24, and Wang Yongxiang and Liu Pinqing, *Weile Zhonghua zhi jueqi*, p. 61. The Chinese Christian Youth Center, built in 1902, was a popular gathering place for Chinese students in Tokyo. It had meeting rooms, a library, a bookstore, and a restaurant. Interview with Sanetō Keishū, Tokyo, July 29, 1983.

61. As quoted in Liu Jianqing, "Zhou Enlai liurishiqide sixiang bianhua." When Zhou Enlai left Tianjin in 1917, one of his friends gave him a copy of *Xinqingnian*. In his diary Zhou said that while at Nankai Middle School he had been too busy to read the journal carefully but that he continued to read it in Japan. See Jin Chongji, ed., *Zhou Enlai zhuan*, p. 28.

62. Xu Kuijiu, "Huiyi zairiben yu Zhou Enlai tongzhi." Half a century later, Zhou asked his Japanese friends whether there were still old bookstores in the Kanda district.

63. See Jansen, *Japan and China*, pp. 221–23, and Shinobu Seisaburō, *Taishō seijishi*, pp. 364–76. As Duan's minister of finance, Liang Qichao was instrumental in receiving the Japanese loans.

64. As quoted in Young, "Chinese Leaders and Japanese Aid," p. 126.

65. For daily police reports on Chinese student activities, see the Diplomatic Archives of the Japanese Ministry of Foreign Affairs, Tokyo.

66. For a detailed report, see Sanetō Keishū, *Nitchū hiyūkō no rekishi*, pp. 43–46, 321–32, and 359–71. National Humiliation Day recalled May 7, 1915, the day on which the Japanese government issued an ultimatum that forced the Yuan Shikai government to accept a substantial portion of the Twenty-One Demands.

67. See the texts of Yoshino's and Terao's letters to *Tokyo Nichinichi Shimbun* in ibid., pp. 359–62.

68. See Zhou Fohai, *Wangyiji*, pp. 18–19, and *Guo Moruo nianpu*, 1: 72.

69. For the text of the memorandum, see Sanetō Keishū, *Nitchū hiyūkō*, pp. 367–68.

70. Wang Jingru, *Zhou Enlai tongzhi*, p. 113.

71. See the texts of the proclamations dated May 22, 28, and 29, in Lin Zexun, *Zhongguo liuxue jiaoyushi*, pp. 417–19.

72. For these claims, see Wang Jingru, *Zhou Enlai tongzhi*, p. 113, Hu Hua, *Early Life of Zhou Enlai*, p. 22, and Huai En, *Zhou zonglide qingshaoniandai*, p. 64. Gong Debai, from Hunan province, was a student at the First Higher School and very active politically. In May 1919 when Chinese students in Japan organized demonstrations in support of the May Fourth Movement, he was one of about 30 Chinese leaders included in a list of wounded students. He went to Taipei in 1949 and published a newspaper. In 1950 he was imprisoned for his criticisms of the Chiang Kai-shek government. He was released from prison seven years later and became a member of the National Assembly. See *Gendai Chūgoku jinmei jiten*, p. 120.

73. As reported in Matsuno Tanio, *Harukanaru Shū Onrai*, p. 58.

74. I have thoroughly reviewed the materials in the Diplomatic Archives of the Japanese Ministry of Foreign Affairs in Tokyo.

75. As quoted in Jin Chongji, ed., *Zhou Enlai zhuan*, p. 32.

76. *Zhou Enlai nianpu*, pp. 25–26.

77. As quoted in Okamoto Ryūzo, "Shū Onrai shushō," p. 175. In the summer of 1968 when Motoki, then a member of the editorial board for Hokkaido history, was in the process of compiling material for the Hokkaido centennial publication, he looked back at his diary for the year of Hokkaido's fiftieth anniversary, 1918. In it he found Zhou Enlai's calling card, and he read his diary entry dated July 29, 1918; he had completely forgotten about the encounter with Zhou Enlai. He wanted to visit with Zhou Enlai once again, but both died before they could meet.

78. *Zhou Enlai nianpu*, p. 27.

79. Ibid. Interview with Professor Jin Chongji, deputy director, Department of Party Archives, Central Committee of the Chinese Communist Party, Oct. 9, 1988, Tianjin, China.

80. *TJ* 15 (1981): 23.

81. Wang Yongxiang and Liu Pinqing, *Weile Zhonghua zhi jueqi*, p. 63.

82. *Zhou Enlai nianpu*, pp. 26–27.

83. Xu Kuijiu, "Huiyi zairiben yu Zhou Enlai tongzhi."

84. As quoted in *Zhou Enlai nianpu*, p. 26.

85. Shinobu Seisaburō, *Taishō seijishi*, p. 411.

86. Meisner, *Li Ta-chao*, p. 56.

87. Shinobu Seisaburō, *Taishō seijishi*, pp. 558–651. For the rice riots,

see Inoue Kiyoshi and Watanabe Tōru, eds., *Komesōdō no kenkyū*, and Shoji Kichinosuke, *Komesōdō no kenkyū*.

88. See his statement in *Nankai Rigan* (Nankai Daily) (July 12, 1919), in ZZ, pp. 149–51.

89. See Wang Yongxiang and Liu Pinqing, *Weile Zhonghua zhi jueqi*, pp. 63–64; Wang Jingru, *Zhou Enlai tongzhi*, p. 104; and *Zhou Enlai nianpu*, p. 27.

90. Of particular relevance to China were Kōtoku Shūsui, *Shakaishugi shinzui* (The Essence of Socialism), *Chōkōzetsu* (Harangue), and *Teikoku shugi* (Imperialism). *Shakaishugi shinzui* (1903) opened with a quotation from the Communist Manifesto and relied heavily on the writings of Marx and Engels. For his great influence among Chinese students in Japan during the first decade of the 20th century, see Huang Fuqing, *Qingmo liuri xuesheng*, pp. 248–53.

91. As quoted in Jansen, *Japan and China*, p. 153. See Kōno Hiromichi, *Kōtoku Shūsui*, pp. 210–12.

92. For an example of an anarchist belief among Chinese students in Japan during the 1910's, see the recollection of Yu Shude (a schoolmate of Li Dazhao at Beiyang School of Law and Politics, a member of the New China Study Society, a student of Kawakami Hajime at Kyoto Imperial University, and a prominent leader of the Chinese Communist Party in the 1920's) in "Wo suozhidaode Li Dazhao tongzhi."

93. Xu Kuijiu, "Huiyi zairiben yu Zhou Enlai tongzhi," p. 152. Matsumoto Shigeharu erroneously mentions that Zhou Enlai attended Waseda University for a year and a half and listened to Kawakami Hajime's lectures on *Das Kapital* at Kyoto Imperial University. See Matsumoto Shigeharu, *Shanghai jidai*, 3: 334.

94. Zhou Enlai said that he had read *The Tale of Poverty, Social Organization and Social Revolution* (1922), and *The Historical Development of Capitalist Economics* (1923). See Ikkai Tomoyoshi, *Kawakami Hajime soshite Chūgoku*, pp. 182–84.

95. Sanetō lists eighteen books written by Kawakami that were translated into Chinese and published in China. See Sanetō Keishū, *Chūgokujin Nihon ryūgaku shi*, pp. 288–89. For Kawakami's influence on Mao Zedong, Li Dazhao, Guo Moruo, Peng Zhen, and others, see Ikkai Tomoyoshi, *Kawakami Hajime*, pp. 173–206. For Guo Moruo's introduction to and translation of Kawakami's *Social Organization and Social Revolution*, see Roy, *Kuo Mo-jo*, pp. 133–65.

96. As quoted in Ikkai Tomoyoshi, *Kawakami Hajime*, pp. 173–74.

97. See Bernstein, *Japanese Marxist*, pp. 87–98. *The Tale of Poverty* is reprinted in *Kawakami Hajime chosakushū*, 2: 3–121. For Kawakami's thesis, see Lee, "Zhou Enlai zai ribende jingli."

98. Xu Kuijiu, "Huiyi zairiben yu Zhou Enlai tongzhi," p. 152.
99. *Kawakami Hajime chosakushū*, 2: 74.
100. Ibid., pp. 61–62.
101. Sumiya Etsuji, *Kawakami Hajime*, p. 162.
102. Bernstein, *Japanese Marxist*, pp. 92–93.
103. *Kawakami Hajime chosakushū*, 2: 83–87.
104. Ibid., pp. 125–334.
105. Sumiya Etsuji, *Kawakami Hajime*, p. 167.
106. The last four parts of this series appeared later in 1919 in numbers 6 (June 1), 7 (July 15), 8 (Sept. 8), and 10 (Nov. 20).
107. See Ikkai Tomoyoshi, *Kawakami Hajime*, pp. 177–79.
108. Hsu, *Chou En-lai*, pp. 20–21.
109. Hu Hua, *Early Life of Zhou Enlai*, pp. 23–24.
110. Spence, *The Gate of Heavenly Peace*, p. 121.
111. For Zhou's praise of the Korean Independence Movement, see *Nankai Rigan*, July 12, 1919, in *ZZ*, p. 149. For the Korean student demonstrations in the Kanda district during 1918 and 1919, see Kamigaito Kenichi, *Nihon ryūgaku to kakumei undō*, pp. 204–6.
112. Xu Kuijiu, "Huiyi zairiben yu Zhou Enlai tongzhi," pp. 150–55.
113. See Lin Zexun, *Zhongguo liuxue jiaoyushi*, pp. 420–21.
114. For Zhou's intention to enter Qinghua School or Beijing University, see *Xiaofeng*, Apr. 30, 1919. At this time the Qinghua School still had a four-year middle school and a four-year higher school; the last two years of the higher school were comparable to an American junior college. In 1921 the eight-year program was divided into a three-year middle school, a three-year high school, and a two-year junior college.
115. Zhang Honggao, "Huiyi xuesheng shidaide Zhou Enlai tongzhi." Other friends present were Wang Ziyu and Mu Mutian, who had been members of the editorial board of the *Jingye Review* at Nankai.
116. See *ZZ*, p. 135. The calligraphy is on display in the Zhou Enlai Memorial Museum in Tianjin.
117. As quoted in *Zhou Enlai nianpu*, p. 28.
118. Interview with Wang Yongxiang (Nankai University professor) in June 1982 at Tianjin.
119. Three of the poems are dated April 5, and the fourth, April 9, 1919. All four poems were first published in the inaugural issue of *Juewu* (Awakening), Jan. 20, 1920.
120. Quoted from N. Lin, *In Quest*. In April 1979 when Zhou Enlai's widow, Deng Yingchao, visited Kyoto, a monument was dedicated at Arashiyama Mountain in memory of Zhou's visit 61 years earlier. When an anti-Communist group defaced the monument in June 1987, Japanese Prime Minister Nakasone Yasuhiro issued an apology to China. See *Renmin Ribao*, June 26, 1987.

121. See Wei Hongyun, "Zhou Enlai tonzhi wusi shiqi geming huodong jiyao," and Ogawa Heishirō, *Chūgoku saihō*, pp. 118–19.

122. As quoted in Wang Yongxiang, "Guanyu Zhou Enlai tongzhi canjia, wusiyundongde shijian."

123. See Meisner, *Li Ta-chao*, p. 56.

124. Liu Jianqing, "Zhou Enlai liurishiqide sixiang bianhua."

125. As quoted in Tamashima Shinji, *Chūgoku no Nihonkan*, p. 168.

Chapter Four

1. "My Old Home," in *Selected Works of Lu Hsun*, vol. 1.

2. Many years later, in January 1971, Zhou Enlai told a Japanese visitor that shortly after his return from Japan the May Fourth Movement had erupted. As quoted by Wang Yongxiang, in *TJ* 15 (1981): 195–99.

3. See the text of Zhou's undated letter in *ZZ*, pp. 147–48. The Nankai Alumni Association in Japan attached this letter to its report dated May 21, 1919, to the American Branch of the Nankai Alumni Association and it was preserved by Feng Liuqi, Zhou Enlai's Nankai classmate, who was studying at Grinnell College.

4. For a general discussion of the May Fourth Movement in China, see Chow Tse-tsung, *The May Fourth Movement*. For written materials about the May Fourth Movement in Tianjin, see *Wusiyundong zai Tianjin*. Zhou Enlai was familiar with Xu Shichang and Cao Rulin; Xu had handed out the special certificates to Zhou and other top Nankai graduates in 1917, and Cao was a trustee of Nankai University, which was about to be established. Zhou Enlai had also met Zhang Zongxiang in Tokyo during Yan Xiu's and Zhang Boling's visit to Japan in December 1918.

5. For Vincent Lebbe (1877–1940) and *Yishibao*, see Yu Zhihou, "Tianjin yishibao gaishu," and Boorman, ed., *Biographical Dictionary of Republican China*, 2: 285–88.

6. For the women's movement in Tianjin, see *Deng Yingchao yu Tianjin zaoqi funü yundong*.

7. At this meeting President Zhang Boling spoke on the origin of National Humiliation Day and explained that he had already sent a cable to President Xu Shichang urging him to release patriotic students. See the text of Zhang's cable and the Nankai meeting in *Yishibao*, May 8 and 10, 1919, as reprinted in *WY*, pp. 6 and 16.

8. The six-point resolutions were to protect the nation's territory, to recover the nation's rights, to revenge the national humiliation, to eliminate traitors, to assure security, and to maintain a consistent policy. See *Yishibao*, June 6, 1919, as reprinted in *WY*, pp. 85–89.

9. Liu Qingyang, "Huiyi juewushe."

10. See the text in *ZZ*, pp. 147–48.

11. As cited in Yan Renzeng, "Zhou zongli yu Yan Fanlao."

12. Ma's letter (undated) appeared in *Nankai Rigan* (Nankai Daily) June 30, 1919. It is reprinted in *WY*, p. 150.

13. His visit to Fengtian and Harbin is suggested in *Zhou Enlai nianpu*, p. 28.

14. See Ye Zufu's report, "Zhou Enlai tongzhi yu haerbinshi Donghua Xuexiao." The report is based on Ye's interviews with the children of Donghua School founders and with Zhou Enlai's brother Zhou Enshou.

15. *Nankai Rigan*, July 8, 1919, in *WY*, p. 181.

16. *Nankai Rigan*, July 12, 1919. See the text in *ZZ*, pp. 149–51.

17. Pan Shilun, "Zhou Enlai tongzhi he Tianjin xuesheng lianhe huibao."

18. As cited in Huai En, *Zhou zonglide qingshaoniandai*, pp. 77–78.

19. *ZZ*, pp. 157–58. This translation is a revised version of Hu Hua, *Early Life of Zhou Enlai*, pp. 29–30.

20. See Liu Qingyang's recollections, "Juexingla Tianjin renmin." Ma Jun's heroic activities were documented in *Yishibao*, Aug. 27, 1919, and *Shenbao*, Aug. 31, 1919. For Ma's activities at Beijing, see *WY*, pp. 742–47.

21. For the origin of the Awakening Society, see Chen Xiaochen, "Juewushe ji qichengyuan." The term *juewu* (awakening) was widely used by Chinese intellectuals at that time. For example, Chen Duxiu wrote an article entitled "Shandong wenti yu guomin juewu" (The Shandong Problem and the People's Awakening) in *Meizhou Pinglun*, May 26, 1919. Zhou Enlai himself used the term in his article in the *Nankai Daily* on July 12, 1919.

22. See *WY*, pp. 669–70, and *Zhou Enlai nianpu*, p. 31.

23. See the text of Governor Cao's secret report dated Sept. 13, 1919, in *WY*, pp. 364–65.

24. Ibid., pp. 365–66.

25. Ibid., pp. 366–67.

26. As quoted in *QS* 4 (1983): 34–35.

27. For Wang Zhanggu's confrontation with Ma Jun, Chen Zhidu, Sun Yueqi, and other student leaders, see Sun Yueqi's recollection, "Tianjin wusiyundongde huiyi."

28. See Chen Xiaochen's recollection, "Li Dazhao xiansheng yu juewushe."

29. For the history of Nankai University, see *Nankai daxue liushinian*, and Wang Wentian, *Zhang Boling yu Nankai*.

30. For the ceremony, see *Xiaofeng*, Nov. 6, 1919. The university was organized in three divisions: Liberal Arts, Sciences, and Business. Zhou Enlai was enrolled in Liberal Arts. As Dean of Academic Affairs, Ling Bing, who had graduated from Nankai Middle School and recieved a Ph.D. in the United States, patterned the academic programs at Nankai after the

American type of college and recruited seventeen professors, mostly from the United States.

31. See Pan Shilun's recollection in *QS* 1 (1980): 18–23.

32. Letter dated Dec. 18, 1919; see the text in *ZZ*, pp. 175–77.

33. See Chen Xiaochen, "Juewushe ji qichengyuan," and Guan Yiwen (Guan Xibin), "Wusi shiqi canjia fujing qingyuan huodongde huiyi." Beijing University's Zhang Guotao (a future founding member of the Chinese Communist Party) was one of the student leaders at the demonstration. For Zhang Guotao's participation in the May Fourth Movement, see Chang Kuo-t'ao, *Rise of the Chinese Communist Party*, 1: 53–69.

34. See *Yishibao*, Nov. 8 and 9, 1919. For a participant's recollections, see Feng Fuguang, "Disice jinjing qingyuan."

35. *Yishibao*, Oct. 8, 1919.

36. Ibid., Oct. 12, 1919, and *Shenbao*, Oct. 13, 1919.

37. *Yishibao*, Oct. 13, 1919, as reprinted in *WY*, pp. 424–26.

38. *Shenbao*, Oct. 23, 1919.

39. For Yang Yide's background and career, see Xia Qinxi, "Yang Yide qiren."

40. The list of members is included in *Zhou Enlai shiwenji*, pp. 110–11.

41. See Chen Zhidu's recollections in ibid., pp. 91–94.

42. See the text of the declaration in ibid., pp. 2–3.

43. The guest speakers included Li Dazhao (on Marxism), Qian Xuantong (on *baihua* literature), Xu Jilong (on national salvation), Bao Shijie (on the trends of new thought), Liu Bannong (on *baihua* poetry), Jiang Menglin, Luo Jialun, Sun Jiyi, Lu Xun, and Zhou Zuoren (on the spirit of the new village in Japan). See Wolff, *Chou Tso-jen*. For the activities and influence of Beijing University intellectuals, see Schwarcz, *Chinese Enlightenment*.

44. For Li Dazhao's reliance on Kawakami Hajime's writings, see Ikkai Tomoyoshi, *Kawakami Hajime*, pp. 177–79.

45. For Chen Xiaochen's recollections about Li Dazhao, see *Zhou Enlai shiwenji*, pp. 102–9, and his essay, "Li Dazhao xiansheng yu juewushe."

46. See Liu Qingyang, "Huiyi juewushe."

47. For Polevoy, see Tikhvinsky (member of the USSR Academy of Sciences and president of the Soviet-Chinese Friendship Association), "Zhou Enlai he Sulian"; Chow Tse-tsung, *May Fourth Movement*, p. 244; and Hsu, *Chou En-lai*, p. 24.

48. "Zhou Enlai tong Li Boman." Zhou Enlai also said that at that time he was much influenced by such major intellectual journals as *Xinqingnian*, *Meizhou Pinglun* edited by Hu Shih, and *Xingqi Pinglun* edited by Dai Jitao.

49. *Yishibao*, Dec. 11, 1919. The other co-chairman was Chen Banling, a student leader of Beiyang School of Law and Politics.

50. Zhou Enlai's articles on Japan appeared in the *Bulletin*, no. 16 (Aug. 6, 1919), no. 17 (Aug. 7, 1919), and no. 45 (Sept. 4, 1919).

51. See Jansen, *Japan and China*, pp. 238–40, and *QS* 4 (1983): 20. Miyazake Ryūnosuke was a good friend of Li Dazhao. Along with Nosaka Sanzo (future chairman of the Japanese Communist Party), he was a key member of the New Man Society (*Shinjinkai*) set up in December 1918 under Yoshino's tutelage; it advocated "the new movement for the liberation of humanity" and supported the May Fourth Movement as well as the Korean Independence Movement.

52. *Bulletin*, no. 19 (Aug. 9, 1919), as reprinted in *ZZ*, pp. 161–62.

53. Saari, *Legacies of Childhood*, p. 18.

54. For an example of the daily leaflet, see *Yishibao*, Dec. 8, 1919.

55. Ibid., Nov. 25, 1919.

56. Ibid., Dec. 17, 1919.

57. Ibid., Aug. 12, 1919, as reprinted in *WY*, pp. 258–59.

58. See Usui Chūsan, *Tenshin kyoryū mindan sanju shūnen kinenshi*, pp. 246–48.

59. *Yishibao*, Dec. 21 and 23, 1919.

60. See Zhou Enlai's report, "Jingting juliuji."

61. *Zhou Enlai nianpu*, p. 37.

62. *Yishibao*, Jan. 30, 1920.

63. As quoted in Hu Hua, *Early Life of Zhou Enlai*, p. 45.

64. See Zhou Enlai's report, "Jingting juliuji."

65. *Yishibao*, Feb. 5, 1920.

66. For Zhang Xilu's reminiscences, see his "Zhou Enlai—Nankai zuihaode xuesheng."

67. Just before his departure for Europe in 1920, Zhou Enlai gave "The Record" to Ma Qianli. Ma started serializing it in his newspaper (*Xinminyibao*) on December 4, 1920, with his introduction. Later it was published as a monograph.

68. Zhou Enlai mailed "The Diary" to Ma Qianli from Europe, and Ma Qianli began serializing it in *Xinminyibao* during the spring of 1921. Because this newspaper was suspended, "The Diary" was not completely printed. In 1926, Meng Zhenhou, one of Zhou Enlai's prison inmates, arranged its publication as a monograph. In "Jianting rilu," Zhou Enlai explained that whereas "The Record" was based on a "purely objective method," "The Diary" was prepared by means of a "purely subjective method."

69. See Ling Zhong's recollection in *QS* 4 (1983): 36–37.

70. *Yishibao*, June 14 and 25, 1920. For Liu's assistance for Beijing students, see Chang Kuo-t'ao, *Rise of the Chinese Communist Party*, 1: 68.

71. See the text of this letter in *ZZ*, pp. 260–61.

72. The text of the judge's decisions was carefully recorded by Zhou Enlai, in *ZZ*, pp. 383–96.

73. The celebration is described in *Yishibao*, July 18, 1920. The medallion is displayed in the Zhou Enlai Memorial Museum, Tianjin.

74. See "Zhou Enlai tong Li Boman" and *Zhou Enlai nianpu*, p. 42.

75. The four organizations were the China Youth Association (*Shaonian zhongguo xuehui*), the Young Work-Study Mutual Aid Corps (*Qingnian gongdu huzhutuan*), the Morning Light Society (*Shuguangshe*), and the Humanitarian Society (*Rendaoshe*). The China Youth Association was established in July 1919 under Li Dazhao's influence and it lasted until 1925. It embraced about 120 members and had branches all over China and in Paris. For its membership and activities, see *Wusi shiqide shetuan*, 1: 218–572.

76. For the proceedings, declaration, and charter of the Reform Federation, see ibid., pp. 327–31. For Zhang Shenfu's recollection, see "Yi Shouchang."

77. See Hung, *Going to the People*.

78. See *Zhou Enlai nianpu*, p. 43, and Liu Jiajun, "Xinminyibao yu Zhou Enlai." Another founder of this newspaper, Liu Tieon, was one of Liu Qingyang's brothers. The newspaper published its first issue on August 15, 1920, and lasted until January 1925.

79. N. Lin, *In Quest*, pp. 21–24.

80. Chow Tse-tsung, *May Fourth Movement*, p. 35.

81. Xu Tianliu, "Fufa qingong jianxueqian Zhou Enlai tongzhi duiwode jiaoyu."

82. The original text of the certificate is displayed in the Zhou Enlai Memorial Museum, Tianjin.

83. Levine, "The Found Generation."

84. Jin Chongji, ed., *Zhou Enlai zhuan*, p. 50. According to Kai-yu Hsu (*Chou En-lai*, p. 26), Liu Chongyou also hoped that Zhou Enlai and his daughter would marry.

85. It has been suggested that Deng Xiaoping, Liu Qingyang, and Zhang Shenfu went to France on the same ship with Zhou Enlai; this remains questionable. For Deng Xiaoping's activities in France, see N. Wang, "Deng Xiaoping: The Years in France." Zhang Shenfu and Liu Qingyang left for France toward the end of November 1920. See Schwarcz, *Time for Telling Truth Is Running Out*, p. 28.

86. The postcard, "La Chasse en Cochinchine," showed a huge elephant killed by hunters. See *Zhou Enlai tongzhi liuou wenji*, p. 68.

87. Xie Shuying, "Yu Zhou Enlai tongzhi tongchuan fufade zhuiyi."

88. Li Yuru, for whom Zhou Enlai had written the poem while in prison, remembers her meeting with Zhou Enlai at the Paris railway station

in *QS* 1 (1980): 22. Yan Zhikai was studying at the Ecole des Beaux-Arts.

89. Zhou Enlai used the name John Knight on his British visa; he may have chosen it because it rhymed well with his Chinese name. In France and Germany he signed his name "E. L. Tchow." For his name as "John Knight," see his letter to Yan Xiu dated Feb. 8, 1921, in *SX*, pp. 28–29.

90. See Zhou Enlai's letters dated Jan. 30 and Feb. 23, 1921, to Yan Xiu in *SX*, pp. 17–22, 28–29.

91. See Zhou Enlai's letter dated Jan. 5, 1921, to Zhou Tiaozhi as quoted in *Zhou Enlai nianpu*, p. 45.

92. For the collection of Zhou Enlai's reports to *Yishibao*, see *Liuou tongxin*.

93. See Zhou Enlai's letters dated Jan. 30 and Feb. 23, 1921, to Chen Shizhou in *SX*, pp. 23–27, 30–33.

94. *Zhou Enlai nianpu*, p. 46.

95. As quoted in Snow, *Red Star Over China* (1978), p. 49.

96. See Yan Xiu's diary in *QS* 4 (1983): p. 34.

97. See Zhou Enlai's "thank-you" postcard dated Mar. 25, 1922, to Chang Ceou in *SX*, p. 34.

98. The New People's Study Society included Li Weihan, Cai Chang (who later married Li Fuchun), and Xiang Jingyu (who later married Cai Hesen in France). For its members and activities, see *Wusi shiqide shetuan*, 1: 4–111. Mao Zedong and Liu Shaoqi also intended to go to France at this time, but for some reason or other they did not do so. See He Changgong, *Qingong jianxue shenghuo huiyi*, pp. 8–11.

99. See Scalapino, "Evolution of a Young Revolutionary," pp. 29–61. For Cai-Mao correspondence, see *Cai Hesen wenji*. For Cai Hesen's relationship with Zhou Enlai, see Snow, *Red Star Over China* (1978), pp. 48–49. Another of Cai's associates was Zhao Shiyan, a member of the China Youth Association. Zhao Shiyan's younger sister, Zhao Juntao, was married to Li Shuoxin, another revolutionary leader, who was executed at Hainan Island in 1931. After Li's death, Zhou Enlai took care of his son, Li Peng (who later became China's Premier).

100. For Nie Rongzhen's activities in Lyons, see *Nie Rongzhen huiyilu*, pp. 22–24. Mao Zedong admired Xu Teli, a teacher at the First Normal School at Changsha toward the end of the Qing dynasty, who cut off the tip of his finger and wrote a petition in blood demanding the opening of parliament in Hunan province. In the 1930's Mao appointed Xu commissioner of education in the soviet government.

101. Kai-yu Hsu claims that Zhou Enlai was arrested in Lyons but was able to escape deportation; see Hsu, *Chou En-lai*, pp. 32–33. I find no evidence to support this claim. Zhao Shiyan was arrested, but escaped from a police station.

102. See Zhang Hongxiang and Wang Yongxiang, *Liufa qingong jianxue yundong jianshi*, pp. 96–97. For Zhou Enlai's lengthy reports to *Yishibao*, see *Liuou tongxin*, pp. 29–57.

103. See *Zhou Enlai nianpu*, p. 47, and Liu Xi, "Guanyu Zhou Enlai rudangde shijian wentide shentao."

104. See Zhang Shenfu, "Liufa qianhou wo tong Zhou Enlai," and Schwarcz, *Time for Telling Truth Is Running Out.*

105. Schwarcz, "Out of Historical Amnesia," p. 177.

106. See *Zhou Enlai xuanji*, 1: 357.

107. *Zhou Enlai nianpu*, p. 52.

108. See *TJ* 15 (1981): 66. Some of Zhou's Nankai friends, including Feng Liuqi, who had been in the United States, visited him in Europe.

109. For Zhou Enlai's meeting with Zhu De in Germany, see Smedley, *The Great Road*, pp. 151–52. After Sun Bingwen was assassinated in 1927, Zhou Enlai and Deng Yingchao adopted his daughter, Sun Weishi, who later became an actress and was married to a famous actor (Jin Shan). She died violently during the Cultural Revolution. For this information, see P. Fang and L. Fang, *Zhou Enlai*, pp. 59–65.

110. In 1956, Zhou Enlai confided to one of his relatives that his relationship with Zhang Ruoming had ended in France because he felt that she was not suitable as a lifelong revolutionary companion. See Cheng Hua, ed., *Zhou Enlai he tade mishumen*, p. 306. For Zhang Ruoming's early life and academic work in Europe, see Levine, "Transcending the Barriers," and Yang Zaidao (Zhang Ruoming's son), "Wusi shiqide Zhang Ruoming."

111. Guan Yiwen (Guan Xibin), "Fufa qingong jianxue qianhou."

112. For Zhou Enlai's relationship with Tao in France, see *QS* 5 (1984): 21–22.

113. N. Lin, *In Quest*, pp. 27–29.

114. *Zhou Enlai shiwenji*, pp. 38–41. For Mao Zedong's description of Huang Ai's activities and death in Hunan province, see Snow, *Red Star Over China* (1978), p. 158.

115. Li Weihan, "Huiyi xinminxuehui."

116. Zhou Enlai approached Zhang Shizhao through one of his Nankai friends in France, Xie Chengrui, who was well connected with Zhang Shizhao. See Zhang Shenfu, "Liufa qianhou wo tong Zhou Enlai," p. 234.

117. For Zhou Enlai's report submitted to the Central Executive Committee of the Chinese Socialist Youth League on Mar. 13, 1923, see *SX*, pp. 54–60. It was signed "Wuhao," the secret name used by Zhou in the Awakening Society.

118. For this episode, see Schwarcz, *Time for Telling Truth Is Running Out*, pp. 115–17.

119. For the list of Moscow-bound persons, see Wang Yongxiang, Kong

Binfeng, and Liu Pinqing, *Zhongguo gongchandang liuouzhibu shihua*, pp. 249–54.

120. In October 1978, after Zhou Enlai's death, Premier Hua Guofeng, French President Giscard d'Estaing, and Paris Mayor Jacques Chirac attended a ceremony to unveil a plaque bearing Zhou's bust at the Godefroy Hotel.

121. See Hsu, *Chou En-lai*, p. 37, and Li Huang's Memoirs translated by Lillian Chu Chin, Chinese Oral History Project, East Asian Institute, Columbia University. Li Huang (1895–1992) was a member of the ten-person Chinese delegation who signed the U.N. Charter in San Francisco in 1945. In 1946 he helped Gen. George C. Marshall in CCP-Guomindang negotiations. After the CCP came to power in 1949, he moved to Hong Kong, where he taught. In 1980, he went to Taipei and led the China Youth Party. Zeng Qi (1892–1951) became a cabinet minister in the Guomindang government in Taipei.

122. See He Changgong, *Qingong jianxue shenghuo huiyi*, p. 75. When the French police raided Deng Xiaoping's room in January 1926, they found "two oil-based ink printing kits with plates and rollers and several packets of paper for printing." See N. Wang, "Deng Xiaoping," p. 701.

123. See *Los Angeles Times*, Oct. 19, 1992.

124. See the text of Wang Jingqi's letter in *QS* 6 (1985): 52–53. Enclosed in the same letter was a group photograph of the leaders of the Guomindang's European branch. In 1925 the French police arrested Wang Jingqi on the ground that he had organized an anti-imperialist demonstration, and deported him again to China. He died on the way home.

125. Zhang Shenfu, "Liufa qianhou wo tong Zhou Enlai," p. 236.

126. As quoted in *Zhou Enlai nianpu*, p. 65.

127. For the text of his report written in Hong Kong on Sept. 1, 1924, see *SX*, p. 69. At this time Tan Pingshan (1886–1956) was a member of the Chinese Communist Party's Central Bureau and director of the Guomindang's Organization Department.

128. See Meisner, *Li Ta-chao*, p. 118.

Conclusion

1. Interview with Wu Guozhen.
2. Henry Lieberman's letter to the author dated Dec. 8, 1985.
3. Ibid.
4. Zhou Enlai never wavered in his steadfast personal loyalty and respect to his mentor, Zhang Boling, even when they were on the opposite sides of the political spectrum. As a staunch supporter of Chiang Kai-shek and a member of the Guomindang from 1941 on, Zhang Boling served as

one of the two Vice Speakers of the People's Political Council (1938–47) at Chongqing, as an elected deputy from Tianjin to the National Congress (1947–49), and as president of the Examination Yuan (1948–49) at Nanjing and Chongqing. Even though Zhang considered Zhou Enlai one of his favorite students, he was very critical of his communist activities and questioned Yan Xiu's financial support for Zhou in Europe and subsequently removed Zhou's name from the roster of the Nankai Alumni Association. During the Xian incident (December 1936), Zhang Boling sent cables to Zhou Enlai and Zhang Xueliang (with whom he had good relations) in an attempt to save Chiang Kai-shek's life, and after Zhou Enlai's intervention helped release Chiang from Zhang Xueliang's captivity, Zhang Boling held a celebration party in Tianjin and restored Zhou Enlai's name to the Nankai Alumni Association roster. (The CCP-Guomindang negotiations at Xian agreed upon a list of Chiang's future cabinet ministers, which included Zhang Boling as a possible Minister of Education.) At Chongqing during the Sino-Japanese War, Zhang and Zhou met frequently and argued their political differences. Zhang urged Zhou to use his persuasive powers to convince Mao Zedong that the CCP should accept Chiang's national leadership; Zhou countered with explanations of the CCP's policy. Toward the end of the civil war, Zhou Enlai asked Zhang not to go to Taipei with Chiang Kai-shek. Zhang did not go. In May 1950 Zhou Enlai sent an airplane to bring Zhang Boling and his family from Chongqing to Beijing; at Zhou's request Zhang Boling brought him a photograph of Yan Xiu. That fall, Zhang Boling returned to Tianjin to live with his third son (Zhang Xizu). He died a few months later, in February 1951, at the age of 76. The day after he died, Zhou Enlai went to Tianjin to pay his last respects to his teacher. Zhou praised Zhang as a "progressive and patriotic educator" and became a member of the funeral committee for Zhang. In 1961 when China was suffering from extreme economic hardships, Zhou Enlai sent 500 yuan (more than an average worker's annual salary) to Zhang Boling's widow. For the relationship between Zhou Enlai and Zhang Boling, see Zhang Zhiguang, ed., *Zhang Boling zhuan*, and Huang Yusheng's recollection in *Renmin Ribao*, Apr. 4, 1986.

5. At the Seventh Central Committee of the Chinese Communist Party, at least ten out of 44 regular members (elected in June 1945) were returnees from Europe. They were Zhou Enlai, Zhu De, Deng Xiaoping, Li Fuchun, Li Lisan, Wang Ruofei, Nie Rongzhen, Xu Teli, Chen Yi, and Cai Chang. In the CCP-Guomindang negotiations during 1945, Wang Ruofei served as Zhou Enlai's right-hand man, but he died in 1946. In the People's Republic of China, the European returnees occupied many important positions: Zhou Enlai (Premier and Minister of Foreign Affairs), Zhu De (chairman of the Standing Committee of the National People's Congress and chief of

the General Staff of the People's Liberation Army), Li Fuchun (Vice Premier and Minister of Heavy Industry), Deng Xiaoping (Vice Premier and chairman of the CCP's Central Military Commission), Chen Yi (Shanghai mayor, Vice Premier, and Minister of Foreign Affairs), Li Lisan (Minister of Labor), Xu Teli (member of the CCP's Central Committee), Nie Rongzhen (Beijing mayor and deputy chief of the General Staff of the People's Liberation Army), Cai Chang (chairman of the All-China Democratic Women's Federation), and Li Weihan (director of the CCP's United Front Department).

6. Zhang Shenfu (1893–1986) left the CCP in 1925 and joined the liberal China Democratic League. In the People's Republic of China he worked at the Beijing Library and served as a member of the Chinese People's Political Consultative Committee. Liu Qingyang (1894–1977) left the CCP in 1927 and joined the China Democratic League. In the PRC she took a number of positions—member of the National Committee of the Chinese People's Political Consultative Committee, member of the National People's Congress, vice chairman of the All-China Democratic Women's Federation, and vice president of the China Red Cross. She rejoined the CCP in 1961. After leaving the CCP, Zhao Guangchen served as a member of the Guomindang's Central Inspection Committee. Likewise, Ren Zhuoxuan (Ye Qing: b. 1895) became a deputy director of the Guomindang's propaganda department and taught at a university in Taipei. In 1929 the CCP expelled Yin Kuan because of his Trotskyite activities. Zhang Ruoming (1902–58) left the CCP in 1924 while in France. In the PRC she taught at a university in Yunnan province.

7. Li Dazhao (1889–1927) was arrested and executed by the warlord Zhang Zuolin in Beijing in 1927. Ma Jun (1895–1928) joined the CCP in 1922 and went to Moscow three years later. After his return to China he became a secretary of the CCP's Beijing District Committee. In 1928 he was executed by Zhang Zuolin in Beijing. Upon her return to China, Guo Longzhen (1893–1930) was active in the CCP's Beijing District Committee. In 1927 she was arrested by Zhang Zuolin and was sentenced to a twelve-year imprisonment but was soon released. Three years later she was arrested in Qingdao and executed in Jinan. Sun Bingwen (1880–1927) was assassinated in Shanghai in 1927. Yu Fangzhou (1900–1928), who had been imprisoned with Zhou Enlai in 1920, joined the CCP in 1922 and became the director of the Organization Department of the CCP's Xunzhi Provincial Committee. He was executed in 1928. After his deportation from France, Cai Hesen (1895–1931) became a member of the CCP's Central Committee in 1922. In 1925 he went to Moscow as a representative of the CCP. Upon his return from Moscow in 1927, he was elected to the CCP's Political Bureau (together with Zhou Enlai). In 1931 he was arrested and

liquidated in Hong Kong. After his return to China in 1924, Zhao Shiyan (1901–27) became a secretary of the CCP's Beijing District Committee. He was executed by the Guomindang authorities in Shanghai in 1927. Upon his return to China in 1924, Chen Yannian (1898–1927) was made a secretary of the CCP's Guangdong District Committee and of its Shanghai District Committee. In 1927 he was executed by the Guomindang authorities in Shanghai. His brother, Chen Qiaonian (1902–28), returned to China in 1924 and became a deputy director of the CCP's Organization Department. The Guomindang force executed him in Shanghai in 1928. Xiong Xiong (1892–1927) returned to China in 1925 and became the director of the Military Affairs Department of the CCP's Guangdong District Committee. He was also the director of the Political Department at Whampoa Military Academy—the same position that Zhou Enlai had occupied. Xiong was executed by the Guomindang at Canton in 1927. Mu Qing (1898–1930) returned to China in 1927 and became the director of the Organization Department of the CCP's Guangdong District Committee. The Guomindang executed him in 1930. Xiang Jingyu (1895–1928), Cai Hesen's wife, was executed in Hankou in 1928.

8. The major positions Zhou Enlai assumed from 1925 to 1930 were: director of the Military Affairs Department of the CCP's Guangdong District Committee, and director of the Military Law Department at Whampoa Military Academy (Jan. 1925); director of the Political Department (and Major General) of the Guomindang's First Revolutionary Army (Sept. 1925); director of the General Political Department of the Northern Expedition Force (Sept. 1925); member of the CCP's Central Military Committee and secretary of the CCP's Organization Department (Dec. 1926); secretary of the Military Affairs Committee of the CCP's Shanghai District Committee (Feb. 1927); member of the CCP's Political Bureau and the CCP's Secretary General (Apr. 1927); director of the CCP's Central Military Department (May 1927); member of the Guomindang's Revolutionary Committee (Aug. 1927); editor of the CCP's official magazine, *Bolshevik* (Dec. 1927); director of the CCP's Organization Bureau (Jan. 1928); member of the five-member Standing Committee of the CCP's Political Bureau, the Political Bureau's Secretary General, and director of the CCP's Organization Department (July 1928); and member of the three-member Central Standing Committee of the CCP (Oct. 1930). For this information, see *Zhou Enlai nianpu*.

References Cited

The following abbreviations are used in the Notes and References Cited:

QS *Zhou Enlai qingnian shidai* [Zhou Enlai's Youthful Period]. Tianjin: Zhou Enlai jinianguan, 1980–86.

SX *Zhou Enlai shuxin xuanji* [Selected Writings and Letters of Zhou Enlai]. Beijing: Zhongyang wenxian chubanshe, 1988.

TJ *Tianjin wenshi ziliao xuanji* [Selected Materials of Tianjin History]. Tianjin: Tianjin renmin chubanshe.

WY *Wusiyundong zai Tianjin* [The May Fourth Movement in Tianjin]. Tianjin: Tianjin renmin chubanshe, 1979.

ZZ Huai En, ed. *Zhou zongli qingshaoniandai shiwenshuxinji* [Collection of Premier Zhou's Poems, Essays, and Letters During his Youthful Period]. Vol. 1. Chengdu: Sichuan renmin chubanshe, 1979.

Abe Hiroshi, ed. *Nitchū kankei to bunka masatsu* [Japan-China Relations and Cultural Conflicts]. Tokyo: Gannandō shoten, 1982.

Archer, Jules. *Chou En-lai*. New York: Hawthorn, 1973.

Ayers, William. *Chang Chih-tung and Educational Reform in China*. Cambridge, Mass.: Harvard University Press, 1971.

Bays, Daniel H. *China Enters the Twentieth Century: Chang Chih-tung and the Issues of a New Age, 1895–1909*. Ann Arbor: University of Michigan Press, 1978.

Bernstein, Gail Lee. *Japanese Marxist: A Portrait of Kawakami Hajime, 1879–1946*. Cambridge, Mass.: Harvard University Press, 1976.

Boorman, Howard R., ed. *Biographical Dictionary of Republican China*. 4 vols. New York: Columbia University Press, 1967, 1970, 1971.

Burns, Richard D., and Edward M. Bennett, eds. *Diplomats in Crisis: United States–Chinese–Japanese Relations, 1919–1941*. Santa Barbara, Calif.: ABC-CLIO, 1974.

Cai Hesen wenji [Collected Works of Cai Hesen]. Beijing: Renmin chubanshe, 1980.

Cao Yu. "Huiyi zai Tianjin kaishede xijushenghuo" [Remembering the Drama Life Begun in Tianjin]. In *TJ* 19 (1982): 140–44.

Chang Kuo-t'ao. *The Rise of the Chinese Communist Party, 1921–1927*. Vol. 1. Lawrence: University Press of Kansas, 1971.

Chang Zuochao and Chang Jingchao. "Zhou Enlai yu Chang Ceou de youyi" [Friendship Between Zhou Enlai and Chang Ceou]. In *QS* 6 (1985): 10–14.

Chen Duo. "Zhou Enlai shaoxing jiashi ji zuju kao" [A Study of Zhou Enlai's Shaoxing Family and Ancestral Home]. In *QS* 7 (1986): 58–62.

Chen Xiaochen. "Juewushe ji qichengyuan" [The Awakening Society and Its Members]. In *TJ* 15 (1981): 156–94.

———. "Li Dazhao xiansheng yu juewushe" [Li Dazhao and the Awakening Society]. In *Huiyi Li Dazhao*, pp. 91–97.

Chen Zilai. "Zhou Yigeng de liangfen ziliao" [Two Documents on Zhou Yigeng]. In *QS* 2 (1982): 32–33.

Cheng Hua, ed. *Zhou Enlai he tade mishumen* [Zhou Enlai and His Secretaries]. Beijing: Zhongguo guangbo dianshi chubanshe, 1992.

Chow Tse-tsung. *The May Fourth Movement: Intellectual Revolution in Modern China*. Cambridge, Mass.: Harvard University Press, 1960.

Christie, Dugald. *Thirty Years in Moukden, 1883–1913*. Edited by his wife. London: Constable, 1914.

Cole, James H. *Shaohsing: Competition and Cooperation in Nineteenth-Century China*. Tucson: University of Arizona Press, 1986.

Deng Yingchao yu Tianjin zaoqi funü yundong [Deng Yingchao and the Early Women's Movement in Tianjin]. Beijing: Zhongguo funü chubanshe, 1987.

Erikson, Erik H. *Childhood and Society*. New York: Norton, 1963.

———. *Gandhi's Truth: On the Origins of Militant Nonviolence*. New York: Norton, 1969.

———. *Young Man Luther: A Study in Psychoanalysis and History*. New York: Norton, 1958.

Fairbank, John K., Edwin O. Reischauer, and Albert M. Craig. *East Asia: The Modern Transformation*. Boston: Houghton Mifflin, 1965.

Fang, Percy Jucheng, and Lucy Guinong J. Fang. *Zhou Enlai—A Profile*. Beijing: Foreign Languages Press, 1986.

Feifei. "Wo zhi rengeguan" [My Views on Human Dignity]. In *ZZ*, pp. 95–99.

Feifei and Guzhu yaren. "Benhui chengli xiaoshi" [A Short History of the Establishment of Our Society]. In *ZZ*, pp. 33–37.

Feng Fuguang. "Disice jinjing qingyuan" [The Fourth Petition at Beijing]. In *WY*, pp. 747–51.

Furth, Charlotte. "The Sage as Rebel: The Inner World of Chang Ping-lin." In Charlotte Furth, ed., *The Limits of Change*, pp. 113–50.

———, ed. *The Limits of Change: Essays on Conservative Alternatives in Republican China*. Cambridge, Mass.: Harvard University Press, 1976.

Futami Tsuyoshi. "Senzen Nihon ni okeru Chūgokujin ryūgakusei kyōiku" [The Education of Chinese Students in Prewar Japan]. In Abe Hiroshi, ed., *Nitchū kankei to bunka masatsu*, pp. 161–207.

Garrett, Shirley S. *Social Reformers in Urban China: The Chinese Y.M.C.A., 1895–1926*. Cambridge, Mass.: Harvard University Press, 1970.

Gendai Chūgoku jinmei jiten [Biographical Dictionary of Modern China]. Tokyo: Konan shoin, 1957.

Giles, Herbert A. *A History of Chinese Literature*. New York: D. Appleton, 1931.

Guan Yiwen. "Fufa qingong jianxue qianhou" [Before and After the Work-Study in France]. In *TJ* 4 (1983): 14–16, 21.

———. "Wusi shiqi canjia fujing qingyuan huodongde huiyi" [Remembering My Participation in the Petition Activities at Beijing During the May Fourth Period]. In *TJ* 3 (1979): 44–47.

Guo Moruo. *Shaonian shidai* [Childhood Period]. Shanghai: Haiyan shudian, 1947.

Guo Moruo nianpu [Chronicle of Guo Moruo's Important Events]. Vol. 1. n.p.: Jiangsu renmin chubanshe, 1983.

Guo Rongsheng and Zhang Yuan, eds. *Zhang Boling xiansheng jinianji* [Memorial Collections on Zhang Boling]. Taipei: Wenhai chubanshe, n.d.

Hammond, Ed. *Coming of Grace: An Illustrated Biography of Zhou Enlai*. Berkeley, Calif.: Lancaster-Miller, 1980.

Harrell, Paula. *Sowing the Seeds of Change: Chinese Students, Japanese Teachers, 1895–1905*. Stanford, Calif.: Stanford University Press, 1992.

Hatano Kanichi. *Chūgoku kyōsantōshi* [History of the Chinese Communist Party]. Vol. 1. Tokyo: Jiji tsūshinsha, 1961.

He Changgong. *Qingong jianxue shenghuo huiyi* [Reflections on the Work-Study Life]. Beijing: Gongren chubanshe, 1958.

Hersey, John. "A Reporter at Large: China—Part II." *The New Yorker*, May 17, 1982.

Hirano Hideo. *Matsumoto Kamejirōden* [Biography of Matsumoto Kamejirō]. Shizuoka: Shizuoka kyōiku shuppansha, 1982.

Hsu, Kai-yu. "Chou En-lai." In Chun-tu Hsueh, ed., *Revolutionary Leaders of Modern China*, pp. 517–34.

———. *Chou En-lai: China's Gray Eminence*. Garden City, N.Y.: Doubleday, 1968.

Hsueh, Chun-tu, ed. *Revolutionary Leaders of Modern China*. New York: Oxford University Press, 1971.
Hu Hua. *The Early Life of Zhou Enlai*. Beijing: Foreign Languages Press, 1980.
Hu Shih. "Chang Poling: Educator." In *There Is Another China*, pp. 4–14.
Huai En. *Zhou zonglide qingshaoniandai* [Premier Zhou's Youthful Period]. Chengdu: Sichuan renmin chubanshe, 1979.
Huainian Zhou Enlai [Remembering Zhou Enlai]. Beijing: Renmin chubanshe, 1986.
Huang Fuqing. *Qingmo liuri xuesheng* [Chinese Students in Japan During the Late Qing Period]. Taipei: Academia Sinica, 1975.
Huang Yusheng. "Zaoqide Nankai zhongxue" [The Nankai Middle School in the Early Years]. In *TJ* 8 (1980): 130–49.
Huiyi Li Dazhao [Remembering Li Dazhao]. Beijing: Renmin chubanshe, 1980.
Hung, Chang-tai. *Going to the People: Chinese Intellectuals and Folk Literature, 1918–1937*. Cambridge, Mass.: Harvard University Press, 1985.
Ikkai Tomoyoshi. *Kawakami Hajime soshite Chūgoku* [Kawakami Hajime and China]. Tokyo: Iwanami shoten, 1982.
Inoue Kiyoshi and Watanabe Tōru, eds. *Komesōdō no kenkyū* [Study of the Rice Riots]. Tokyo: Yūhikaku, 1959.
Iriye, Akira, ed. *The Chinese and the Japanese: Essays in Political and Cultural Interactions*. Princeton, N.J.: Princeton University Press, 1980.
Itō Teruo. *Chūgokujin no Nihonjinkan hyakunenshi* [A One Hundred–Year History of the Chinese People's Views on Japanese People]. Tokyo: Jiyugokuminsha, 1974.
Jansen, Marius B. *Japan and China: From War to Peace, 1894–1972*. Chicago: Rand McNally College Publishing, 1970.
Jin Chongji, ed. *Zhou Enlai zhuan 1898–1949* [Biography of Zhou Enlai]. Beijing: Renmin chubanshe, 1989.
Jinian wusiyundong liushizhounian xueshu tulunhui lunwuji [Collection of Papers Presented at the Scholarly Conference in Commemoration of the 60th Anniversary of the May Fourth Movement]. Vol. 3. Beijing: Zhongguo shehuikexue chubanshe, 1980.
Kamigaito Kenichi. *Nihon ryūgaku to kakumei undō* [Study in Japan and Revolutionary Movements]. Tokyo: Tōkyō daigaku shuppankai, 1982.
Kawakami Hajime chosakushū [Collected Works of Kawakami Hajime]. Vol. 2. Tokyo: Chikuma shobō, 1964.
Kissinger, Henry A. *White House Years*. Boston: Little, Brown, 1979.
Kōno Hiromichi. *Kōtoku Shūsui—Hyōron to zuisō* [Kōtoku Shūsui—Commentaries and Essays]. Tokyo: Jiyū hyōronsha, 1950.
Lee, Chae-Jin. "Zhou Enlai zai ribende jingli" [Zhou Enlai's Experience in

Japan]. In Liu Xi, ed., *Zhongwai xuezhe lun Zhou Enlai*, pp. 28–46.
Levine, Marilyn A. "The Found Generation: Chinese Communism in Europe, 1919–1925." Ph.D. diss., University of Chicago, 1985.
———. "Transcending the Barriers: Zhang Ruoming and André Gide." Unpublished paper, 1988.
Li Tien-Min. *Chou En-lai.* Taipei: Institute of International Relations, 1970.
Li Weihan. "Huiyi xinminxuehui" [Remembering the New People's Study Society]. In *Wusi shiqide shetuan*, 1: 609–43.
Liao Yongwu. "Zhou Enlai tongzhi yu Nankai xiaofeng" [Comrade Zhou Enlai and Nankai's *Xiaofeng*]. *Nankai Daxue Xuebao* [Nankai University Journal], January 1979, pp. 24–29.
Liao Yongwu and Jiang Hai. "Zhou Enlai tongzhi zaoqi geming sixiang fazhanchutan" [The Development of Comrade Zhou Enlai's Early Revolutionary Thought]. In *Jinian wusiyundong liushizhounian xueshu tulunhui lunwuji*, pp. 101–32.
Lin, Han-shen. "Chou Fo-hai: The Diplomacy of Survival." In Richard D. Burns and Edward M. Bennett, eds., *Diplomats in Crisis*, pp. 171–93.
Lin, Nancy T. *In Quest: Poems of Chou En-lai.* Hong Kong: Joint Publishing, 1979.
Lin Zexun. *Zhongguo liuxue jiaoyushi* [History of Chinese Students Abroad]. Taipei: Huagang chubanshe, 1976.
Liu Jiajun. "Xinminyibao yu Zhou Enlai" [*Xinminyibao* and Zhou Enlai]. In *QS* 5 (1984): 3–7.
Liu Jianqing. "Zhou Enlai liurishiqide sixiang bianhua" [The Transformation of Zhou Enlai's Thought During His Stay in Japan]. In Liu Xi, ed., *Zhongwai xuezhe lun Zhou Enlai*, pp. 47–53.
Liu Qingyang. "Huiyi juewushe" [Remembering the Awakening Society]. In *Zhou Enlai shiwenji*, pp. 95–99.
———. "Juexingla Tianjin renmin" [The People of Tianjin Were Awakened]. In *WY*, pp. 696–731.
Liu Xi. "Guanyu Zhou Enlai rudangde shijian wentide shentao" [In-Depth Discussion of the Timing of Zhou Enlai's Admission to the (Chinese Communist) Party]. In *QS* 6 (1985): 24–27.
———, ed. *Zhongwai xuezhe lun Zhou Enlai* [Chinese and Foreign Scholars' Studies on Zhou Enlai]. Tianjin: Nankai daxue chubanshe, 1990.
Liuou tongxin [Correspondence from Europe]. Beijing: Renmin chubanshe, 1979.
Ma Cuiguan. "Xianfu Ma Qianli xiansheng shilüe" [The Activities of My Late Father Ma Qianli]. In *TJ* 17 (1981): 157–77.
Ma Ming. "Zhang Pengchun yu Zhongguo xiandaihuaju" [Zhang Pengchun and China's Modern New Drama]. In *TJ* 19 (1982): 112–39.

Ma Shunyi. *Taochura chisede jiating* [Escape from the Red Family]. Taipei: Zhongxing shiyeshe, 1950.
Ma Zhuguan. "Wo de wujiufu" [My Fifth Uncle]. In *Xuefu jiwen—Guoli Nankai daxue*, pp. 178–82.
Maiya Kenichirō, ed. *Shū Onrai Nihon o kataru* [Zhou Enlai Speaks on Japan]. Tokyo: Jitsugyōno nihonsha, 1972.
Malraux, André. *Anti-Memoirs*. New York: Holt, Rinehart and Winston, 1968.
Marsh, Susan. "Chou Fo-hai: The Making of a Collaborator." In Akira Iriye, ed., *The Chinese and the Japanese*, pp. 304–27.
Matsumoto Shigeharu. *Shanghai jidai* [Shanghai Period]. Vol. 3. Tokyo: Chūō kōronsha, 1975.
Matsuno Tanio. *Chūgoku no shidōsha—Shū Onrai to sono jidai* [China's Leader—Zhou Enlai and His Time]. Tokyo: Dōyūsha, 1961.
———. *Harukanaru Shū Onrai* [Faraway Zhou Enlai]. Tokyo: Asahi shimbunsha, 1981.
Meisner, Maurice. *Li Ta-chao and the Origins of Chinese Marxism*. Cambridge, Mass.: Harvard University Press, 1967.
Meng, Chih. *Chinese-American Understanding: A Sixty-Year Search*. New York: China Institute in America, 1981.
Nakano Akira. *Ajia no kaiki—Chūkyō* [Asia's Mystery—Communist China]. Tokyo: Kokumin kyōikusha, 1952.
Nankai daxue liushinian [Sixty Years of Nankai University]. Tianjin: Nankai daxue, 1979.
Nashimoto Yūhei. *Shū Onrai* [Zhou Enlai]. Tokyo: Kyokusa shobō, 1967.
Nie Rongzhen. *Nie Rongzhen huiyilu* [Nie Rongzhen's Memoir]. Beijing: Jiefangjun chubanshe, 1984.
Nishikawa Tsutomu. *Arubamu hyōden—Kawakami Hajime* [Critical Biography in Album—Kawakami Hajime]. Tokyo: Shinhyōron, 1980.
Nixon, Richard M. *Leaders*. New York: Warner Books, 1982.
Ogawa Heishirō, *Chūgoku saihō* [China Revisited]. Tokyo: Simul Press, 1981.
———. "Shūkin joshi to Shū Onrai" [Madame Qiu Jin and Zhou Enlai]. *Tōa* [East Asia], May 1986, pp. 45–49, and October 1987, p. 85.
Okamoto Ryūzo. "Shū Onrai shushō" [Premier Zhou Enlai]. *Ajia Rebyū* [Asia Review], March 1970, pp. 178–96.
Pan Shilun. "Zhou Enlai tongzhi he Tianjin xuesheng lianhe huibao" [Comrade Zhou Enlai and the Tianjin Student Union *Bulletin*]. In *Wusi qianhou Zhou Enlai tongzhi shiwenxuan*, pp. 399–402.
Pye, Lucian W. *Mao Tse-tung: The Man in the Leader*. New York: Basic Books, 1976.

Qi Zhilu. "Tianjin jindai zhuming jiaoyujia Yan Xiu" [Tianjin's Famous Modern Educator—Yan Xiu]. In *TJ* 25 (1983): 1–45.

Quotations from Premier Chou En-lai. New York: Thomas Y. Crowell, 1973.

Roots, John McCook. *Chou: An Informal Biography of China's Legendary Chou En-lai*. Garden City, N.Y.: Doubleday, 1978.

Roy, David Todd. *Kuo Mo-jo: The Early Years*. Cambridge, Mass.: Harvard University Press, 1971.

Saari, Jon L. *Legacies of Childhood: Growing Up Chinese in a Time of Crisis, 1890–1920*. Cambridge, Mass.: Harvard University Press, 1990.

Sanetō Keishū. *Chūgoku ryūgakusei shidan* [Historical Discussions of Chinese Students in Japan]. Tokyo: Daiichi shobō, 1981.

———. *Chūgokujin Nihon ryūgaku shi* [History of Chinese Students in Japan]. Tokyo: Kuroshio shuppan, 1960.

———. *Nitchū hiyūkō no rekishi* [History of Japan-China Unfriendliness]. Tokyo: Asahi shimbunsha, 1973.

Scalapino, Robert A. "The Evolution of a Young Revolutionary—Mao Zedong in 1919–1921." *Journal of Asian Studies*, November 1982, pp. 29–61.

Schiff, Geraldine R. "The Life and Writings of Tsou Jung." In Chun-tu Hsueh, ed., *Revolutionary Leaders of Modern China*, pp. 153–209.

Schwarcz, Vera. *The Chinese Enlightenment: Intellectuals and the Legacy of the May Fourth Movement*. Berkeley: University of California Press, 1986.

———. "Out of Historical Amnesia: An Eclectic and Nearly Forgotten Chinese Communist in Europe." *Modern China*, April 1987, pp. 177–225.

———. *Time for Telling Truth Is Running Out: Conversations with Zhang Shenfu*. New Haven, Conn.: Yale University Press, 1992.

Schwartz, Benjamin. *In Search of Wealth and Power: Yen Fu and the West*. Cambridge, Mass.: Harvard University Press, 1964.

Selected Works of Lu Hsun. Vol. 1. Beijing: Foreign Languages Press, 1956.

Shen Tianmin. "Huiyi yu Zhou Enlai tongban tushude shiqi" [Remembering the Period of Studying with Zhou Enlai in the Same Class]. In *QS* 7 (1986): 12–13.

Shi Zizhou. "Huinian Boling xiansheng" [Remembering Mr. Zhang Boling]. In Guo Rongsheng and Zhang Yuan, eds., *Zhang Boling xiansheng jinianji*, pp. 2–3.

Shinobu Seisaburō. *Taishō seijishi* [History of Taishō Politics]. Tokyo: Kawade shobō, 1968.

Shoji Kichinosuke, *Komesōdō no kenkyū* [Study of the Rice Riots]. Tokyo: Miraisha, 1957.

Shu Xincheng. *Jindai zhongguo liuxueshi* [Contemporary History of Chinese Students Abroad]. Shanghai: Zhonghua shuju, 1927.

Smedley, Agnes. *The Great Road: The Life and Times of Chu Teh*. New York: Monthly Review Press, 1956.

Snow, Edgar. *Red Star Over China*. New York: Grove Press, 1961 [1938].

———. *Red Star Over China*. First revised and enlarged ed. New York: Bantam Books, 1978.

Spence, Jonathan D. *The Gate of Heavenly Peace: The Chinese and Their Revolution, 1895–1980*. New York: Viking, 1981.

Stuart, J. Leighton. "Introduction." In *There Is Another China*, pp. 1–3.

Su Shuyang. *Dadide erzi—Zhou Enlai de gushi* [The Son of the Great Earth—Stories About Zhou Enlai]. Beijing: Zhongguo shaonian ertong chubanshe, 1983.

Sumiya Etsuji. *Kawakami Hajime* [Kawakami Hajime]. Tokyo: Yoshikawa kōbunkan, 1962.

Sun Limin and Xin Gongxian. "Tianjin rizujie gaikuang" [An Outline of the Japanese Concession in Tianjin]. In *TJ* 18 (1982): 111–52.

Sun Yueqi. "Tianjin wusiyundongde huiyi" [Remembering the May Fourth Movement in Tianjin]. In *TJ* 3 (1979): 27–33.

Sun Zhiyao. "Zhou Enlai jiashi tongnian he guxiang yanjiu zhongde jigewenti" [Some Questions About Zhou Enlai's Family, Childhood, and Hometown]. In Liu Xi, ed., *Zhongwai xuezhe lun Zhou Enlai*, pp. 1–8.

Tamashima Shinji. *Chūgoku no Nihonkan* [China's Views on Japan]. Tokyo: Kōbūndō shinsha, 1967.

There Is Another China: Essays and Articles for Chang Poling of Nankai. New York: King's Crown Press, 1948.

Tikhvinsky, S. L. "Zhou Enlai he Sulian" [Zhou Enlai and the Soviet Union]. In Liu Xi, ed., *Zhongwai xuezhe lun Zhou Enlai*, pp. 13–27.

Usui Chūsan, *Tenshin kyoryū mindan sanjū shūnen kinenshi* [The 30th Year Commemorative Volume on the (Japanese) Residence Association in Tianjin]. Tianjin: Tenshin kyoryū mindan, 1941.

Waley, Arthur. *The Analects of Confucius*. London: Allen and Unwin, 1938.

Wang, Nora. "Deng Xiaoping: The Years in France." *China Quarterly*, December 1982, pp. 698–705.

Wang, Y. C. *Chinese Intellectuals and the West, 1892–1949*. Chapel Hill: University of North Carolina Press, 1966.

Wang Jingru. *Zhou Enlai tongzhi qingshaonian shidai* [Comrade Zhou Enlai's Childhood and Youth]. n.p.: Henan renmin chubanshe, 1980.

Wang Wenjun, ed. *Zhang Boling jiaoyu yanlun xuanji* [Zhang Boling's Selected Speeches on Education]. Tianjin: Nankai daxue chubanshe, 1984.

Wang Wentian. *Zhang Boling yu Nankai* [Zhang Boling and Nankai]. Taipei: Zhuanji wenxue chubanshe, 1968.

Wang Yongxiang. "Guanyu Zhou Enlai tongzhi canjia wusiyundongde shijian" [Concerning the Timing of Comrade Zhou Enlai's Participation in the May Fourth Movement]. In *TJ* 15 (1981): 195–98.

Wang Yongxiang, Kong Binfeng, and Liu Pinqing. *Zhongguo gongchandang liuouzhibu shihua* [A History of the European Branch of the Chinese Communist Party]. Beijing: Zhongguo qingnian chubanshe, 1985.

Wang Yongxiang and Liu Pinqing. *Weile Zhonghua zhi jueqi—Zhou Enlai qingnian shiqide shenghuo yu douzhan* [For China's Soaring: Zhou Enlai's Life and Struggle During His Youth]. Tianjin: Tianjin renmin chubanshe, 1980.

Wei Hongyun. "Zhou Enlai tongzhi wusi shiqi geming huodong jiyao" [The Record of Comrade Zhou Enlai's Revolutionary Activities During the May Fourth Period]. *Nankai Daxue Xuebao* [Nankai University Journal], January 1979, pp. 16–23.

Wei Yuanjin. "Youguan daze buxi xuexiao de yiduan huiyi" [Remembering the Daze Preparatory School]. In *QS* 5 (1984): 2.

Weidenbaum, Rhoda Sussman. "Chou En-lai: Creative Revolutionary." Ph.D. diss., University of Connecticut, 1981.

White, Theodore H. *In Search of History: A Personal Adventure*. New York: Harper & Row, 1978.

Who's Who in Communist China. Hong Kong: 1966.

Wilson, Dick. *Zhou Enlai: A Biography*. New York: Viking, 1984.

Wolff, Ernst. *Chou Tso-jen*. New York: Twayne, 1971.

Wusi qianhou Zhou Enlai tongzhi shiwenxuan [Selected Writings of Comrade Zhou Enlai Before and After the May Fourth Movement]. Tianjin: Tianjin renmin chubanshe, 1979.

Wusi shiqide shetuan [Organizations During the May Fourth Movement]. 4 vols. Beijing: Shenghuo dushu xinzhi sanlianshudian, 1979.

Wusiyundong huiyilu [Reminiscences of the May Fourth Movement]. Beijing: Zhongguo shehuikexue chubanshe, 1979.

Xia Jianshan, ed. *Nankai huoju yundong shiliao* [Historical Materials on the Drama Movement at Nankai]. Tianjin: Nankai daxue chubanshe, 1984.

Xia Qinxi. "Yang Yide qiren" [On Yang Yide]. In *TJ* 3 (1979): 54–65.

Xie Shuying. "Yu Zhou Enlai tongzhi tongchuan fufade zhuiyi" [Remembering the Travel to France with Comrade Zhou Enlai on the Same Ship]. In *QS* 1 (1980): 9–10.

Xu Kuijiu. "Huiyi zairiben yu Zhou Enlai tongzhi xiangchude rizi" [Remembering the Days When I Had Close Relations with Comrade Zhou Enlai in Japan]. In *QS* 15 (1981): 150–55.

Xu Tianliu. "Fufa qingong jianxueqian Zhou Enlai tongzhi duiwode jiaoyu" [Comrade Zhou Enlai's Teaching to Me Before Going to France for the Work-Study Program]. In *QS* 1 (1980): 7–8.

Xuefu jiwen—Guoli Nankai daxue [Educational Annals—National Nankai University]. Taipei: Nanjing chubangongse, 1981.

Xuefu jiwen—Guoli Qinghua daxue [Educational Annals—National Qinghua University]. Taipei: Nanjing chubangongse, 1981.

Yan Jingwen. *Zhou Enlai pingzhuan* [Critical Biography of Zhou Enlai]. Hong Kong: Bowen shuju, 1974.

Yan Renzeng, ed. *Yan Fansun xiansheng nianpu* [Chronicle of Yan Fansun's Important Events]. Tianjin: Tianjinshi wenshi yangjiuguan, 1980.

———. "Zhou zongli yu Yan Fanlao" [Premier Zhou and Mr. Yan Fansun]. In *QS* 2 (1982): 3–4.

Yang Fuqing. "Xinzhongxuehui jiyao" [The Record of the New China Study Society]. In *Wusiyundong huiyilu*, pp. 460–67.

Yang Zaidao. "Wusi shiqide Zhang Ruoming" [Zhang Ruoming During the May Fourth Period]. Unpublished paper, 1987.

Ye Zufu. "Zhou Enlai tongzhi yu haerbinshi Donghua Xuexiao" [Comrade Zhou Enlai and the Donghua School in Harbin City]. In *TJ* 15 (1981): 199–201.

Young, Ernest P. "Chinese Leaders and Japanese Aid in the Early Republic." In Akira Iriye, ed., *The Chinese and the Japanese*, pp. 124–39.

———. "Problems of a Late Ch'ing Revolutionary: Ch'en T'ien-hua." In Chun-tu Hsueh, ed., *Revolutionary Leaders of Modern China*, pp. 210–47.

Yu Shude. "Wo suozhidaode Li Dazhao tongzhi" [Comrade Li Dazhao Whom I Knew]. In *Huiyi Li Dazhao*, pp. 23–27.

Yu Zhihou. "Tianjin Yishibao gaishu" [General Outline of Tianjin's *Yishibao*]. In *TJ* 18 (1982): 70–93.

Zhang Boling xiansheng bainian danchen jiniance [The Memorial Volume on Zhang Boling's Centennial Birthday]. Taipei: Taiwan nankai xiaoyuhui, 1975.

Zhang Honggao. "Huiyi xuesheng shidaide Zhou Enlai tongzhi" [Remembering Comrade Zhou Enlai During his Student Period]. In *Wusi qianhou Zhou Enlai tongzhi shiwenxuan*, pp. 391–98.

———. "Huiyi Zhou Enlai zai Nankai xuexiao he liuri shiqide xuexi yu shenghuo" [Remembering Zhou Enlai's Study and Life at Nankai School and in Japan]. In *QS* 7 (1986): 6–11, 42.

Zhang Hongxiang and Wang Yongxiang. *Liufa qingong jianxue yundong jianshi* [A Short History of the Work-Study Movement in France]. Harbin: Heilongjiang renmin chubanshe, 1982.

Zhang Lunyuan. "Huiyi Zhou zongli zai Nankai yu shisheng changyan xinju jilüe" [Recollections of Premier Zhou at Nankai and Records of the New Drama Created and Played by Teachers and Students]. In *QS* 2 (1982): 4–5.

Zhang Shenfu. "Liufa qianhou wo tong Zhou Enlai tongzhide yixie jeichu he jiaowang" [My Contact and Exchanges with Comrade Zhou Enlai Before and After the French Sojourn]. In *Huainian Zhou Enlai*, pp. 232–36.

———. "Yi Shouchang" [Remembering Li Dazhao]. In *Huiyi Li Dazhao*, pp. 61–66.

Zhang Xilu. "Zhou Enlai—Nankai zuihaode xuesheng" [Zhou Enlai—The Best Student of Nankai]. In *QS* 1 (1980): 3–4.

Zhang Xizuo. "Zhang Boling xiansheng zhuanlüe" [A Brief Biography of Mr. Zhang Boling]. In *TJ* 8 (1980): 75–118.

Zheng Zhiguang, ed. *Zhang Boling zhuan* [Biography of Zhang Boling]. Tianjin: Tianjin renmin chubanshe, 1989.

Zhou Enlai. "Jianting rilu" [The Diary in the Public Prosecution Prison]. In *ZZ*, pp. 262–396.

———. "Jingting juliuji" [The Record of Detention in the Police Station]. In *ZZ*, pp. 187–253.

———. "Woxiao xinjuguan" [Views on Our School's New Drama]. In *ZZ*, pp. 67–74.

Zhou Enlai nianpu [Chronicle of Zhou Enlai's Important Events]. Beijing: Renmin chubanshe, 1989.

Zhou Enlai qingnian shidai [Zhou Enlai's Youthful Period]. Beijing: Wenwu chubanshe, 1988.

Zhou Enlai shiwenji—Juewu Jueyou [Collection of Zhou Enlai's Poems and Writings—Awakening and Awakening Letters]. Tianjin: Nankai daxue yinshuating, 1980.

"Zhou Enlai tong Li Boman tan geren jingli" [Zhou Enlai Discusses His Personal History with Lieberman]. *Liaowang*, Jan. 9, 1984, pp. 26–29.

Zhou Enlai tongzhi liuou wenji [Collection of Comrade Zhou Enlai's Writings in Europe]. Beijing: Wenwu chubanshe, 1979.

Zhou Enlai tongzhi qingnianshiqi zai Tianjinde xijuhuodong ziliao huipian [Collection of Materials on Comrade Zhou Enlai's Drama Activities During his Youth in Tianjin]. Tianjin: Zhou Enlai jinianguan, 1981.

Zhou Enlai tongyi zhanxian wenxuan [Zhou Enlai's Selected Works on United Front Struggles]. Beijing: Renmin chubanshe, 1984.

Zhou Enlai zongli bashidanchen jinian shiwenxuan [Selected Memorial Essays on Zhou Enlai's 80th Birthday]. Beijing: Renmin chubanshe, 1978.

Zhou Enlai xuanji [Selected Works of Zhou Enlai]. Vol. 1. Beijing: Renmin chubanshe, 1980.
Zhou Enzhu. "Wode tangxiong—Zhou Enlai" [My Older Cousin—Zhou Enlai]. In *QS* 2 (1982): 1–3.
Zhou Fohai. *Wangyiji* [A Collection of Past Events]. Hong Kong: Hezhong chubanshe, 1955.
Zhou zongli yu guxiang [Premier Zhou and His Hometown]. n.p.: Jiangsu renmin chubanshe, 1979.

Character List

baisuitang 百歲堂
Baohuanghui 保皇會
Bian Yueting 卞月庭
Bimbō monogatari 貧乏物語
Cai Chang 蔡暢
Cai Hesen 蔡和森
Cai Yuanpei 蔡元培
Cao Kun 曹昆
Cao Rui 曹銳
Cao Rulin 曹汝霖
Chang Ceou 常策歐
Chen Borong 陳伯榮
Chen Duxiu 陳獨秀
Chen Gongpei 陳公培
Chen Jingfu 陳鏡芙
Chen Qiaonian 陳喬年
Chen Shizhou 陳式周
Chen Songyan 陳頌言
Chen Tianhua 陳天華
Chen Yannian 陳延年
Chen Yuan 陳源
Chen Zhidu 諶志篤
Chiguang 赤光
chongxi 冲喜
Chūō Kōron 中央公論
Dagongbao 大公報
Dai Jitao 戴季陶
Daiichi Kōtō Gakkō
第一高等學校
Daini bimbō monogatari
第二貧乏物語
Daluan 大鸞
dao minjian qu 到民間去
Daze yingwen suanxue buxi xuexiao
大澤英文算學補習學校
Deng Yingchao (Deng Wenshu) 鄧穎超(鄧文淑)
dengmi 燈謎
Dongfang Zazhi 東方雜誌
Duan Molan 段茂瀾
Duan Qirui 段祺瑞
Fan Jingsheng (Fan Yuanlian)
範靜生(範源廉)
feifei 飛飛
Feng Guozhang 馮國璋
Feng Liuqi (Feng Wenqian)
馮柳猗(馮文潛)
Fu Zengxiang 傅增湘
fuqiang 富强

funü duli 婦女獨立
gaige 改革
gaizao 改造
Gaizao lianhe 改造聯合
ganma 乾媽
Gao Gewu 高戈吾
geming 革命
Gemingjun 革命軍
gexin 革新
Gong Debai 龔德柏
Gong Yinsun 龔蔭蓀
Gong Zhiru 龔志如
gongneng 公能
Gotō Shimpei 後滕新平
Gu Shaochuan 顧少川
Guan Tianpei 關天培
Guan Xibin (Guan Yiwen) 管錫斌(管易文)
guanfei 官費
Guo Longzhen 郭隆眞
Guo Moruo 郭沫若
Guo Qinguang 郭欽光
Guocui Xuebao 國粹學報
guojia zhuyi 國家主義
guojipai 過激派
guwen 古文
Han Zhifu 韓質夫
hanjian 漢奸
hanlin 翰林
He Dianjia 何殿甲
Hongloumeng 紅樓夢
Hu Hua 胡華
Hu Shih 胡適
Hua Wuqing 華午晴
Huang Xing 黃興
Huang Yusheng 黃鈺生
Huang Zhengpin (Huang Ai) 黃正品(黃愛)
Huangpu [Whampoa] 黃埔
Ishingō 維新號
Jiang Gengsheng 姜更生
Jiang Jiang 蔣江
Jiang Menglin 蔣夢麟
jiangzhe tongxuehui 江浙同學會
Jianting rilu 檢廳日錄
Jiao Tianmin 矯天民
Jiayin Zazhi 甲寅雜誌
jiguan 籍貫
Jin Bangzheng 金邦正
Jinghuayuan 鏡花綠
Jingting juliuji 警廳拘留記
Jingye lequnhui 敬業樂群會
jinshi 進士
Juewushe 覺悟社
Jueyou 覺郵
junguo zhuyi 軍國主義
Kaihō 鮮放
Kaizō 改造
Kang Nairu 伉乃如
Kang Youwei 康有為
Kawakami Hajime 河上肇
keyuan 科員
Kōbun Gakuin 宏文學院
komesōdō 米騷動
Kōtō Daidō Gakkō 高等大同學校
Kōtoku Shūsui 幸德秋水
langdang nianyu 浪蕩年余
laodong jieji 劳働階級

Li Dazhao (Li Shouchang) 李大釗(李守常)
Li Fuchun 李富春
Li Fujing 李福景
Li Huang 李璜
Li Mingxun 李銘勛
Li Shizeng 李石曾
Li Weihan 李維漢
Li Yuanhong 黎元洪
Li Yuru 李愚如
Liao Zhongkai 廖仲愷
Lin Wei 林蔚
Ling Bing 凌冰
Ling Zhong 凌鍾
Liu Chongyou 劉崇佑
Liu Junqing 劉俊卿
Liu Qingyang 劉清楊
Lu Muzhai 盧木斋
Lu Zongyu 陸宗輿
luodi 落第
Ma Jun 馬駿
Ma Liang 馬良
Ma Qianli 馬千里
Ma Shunyi 馬順宜
Ma Yunting 馬雲亭
Matsumoto Kamejirō 松本亀次郎
Mei Lanfang 梅蘭芳
Mei Yibao 梅貽寶
Mei Yilin 梅貽琳
Mei Yiqi 梅貽琦
Meizhou Pinglun 每週評論
Meng Chih [Meng Zhi] 孟治
Meng Jinrang 孟進襄
Meng Zhenhou 孟震侯
minquan 民權
Minquanbao 民權報
Miyazaki Ryūnosuke 宮崎龍之介
Miyazaki Tōten 宮崎滔天
Motoki Shōgo 元木省吾
Mu Qing 穆清
Muyang aihua 牧羊哀話
Nagashima Masao 長島善雄
Nankai Sichao 南開思潮
Nankai Xingqibao 南開星期報
Natsume Sōseki 夏目漱石
niang 娘
Nie Rongzhen 聶榮臻
Nikka Gakudō 日華學堂
nükui 女魁
Ogawa Heishirō 小川平四郎
Ōkuma Shigenobu 大隈重信
Pan Shilun (Pan Shuon) 潘世綸(潘述庵)
pingdeng 平等
pingmin 平民
Qingnian gongdu huzhutuan 青年工讀互助團
qingong jianxue 勤工儉學
qinjian pushi 勤儉樸實
Qiu Jin 秋瑾
Quanxuepian 勸學篇
qushe quliu 取舍去留
ren 仁
Ren Zhuoxuan 任卓宣
Rendaoshe 人道社
rensheng wuchang 人生無常
riren lingwo 日人凌我
ronin 浪人

Seijō Gakkō 成城學校
Shakai mondai kenkyū 社會問題研究
Shanyang 山陽
Shaonian 少年
Shaonian zhongguo xuehui 少年中國學會
shehui heian 社會黑暗
Shi Zizhou (Shi Zuoxin) 時子周(時作新)
Shinjinkai 新人會
Shinshakai 新社會
shiye 師爺
Shuguangshe 曙光社
Shuihuzhuan 水滸傳
Sili zhongxuetang 私立中學堂
Sumiya Etsuji 住谷悅治
Sun Bingwen 孫炳文
Sun Huijuan 孫慧娟
Sun Weishi 孫維世
Sun Ziwen 孫子文
Taiwushibao 泰晤士報
Takahashi Motokichi 高橋本吉
Tamatsukan 玉津館
Tan Pingshan 譚平山
Tao Menghe 陶孟和
Tao Shangzhao 陶尚釗
Terao Tōru 寺尾亨
Terauchi Masatake 寺內正毅
teyuesheng 特約生
Tianjin xuesheng lianhehui 天津學生聯合會
Tianjin xuesheng lianhehuibao 天津學生聯合會報
Tianyanlun 天演論
Tianyuhua 天雨花
Tōa Kōtō Yobigakkō 東亞高等予備學校
Tōa Shōgyō Gakkō 東亞商業學校
Tōkyō Dōbun Shoin 東京同文書院
Tōkyō Kōtō Shihan Gakkō 東京高等師範學校
Tong Qiyan 童啓顏
tongzibu 童子部
tuanti 團體
Uchiyama Kanzō 內山完造
Wan Donger 萬冬兒
Wan Qingxuan 萬青選
Wang Dazhen 王大楨
Wang Jingqi 王景岐
Wang Pushan 王樸山
Wang Ruofei 王若飛
Wang Shiyu 王世裕
Wang Xiying 王錫瑛
Wang Zhanggu 王章祜
wenhepai 溫和派
wenshu 文書
woguo 倭國
Wu Guobing 吳國柄
Wu Guozhen 吳國禎
Wu Hantao 吳瀚濤
Wu Peifu 吳佩孚
Wu Yuzhang 吳玉章
Wu Zhihui 吳稚暉
wubing 五病
Wugengzhong 五更鍾
Wuhao 伍豪
wusiyundong 五四運動
Xia Qinxi 夏琴西

Xiang Jingyu 向警予
xianren zhengce 賢人政策
xiaobailian 小白臉
Xiaofeng 校風
Xingqi Pinglun 星期評論
xingshu 行書
Xinhua Ribao 新華日報
xinju 新劇
Xinmin xuehui 新民學會
Xinminyibao 新民意報
Xinqingnian 新青年
xinsichao 新思潮
Xinzhongxuehui 新中學會
Xiong Bingsan 熊秉三
Xiong Xiong 熊雄
xiushen 修身
Xiyouji 西游記
Xu Deheng 許德珩
Xu Kuijiu 徐逵九
Xu Shichang 徐世昌
Xu Teli 徐特立
Xue Zhuodong 薛卓東
xuebu shilang 學部侍郎
xuezheng 學政
Yan Fu 嚴復
Yan Renzeng 嚴仁曾
Yan Xiu (Yan Fansun) 嚴修(嚴範孫)
Yan Zhian 嚴智安
Yan Zhichong 嚴智崇
Yan Zhikai 嚴智開
Yang Mingseng 楊明僧
Yang Yide 楊以德
yi 義
yideng keyuan 一等科員
yiju yidong 一舉一動
Yin Kuan 尹寬
Yiniancha 一念差
Yingang shuyuan 銀岡書院
yinming 隱名
yinshi qiju 飲食起居
Yishibao 益世報
Yiyuanqian 一圓錢
Yoshino Sakuzō 吉野作造
Yu Fangzhou 于方舟
Yu Shude 于樹德
Yue Fei 岳飛
yulun 輿論
Zaishengyuan 再生緣
Zeng Qi 曾琦
Zhang Binglin 章炳麟
Zhang Boling 張伯嶺
Zhang Gaoru 張皞如
Zhang Guotao [Chang Kuo-t'ao] 張國燾
Zhang Honggao 張鴻誥
Zhang Pengchun 張彭春
Zhang Ruifeng (Zhang Pengxian) 張瑞峯(張蓬仙)
Zhang Ruoming 張若名
Zhang Shenfu 張申府
Zhang Shiling 張詩嶺
Zhang Shizhao 章士釗
Zhang Xilu 張希陸
Zhang Xueliang 張學良
Zhang Zhidong 張之洞
Zhang Zongxiang 章宗祥
Zhang Zuolin 張作霖
Zhao Guangchen 趙光宸
Zhao Shiyan 趙世炎
Zhao Xiwen 趙希文
Zheng Daoru 鄭道儒

zhengsi shuguan 正司書官
zhixian 知縣
zhixing heyi 知行合一
Zhou Bingjian 周秉建
Zhou Dunyi 周敦頤
Zhou Enlai (Xiangyu) 周恩來(翔宇)
Zhou Enpu (Boyu) 周恩溥(博宇)
Zhou Enshou (Tongyu) 周恩壽(同宇)
Zhou Enshuo (Panyu) 周恩碩(潘宇)
Zhou Enzhu (Runmin) 周恩霔(潤民)
Zhou Erhui 周爾輝
Zhou Erliu 周爾流
Zhou Fohai 周佛海
Zhou Guizhen 周桂珍
Zhou Jianren 周建人
Zhou Junang (Haixiang) 周駿昂(亥祥)
Zhou Junlong (Panlong) 周駿龍(攀龍)
Zhou Mao 周茂
Zhou Qiaoshui 周樵水
Zhou Songyao 周嵩堯
Zhou Yikang (Tiaozhi) 周貽康(調之)
Zhou Yigan 周貽淦
Zhou Yigeng 周貽賡
Zhou Yikui 周貽奎
Zhou Yineng (Mouchen) 周貽能(懋臣)
Zhou Yiqian 周貽謙
Zhou Zuoren 周作人
zhushi 主事
ziqiang zhi dao 自強之道
ziyou guxiang 自由故鄉
zizhilixuehui 自治勵學會
zongguo 宗國
zuixin sichao 最新思潮

Index

In this index an "f" after a number indicates a separate reference on the next page, and an "ff" indicates separate references on the next two pages. A continuous discussion over two or more pages is indicated by a span of page numbers, e.g., "57–59." *Passim* is used for a cluster of references in close but not consecutive sequence.

Library of Congress Cataloging-in-Publication Data

Lee, Chae-Jin, 1936–
Zhou Enlai : the early years / Chae-Jin Lee.
p. cm.
Includes bibliographical references and index.
ISBN 0-8047-2302-8 (cl.) : ISBN 0-8047-2700-7 (pbk.)
1. Chou, En-lai, 1898–1976—Childhood and youth.
2. Prime ministers—China—Biography. I. Title.
DS778.C593L44 1994
951.05'092—dc20 93-33525
CIP

∞ This book is printed on acid-free paper.

Original printing 1994
Last figure below indicates year of this printing:
05 04 03 02 01 00 99 98 97 96